The Meditative
Readings in the Theory
of Buddhist Meditation

The Meditative Way

Readings in the Theory and Practice
of Buddhist Meditation

compiled by
Rod Bucknell and Chris Kang

CURZON

First published in 1997
by Curzon Press
St John's Studios, Church Road, Richmond
Surrey, TW9 2QA

© 1997 Rod Bucknell and Chris Kang

Typeset in Baskerville by LaserScript, Mitcham, Surrey
Printed in Great Britain by
TJ Press (Padstow) Limited, Padstow, Cornwall

British Library Cataloguing in Publication Data
A catalogue record for this book is available from the British Library

Library of Congress Cataloguing in Publication Data
A catalogue record for this book has been requested

ISBN 0 7007 0677 1 (Hbk)
ISBN 0 7007 0678 X (Pbk)

Contents

Acknowledgements   vii
Sources and Permissions   viii
General Introduction   1

Section I   Pali Sources

Introduction   7
1 *The Middle Way,* Dhamma-cakka-ppavattana Sutta   11
2 *The Eightfold Path Explained,* Sacca-vibhanga Sutta   12
3 *The Subduing of Thoughts,* Vitakka-santhāna Sutta   14
4 *The Sublime States,* Udumbarika-sīhanāda Sutta   17
5 *The Foundations of Mindfulness,* Satipaṭṭhāna Sutta   19
6 *Mindfulness of Breathing,* Ānāpāna-sati Sutta   26
7 *The Jhānas,* Sallekha Sutta   29
8 *The Meditator's Progress,* Sāmañña-phala Sutta   30

Section II   Classical Masters

Introduction   41
9   *Concentration on the Earth Disk,* Buddhaghosa   43
10 *Self-Protection through Mindfulness,* Śāntideva   50
11 *Calm and Insight,* Zhiyi   55
12 *Seated Meditation,* Dōgen   64
13 *Some Zen Kōans,* Mumon   66
14 *Fastening the Mind,* Tsongkhapa   69

Section III   Contemporary Masters

Introduction   81

15 *A Spectrum of Meditative Practices*, Dhammika Bhikkhu   85
16 *Observing Your Mind*, Achaan Chah   97
17 *Insight by the Nature Method*, Buddhadasa Bhikkhu   106
18 *Insight through Mindfulness*, Mahasi Sayadaw   113
19 *The Meditative Mind*, Dhiravamsa   123
20 *Watching Thoughts and Emotions*, Godwin Samararatne   136
21 *Zen Mind*, Shunryu Suzuki   146
22 *Some Tibetan Practices*, Kathleen McDonald   159
23 *Meditation in Tantra*, Lama Yeshe   175

Section IV   Personal Accounts

Introduction   195

24 *Experiences in Meditation*, Chris Kang   197
25 *From a Meditator's Diary*, Jane Hamilton-Merritt   208
26 *A Student's Response to Meditation*, Donald K. Swearer   219
27 *Initial Meditative Experiences*, Roger Walsh   228
28 *Experiments in Insight Meditation*, Rod Bucknell   244

Abbreviations   265
Notes   266
Index   270

Acknowledgements

The many authors, publishers, and journal editors who gave permission to reprint materials in this volume are listed in full in the following section, where they are identified by the annotation "Reprinted with permission." We, the compilers, wish to express here our sincere thanks to them all, and especially to those who wrote personally to encourage us in this project.

We also wish to thank Dr. Edward Crangle for his valuable assistance in scanning the original materials and preparing the Index.

Rod Bucknell and Chris Kang,
"Veluvana," Brisbane, Australia.
July, 1995

Sources and Permissions

The following are the sources of the twenty-eight readings. Unless otherwise indicated, translations are by the compilers of this volume.

1 *Dhamma-cakka-ppavattana Sutta.* S5.12.11 = S v 421.
Translated from the Pali.
2 *Sacca-vibhanga Sutta.* M141 = M iii 248–252.
Translated from the Pali.
3 *Vitakka-santhāna Sutta.* M20 = M i 118–122.
Translated from the Pali.
4 *Udumbarika-sīhanāda Sutta.* D25 = D iii 49–50.
Translated from the Pali.
5 *Satipaṭṭhāna Sutta.* M10 = M i 55–63; D22 = D ii 290–315.
Translated from the Pali.
6 *Ānāpāna-sati Sutta.* M118 = M iii 78–88.
Translated from the Pali.
7 *Sallekha Sutta.* M8 = M i 40–46.
Translated from the Pali.
8 *Sāmañña-phala Sutta.* D2 = D i 47–86.
Translated from the Pali.
9 Buddhaghosa, *Visuddhimagga.* Vism 123–166.
Translated from the Pali.
10 Śāntideva, *Śikṣā-samuccaya.*
Cecil Bendall (ed.), *Çikshāsamuccaya, A Compendium of Buddhistic Teaching Compiled by Çāntideva.* 's-Gravenhage: Mouton, 1957, pp. 118–124, 228–237.
Translated from the Sanskrit.
11 Zhiyi, *Tongmen Zhiguan = Xiuxi Zhiguan Zuochan Fayao = Xiao Zhiguan.* T1915 = T xlvi 462–474.
Translated from the Chinese.

12 Dōgen, *Fukan Zazen Gi.* Okubo Dōshū (ed.), *Dōgen Zenji Zenshū* (Tokyo: Chikuma Shobō, 1969–70), vol. 2, pp. 3–5.
Translated from the Japanese.

13 Mumon, *Mumonkan.*
Sekida Katsuki (trans.), A. V. Grimstone (ed.), *Two Zen Classics* (New York and Tokyo: Weatherhill, 1977), pp. 27–28, 44, 73, 128.
Reprinted with permission.

14 Tsong-kha-pa, *Lam rim chen mo.*
Alex Wayman (trans.), *Calming the Mind and Discerning the Real: Buddhist Meditation and the Middle View* (New Delhi: Motilal Banarsidass, 1978), pp. 117–126, 446–447.
Reprinted with permission.

15 Dhammika Bhikkhu, *All About Buddhism: A Modern Introduction to an Ancient Spiritual Tradition* (Singapore: Buddha Dhamma Mandala Society, 1962), pp. 142–147, 153–164, 173–180, 253–254.
Reprinted with permission.

16 Achaan Chah.
Jack Kornfield and Paul Breiter, *A Still Forest Pool: The Insight Meditation of Achaan Chah* (Wheaton: Theosophical Publishing House, 1985), pp. 81–103.
Reprinted with permission.

17 Buddhadasa Bhikkhu, *Khū-mȳ Manut* (Bangkok: Ongkān Fȳnfū Phutthasāsanā, no date), pp. 97–115.
Rod Bucknell (trans.), "Insight by the Nature Method," in *Me and Mine: Selected Essays of Bhikkhu Buddhadāsa*, ed. Donald K. Swearer (Albany, N.Y.: State University of New York Press, 1989), pp. 34–39.
Reprinted with permission.

18 Mahasi Sayadaw, talk given on 27 July 1951 and tape recorded by Buddha Sasananuggaha Association.
U Pe Thin (trans.), *Satipaṭṭhāna Vipassanā: Insight through Mindfulness* (Kandy: Buddhist Publication Society, 1990; *Wheel* No. 370/371), pp. 21–35, 38–40, 44–49.
Reprinted with permission.

19 Dhiravamsa, *The Way of Non-Attachment: The Practice of Insight Meditation* (Wellingborough, U.K.: Crucible, 1989), pp. 13–19, 28–32, 104–107.
Reprinted with permission.

20 Godwin Samararatne, tape recording of a guided meditation and discussion conducted at the Buddhist Library, Singapore in 1992.
Transcribed with permission.

21 Shunryu Suzuki, *Zen Mind, Beginner's Mind* (New York: Weather-hill, 1991), pp. 25–37, 80–83.
Reprinted with permission.

22 Kathleen McDonald, *How to Meditate* (London: Wisdom Publications, 1984), pp. 56–62, 110–125, 134–138.
Reprinted with permission.

23 Lama Yeshe, *Introduction to Tantra: A Vision of Totality,* comp. & ed. Jonathan Landaw (London: Wisdom Publications, 1987), pp. 81–93, 98–107, 111–113.
Reprinted with permission.

24 Chris Kang, "Experiences in Meditation," unpublished manuscript, 1992.

25 Jane Hamilton-Merritt, *A Meditator's Diary: A Western Woman's Unique Experiences in Thailand Monasteries* (London: Unwin, 1966), pp. 37–50.
Reprinted with permission.

26 Donald K. Swearer, *Secrets of the Lotus* (New York: Macmillan, 1971), pp. x, 6–8, 212–222.
Reprinted with permission.

27 Roger Walsh, "Initial Meditative Experiences," Parts I and II, *Journal of Transpersonal Psychology,* 9 (1977), 151–192; and 10 (1978), 1–28.
Reprinted with permission.

28 Roderick S. Bucknell, "Experiments in Insight Meditation," *Australian Journal of Transpersonal Psychology,* 3 (1983), 96–117.
Reprinted with permission.

General Introduction

The continuing growth of interest in Eastern techniques of meditation has generated a wide range of relevant writings: self-help manuals for aspiring meditators; research papers on the psychological and physiological effects of meditation; linguistic/hermeneutic analyses of the relevant classical texts; and, occasionally, intimate personal accounts of the actual experiences of practising meditators.

Buddhist meditation, while attracting less popular attention than some other meditative disciplines, has given rise to a particularly rich literature in recent years. Despite differences in style and terminology, these modern writings on Buddhist meditation serve much the same purposes as did the manuals and commentaries of the classical masters: to explicate and interpret the Buddha's teachings on meditation, to clarify the nature and value of the various meditative techniques and attainments, and/or to offer advice on the actual practice of meditation.

The demand for such writings grows as practitioners of Buddhist meditation become more numerous. This has led to the appearance of some books of questionable quality. Overall, however, the trend has been toward constantly improving standards and a more critical, discriminating approach among both meditators and those who write for them. Meditators are increasingly inclined to compare and evaluate critically what the different contemporary meditation masters have to say, to weigh up the results of relevant scientific studies, or to consult translations of the primary texts in search of the Buddha's "original" teachings on meditation. Writers on meditation are also increasingly adopting an appropriately critical approach, particularly as regards the reliability of textual accounts. Relatively few still commit the old error of assuming that the Pali canon is a complete and faithful record of what the Buddha said on the subject, or that the classical commentators were infallible authorities.

1

It is increasingly common for those doing research on meditation to be meditators themselves. Such people are far better equipped than non-meditator researchers to arrive at balanced and well informed conclusions. Textual scholars who meditate are in a position to interpret the textual accounts of meditation intelligibly and realistically, and perhaps to correlate otherwise obscure statements with actual meditative techniques and attainments. Psychologist-meditators, with their training in detached observation and their technical vocabulary, are in a position to formulate accurate and insightful descriptions and interpretations of what they experience in their meditation. Such factors have contributed to the recent rapid growth of well informed writings on Buddhist meditation.

The present collection of twenty-eight readings is designed to give meditators, researchers, and general readers ready access to representative samples of those writings, and to the principal relevant texts.

The readings are grouped under four headings, arranged in roughly chronological order, as follows.

Section I. Pali Sources

The historically earliest source of information on Buddhist meditation is the *suttas*, or discourses of the Buddha, preserved principally in the canonical texts of Theravāda Buddhism. Excerpts from eight *suttas* containing important teachings on meditation are presented in this first section.

Section II. Classical Masters

In this section are presented six samples of the writings of highly regarded classical authorities on meditation. They cover a wide historical and geographical range, from fifth-century Sri Lanka to thirteenth-century Japan and fifteenth-century Tibet. These readings contain much information on the types of meditation traditionally practised in the diverse schools of Buddhism which they represent.

Section III. Contemporary Masters

Nine well-known meditation teachers of the modern era, both Asians and Westerners and from various schools of Buddhism, are represented here. These readings present their most characteristic teachings, and cover most of the currently practised meditative techniques.

Section IV. Personal Accounts

Practising meditators' reports on their actual experiences represent a valuable but relatively rare genre of meditation literature. Five such reports are reproduced here.

In the selecting of these readings, every effort was made to ensure adequate and even representation of the major Buddhist schools, meditative techniques, and interpretive styles. However, this ideal could not be fully realized, for various reasons. Difficulty in obtaining permission to reprint resulted in the absence of the Tibetan Dzogchen and Mahāmudrā traditions from Section II, and of some well-known present-day masters from Section III. In Section IV, *Personal Accounts*, only Theravāda is represented because of a shortage of satisfactory material of this type for other schools. And Section I is explicitly limited to translations from the Pali Tipiṭaka (the canon of Theravāda Buddhism) because of the inaccessibility of comparably early material on meditation in non-Hīnayāna schools. Such incompleteness or unevenness in the representation of the different traditions is, however, made up for by a maximally even and comprehensive coverage of the recognized types and styles of meditative practice.

As regards their sources, the readings are of several types. Most of the textual selections are new translations from the original Pali, Chinese, etc. Most of the contemporary materials have already been published elsewhere, as book chapters or journal articles, and are reproduced here with permission (see Sources and Permissions). A few are published here for the first time. Some of the items have been abbreviated to varying degrees by deleting sections that seemed to have no direct bearing on meditation.

Each of the four sections is provided with an introduction, which supplies background to the readings it contains, and comments on their significance. The Notes section near the end of the book brings together the footnotes and references that originally accompanied many of the individual items, and includes also some editorial comments. Finally, there is a fairly detailed Index, which, together with the references in the Notes, will provide guidance for readers wishing to pursue particular topics in greater depth.

Rendering information about meditation accessible in this way is one aspect of the ongoing demystification of meditation. It is a contribution to the process whereby meditation is steadily losing its exotic, alien image and gaining recognition as an attainable and relevant skill for ordinary people. One of the preliminary stages on the meditative path is the gaining of an intellectual understanding of the nature and rationale of meditation. It is hoped that this collection of readings will do something to facilitate such understanding.

Section I

Pali Sources

INTRODUCTION

This first section presents some of the Buddha's most important teachings on meditation, as preserved in the Sutta Piṭaka of the Buddhist canon in Pali language.

The formerly widespread view that the Pali suttas (discourses) are a largely complete and reliable record of the Buddha's teaching can no longer be sustained. The Pali canon was not written down until the first century B.C., some five centuries after the death of the Buddha. Also, as the canon of the Theravāda (Teaching of the Elders), it represents just one of the many schools into which the Buddhist tradition had split by that time. It is, therefore, likely to be to some extent sectarian and unrepresentative of the original teaching. However, for the other schools of the Hīnayāna (the more conservative of the two major derivatives of early Buddhism) we have only a partial record, mainly in Chinese translations; and for the schools that constitute the Mahāyāna the available texts are in many cases demonstrably late creations, much of whose content cannot plausibly be attributed to the Buddha himself. It therefore remains true that the Pali suttas are a crucially important source of information on the basic teachings and practices of early Buddhism.

In reading the following sutta extracts, one has to bear in mind that they are modern translations of ancient texts and, as such, certainly fallible. This is particularly the case with the technical terminology. For example, the term *āsava*, here fairly literally translated "influence," has often been rendered by other translators as "deadly flood," "intoxicant," "canker," "defilement," and so on. The truth is that we are, in many cases, still far from sure what such technical terms really refer to, and how they ought to be translated. Another point to note is that some of the sutta translations offered here have been rendered more readable by deleting irrelevant material and abbreviating some repeated sections. Enough repetitions remain, however, to give a good idea of the often singsong style of the original texts.

While often repetitive and wordy in style, the texts are in many cases tantalizingly short on detail. They usually describe meditative practices only in broad outline, while giving little guidance on practical technique – hence the value of the later commentaries and modern meditation guides. Despite such difficulties, however, the eight sutta extracts presented here provide a wealth of essential information on the Buddha's meditative teaching. The first is, appropriately, from the first discourse the Buddha delivered following his enlightenment.

The Middle Way (Reading 1) is taken from the "Discourse that Set the Dharma-Wheel Turning." In it the Buddha provides some fundamental guidelines for practice and a straightforward statement of his most essential doctrines. First he speaks of the middle way, the path of practice that avoids the extremes of sensual indulgence on the one hand, and severe asceticism on the other. He identifies this way specifically as the noble eightfold path, a course of practice in eight stages, of which the last three relate explicitly to meditation. Then follows a brief introduction to the four noble truths: the existence of suffering (*dukkha*), the cause of suffering, the cessation of suffering, and the way of practice that brings about the cessation of suffering. That way of practice is then spelled out; it is again the noble eightfold path.

The path of practice, outlined briefly in the first teaching (Reading 1), is described in more detail in *The Eightfold Path Explained* (Reading 2), an extract from a discourse entitled "Analysis of the Truths." Of particular relevance here are the definitions given for those stages of the path that pertain to meditation, namely right effort, right mindfulness, and right concentration.

The Subduing of Thoughts (Reading 3), from a sutta of the same name, explains one aspect of the practice of right effort. It describes various techniques whereby the beginning meditator can gain control over "unwholesome" (or "unskilful") mental states and thereby become a "master of the pathways of thought."

As well as putting down unwholesome states, the practitioner of right effort seeks to cultivate wholesome states. A set of four such states is particularly recommended, namely: loving-kindness, compassion, empathic joy, and equanimity. These four, and the practice for developing them, are outlined briefly in *The Sublime States* (Reading 4), an extract from "The 'Lion's Roar' to the Udumbari-kans."

The Foundations of Mindfulness (Reading 5) is virtually the full text of two nearly identical discourses of the same name. In it the Buddha describes how the meditator develops mindfulness with respect to four objects: the body, feelings, mental states, and mental contents. Each of these four categories of mindfulness is described fully and clearly – though the description of the fourth, mindfulness of mental contents, raises serious problems of interpretation. Some present-day systems of meditative practice are based on a belief that the techniques described in this sutta are to be identified as *vipassanā-*

bhāvanā, insight meditation. While this understanding is perhaps an over-simplification, the value of mindfulness meditation is beyond question.

Along one line of development mindfulness practice leads to concentration; along another it leads to insight. For meditators proceeding in the direction of concentration, a practice strongly advocated by the Buddha is mindfulness based on the breathing (*ānāpāna-sati*). This practice is described in *Mindfulness of Breathing* (Reading 6), an extract from the discourse of the same name.

The Jhānas (Reading 7) describes the stages of progressively deepening mental concentration (*jhānas*) attainable through mindfulness of breathing and similar techniques. The source is the "Discourse on Effacement"; however, this is a stereotyped description, repeated with little variation in many different suttas. The present account covers all eight stages: four material jhānas followed by four non-material jhānas. In many suttas the last four are omitted, a situation suggesting that the non-material jhānas were not considered essential as a basis for the development of insight. In another variant version, a ninth stage, "cessation," is added.

The final item in this section, *The Meditator's Progress* (Reading 8), is extracted from the lengthy "Discourse on the Fruits of the Homeless Life." It describes the entire course of practice to be followed by the Buddhist practitioner, and coincides broadly with the noble eightfold path. The series of stages listed begins with the first hearing of the teaching and concludes with the attainment of enlightenment and liberation. Several early suttas set out the very same list of stages. A few others give a list that differs only in omitting three of the stages: supernormal powers, divine ear, and knowledge of others' minds. That shorter listing has the practitioner (including the Buddha himself on the night of his enlightenment) advancing directly from the jhānas to a set of three knowledges, namely: recollection of former existences, observing the death and rebirth of beings according to their karmas, and destruction of the influences. With the perfection of the third of these knowledges comes the ending of delusion and suffering, and the fulfilment of the spiritual life.

Some of the stages on the Buddhist path of practice appear, from the sutta descriptions, to be truly superhuman achievements – unless, perhaps, they are meant to be understood in some non-literal sense. Otherwise, however, the path is a series of clearly defined and seemingly attainable stages consisting, at the more advanced levels, in increasingly sophisticated types of meditative practice.

Reading 1

The Middle Way

From Dhamma-cakka-ppavattana Sutta

There are, monks, two extremes that a practitioner should avoid. One is attachment to sensual pleasures, which is low, common, worldly, unworthy, and without benefit. The other is attachment to self-mortification, which is painful, unworthy, and without benefit. Avoiding these two extremes, I have realized a middle way, which produces insight and knowledge, and which leads to serenity, supernormal knowledge, full enlightenment, and nirvana.

And what is this middle way that I have realized . . .? It is none other than this noble eightfold path, namely: right view, right thought, right speech, right action, right livelihood, right effort, right mindfulness, right concentration. This is the middle way that I have realized, which produces insight and knowledge, and which leads to serenity, supernormal knowledge, full enlightenment, and nirvana.

Now, this is the noble truth of suffering:[1] birth is suffering, ageing is suffering, sickness is suffering, death is suffering, association with what one dislikes is suffering, separation from what one likes is suffering, not getting what one desires is suffering. In short, the five clinging aggregates[2] are suffering.

This is the noble truth of the arising of suffering: desire which leads to rebirth, which is associated with passionate delight, which finds pleasure now here now there, namely desire for sense pleasures, desire for becoming, and desire for non-becoming.

This is the noble truth of the cessation of suffering: the total fading away and cessation of that very desire, giving it up, relinquishing it, release from it, non-attachment to it.

And this is the noble truth of the way to the cessation of suffering: it is none other than this noble eightfold path, namely: right view, right thought, right speech, right action, right livelihood, right effort, right mindfulness, right concentration.

The Eightfold Path Explained

From Sacca-vibhanga Sutta

What, monks, is the noble truth of the way to the cessation of suffering? It is none other than this noble eightfold path, namely: right view, right thought, right speech, right action, right livelihood, right effort, right mindfulness, right concentration.

And what is right view? It is knowledge of suffering, knowledge of the arising of suffering, knowledge of the cessation of suffering, and knowledge of the way to the cessation of suffering. This is called right view.

And what is right thought? Thought of renunciation, thought free from ill-will, thought free from harming. This is called right thought.

And what is right speech? Abstaining from lying, abstaining from slander, abstaining from harsh talk, abstaining from frivolous talk. This is called right speech.

And what is right action? Abstaining from killing, abstaining from stealing, abstaining from sexual misconduct. This is called right action.

And what is right livelihood? Here the noble disciple, giving up wrong livelihood, makes a living by right livelihood. This is called right livelihood.

And what is right effort? Here the monk arouses his will, puts forth effort, generates energy, exerts his mind, and strives to prevent the arising of evil and unwholesome mental states that have not yet arisen. He arouses his will . . . and strives to eliminate evil and unwholesome mental states that have already arisen. He arouses his will . . . and strives to generate wholesome mental states that have not yet arisen. He arouses his will, puts forth effort, generates energy, exerts his mind, and strives to maintain wholesome mental states that have already arisen, to keep them free of delusion, to develop, increase, cultivate, and perfect them. This is called right effort.

And what is right mindfulness? Here the monk remains

contemplating the body as body, resolute, aware and mindful, having put aside worldly desire and sadness; he remains contemplating feelings as feelings . . .; he remains contemplating mental states as mental states . . .; he remains contemplating mental objects as mental objects, resolute, aware and mindful, having put aside worldly desire and sadness. This is called right mindfulness.

And what is right concentration? Here, the monk, detached from sense-desires, detached from unwholesome states, enters and remains in the first *jhāna* (level of concentration), in which there is applied and sustained thinking,[3] together with joy and pleasure born of detachment. And through the subsiding of applied and sustained thinking, with the gaining of inner stillness and oneness of mind, he enters and remains in the second jhāna, which is without applied and sustained thinking, and in which there are joy and pleasure born of concentration. And through the fading away of joy, he remains equanimous, mindful and aware, and he experiences in his body the pleasure of which the noble ones say: "equanimous, mindful, and dwelling in pleasure," and thus he enters and remains in the third jhāna. And through the giving up of pleasure and pain, and through the previous disappearance of happiness and sadness, he enters and remains in the fourth jhāna, which is without pleasure and pain, and in which there is pure equanimity and mindfulness. This is called right concentration.

And that, monks, is the noble truth of the way to the cessation of suffering.

Reading 3

The Subduing of Thoughts

From Vitakka-santhāna Sutta

When a monk is pursuing higher mental states, there are five practices that he should attend to from time to time. What are these five?

If, owing to some mental image to which he is attending, there arise in him evil, unwholesome thoughts associated with desire, hatred, or delusion, then he should attend instead to some other image associated with what is wholesome. When he attends instead to some other image associated with what is wholesome, then those evil, unwholesome thoughts associated with desire, hatred, and delusion are eliminated and cease. And by eliminating them his mind becomes inwardly calmed, quiet, one-pointed, concentrated.

It is just like a skilled joiner or his apprentice using a thin peg to knock out, drive out, and remove a thick peg. In the same way, if, owing to some image to which he is attending, there arise in him evil, unwholesome thoughts, . . . by eliminating them his mind becomes inwardly calmed, quiet, one-pointed, concentrated.

If, while he is attending instead to that other image which is associated with what is wholesome, there still arise in him evil, unwholesome thoughts associated with desire, hatred, or delusion, then he should ponder the danger in those thoughts, reflecting: "These thoughts are unwholesome, blameworthy, and conducive to suffering." When he thus ponders the danger in those thoughts, then those evil, unwholesome thoughts associated with desire, hatred, and delusion are eliminated and cease. And by eliminating them his mind becomes inwardly calmed, quiet, one-pointed, concentrated.

It is just like a young man or woman fond of ornaments, who would be horrified, ashamed, and disgusted if the carcase of a snake or a dog or a human being were hung round their neck. In the same way, . . . his mind becomes inwardly calmed, quiet, one-pointed, concentrated.

If, while he is pondering the danger in those thoughts, there still arise in him evil, unwholesome thoughts associated with desire, hatred, or delusion, then he should try to ignore those thoughts, paying no attention to them. When he tries to ignore those thoughts, paying no attention to them, then those evil, unwholesome thoughts associated with desire, hatred, and delusion are eliminated and cease. And by eliminating them his mind becomes inwardly calmed, quiet, one-pointed, concentrated.

It is just like a man with good eyes who does not want to see certain objects that have come into view, who then either shuts his eyes or looks away. In the same way, . . . his mind becomes inwardly calmed, quiet, one-pointed, concentrated.

If, when he tries to ignore those thoughts, paying no attention to them, there still arise in him evil, unwholesome thoughts associated with desire, hatred, or delusion, then he should attend to calming the emotions related to those thoughts. When he attends to calming the emotions related to those thoughts, then those evil, unwholesome thoughts associated with desire, hatred, and delusion are eliminated and cease. And by eliminating them his mind becomes inwardly calmed, quiet, one-pointed, concentrated.

It is just like a man walking quickly who thinks: "Why am I walking quickly? What if I were to walk slowly?" and so walks slowly instead; and who then thinks: "Why am I walking slowly? What if I were to stand still? . . . What if I were to sit down? . . . What if I were to lie down?" and so he lies down; for by so doing he is replacing each more strenuous posture with a more relaxed one. In the same way, . . . his mind becomes inwardly calmed, quiet, one-pointed, concentrated.

If, when he attends to calming the emotions related to those thoughts, there still arise in him evil, unwholesome thoughts associated with desire, hatred, or delusion, then with teeth clenched and tongue pressed against the palate he should subdue, restrain, and suppress mental states with mental states. When with teeth clenched and tongue pressed against the palate he subdues, restrains, and suppresses mental states with mental states, then those evil, unwholesome thoughts associated with desire, hatred, and delusion are eliminated and cease. And by eliminating them his mind becomes inwardly calmed, quiet, one-pointed, concentrated.

It is just like a strong man who seizes a weaker one by the head or shoulders and subdues, restrains, and suppresses him. In the same way, if, when he attends to calming the emotions related to those thoughts, there still arise in him evil, unwholesome thoughts associated with desire, hatred, or delusion, then with teeth clenched and tongue pressed against the palate he should subdue, restrain, and suppress mental states with mental states. When with teeth clenched and tongue pressed against the palate he subdues, . . . his mind becomes inwardly calmed, quiet, one-pointed, concentrated.

When the monk does this, and his mind becomes inwardly calmed, quiet, one-pointed, concentrated, then he is called a master of the pathways of thought. He can then think such thoughts as he wishes to think, and not think thoughts that he does not wish to think. He has cut out desire, cast off the fetters, mastered conceit, and truly made an end of suffering.

The Four Sublime States

From Udumbarika-sīhanāda Sutta

He [the monk/meditator] selects a deserted place: in the forest, at the base of a tree, in a mountain cave or ravine, a charnel ground, a jungle thicket, or on a heap of straw in the open. Then, after having returned from the alms round and eaten his meal, he sits down with legs crossed and body erect, and establishes mindfulness in the present. Putting aside worldly desire, he remains with his mind free of desire, and purifies his mind of it. Putting aside ill-will and hatred, he remains with his mind free of hatred; and by cultivating compassion and benevolence for all living beings, he purifies his mind of ill-will and hatred. Putting aside slackness and drowsiness, he remains with his mind free of slackness and drowsiness; and by practising light-perception, mindfulness, and awareness, he purifies his mind of slackness and drowsiness. Putting aside distraction and worry, he remains undistracted; and with the mind inwardly calm, he purifies his mind of distraction and worry. Putting aside doubt, he remains with doubt left behind; and free of uncertainty as to what things are wholesome, he purifies his mind of doubt.

Having put aside these five hindrances,[4] and in order to weaken the mental defilements by means of insight, he remains causing his mind, filled with loving-kindness,[5] to pervade one quarter, then a second, then a third, then the fourth. In the same way he remains pervading the whole wide world, above, below, across, and everywhere with a mind filled with loving-kindness, abundant, grown great, beyond measure, free from hatred and ill-will.

And he remains causing his mind, filled with compassion, . . .

And he remains causing his mind, filled with empathic joy, . . .

And he remains causing his mind, filled with equanimity, to pervade one quarter, then a second, then a third, then the fourth. In the same way he remains pervading the whole wide world, above, below, across, and everywhere, with a mind filled with equanimity, abundant, grown great, beyond measure, free from hatred and ill-will.

Reading 5

The Foundations of Mindfulness

From Satipaṭṭhāna Sutta

There is, monks, this one way for purifying beings, overcoming sorrow and distress, eliminating pain and sadness, attaining the right path, and realizing nirvana, namely the four foundations of mindfulness.[6]

What are these four? Here, a monk remains observing the body as body, resolute, aware and mindful, having put aside worldly desire and sadness; he remains observing feelings as feelings . . .; he remains observing mental states as mental states . . .; he remains observing mental objects as mental objects, resolute, aware and mindful, having put aside worldly desire and sadness.

1. The Body

(a) The Breathing:[7] And how does the monk remain observing the body as body? In this case, the monk, having gone into the forest, or to the base of a tree, or to a deserted place, sits down with legs crossed and body erect, and establishes mindfulness in the present.

Mindfully he breathes in; mindfully he breathes out. When breathing in a long breath, he knows he is breathing in a long breath; and when breathing out a long breath, he knows he is breathing out a long breath. When breathing in a short breath, he knows he is breathing in a short breath; and when breathing out a short breath he knows he is breathing out a short breath. He practises experiencing the whole body while breathing in; . . . while breathing out. He practises calming the bodily activities while breathing in; . . . while breathing out.

He is just like a skilled turner or his apprentice who, when making a long turn, knows that he is making a long turn, and when making a short turn, knows that he is making a short turn. In the same way, the monk, when breathing in a long breath, knows that he is breathing in a long breath . . .

Thus he remains observing the body as body inwardly, or . . . outwardly, or . . . both inwardly and outwardly.[8] He remains observing the arising of phenomena[9] in the body, or the ceasing . . . , or the arising and ceasing of phenomena in the body. Or he is mindful that the body exists, just to the extent necessary for knowledge and awareness. And he remains detached, grasping at nothing in the world. This is how the monk remains observing the body as body.

(b) The Postures: Again, the monk when walking knows that he is walking, when standing still knows that he is standing still, when seated knows that he is seated, when lying down knows that he is lying down. However his body is disposed, he knows it. Thus he remains observing the body as body inwardly, . . . And he remains detached, grasping at nothing in the world. This is how the monk remains observing the body as body.

(c) Bodily Movements: Again, the monk acts with awareness in going back and forth, in looking ahead or behind, in bending and stretching, in wearing his robes and carrying his bowl, in eating and drinking, in chewing and swallowing, in defecating and urinating, in walking, standing, and sitting, in going to sleep and waking up, in speaking and keeping silent; always he acts with awareness. Thus he remains . . . observing the body as body.

(d) The Repulsiveness of the Body: Again, the monk reviews the body, upward from the soles of the feet and downward from the crown of the head, seeing it as a skinful of impurities of every sort; and he reflects: "This body is composed of hair, nails, teeth, skin, flesh, sinews, bones, marrow, kidneys, heart, liver, membranes, spleen, lungs, mesentery, bowels, stomach, excrement, bile, phlegm, pus, blood, sweat, fat, tears, serum, saliva, mucus, synovial fluid, and urine."

It is just like a sack with an opening at each end, filled with various kinds of grain, such as hill-paddy, paddy, beans, peas, sesame, and husked rice; and he is like a man with good eyes who opens it up and reflects: "This is hill-paddy, this is paddy, . . ." In the same way the monk reviews the body . . . and reflects: "This body is composed of hair, nails, . . . urine." Thus he remains . . . observing the body as body.

(e) The Elements:[10] Again, the monk reflects on the body, however located or disposed, in terms of the four elements: "This body is composed of the elements of earth, water, fire, and air." He is just like a skilled butcher or his apprentice, who has slaughtered a cow and sits at the intersection of four major roads dividing the portions among them. In the same way the monk reflects on the body . . . in terms of the four elements: ". . . earth, water, fire, and air." Thus he remains . . . observing the body as body.

(f-i) The Cemetery Meditations: Again, the monk compares his body to a corpse such as one might see thrown aside in a charnel ground, one, two, or three days dead, bloated, discoloured, decomposing; and he reflects: "My body is of a similar nature, a similar make-up, and is not above such a fate." Thus he remains . . .

Again, the monk compares his body to a corpse such as one might see thrown aside in a charnel ground, being fed upon by crows, hawks, vultures, dogs, jackals, or various small creatures; and he reflects: "My body is of a similar nature, a similar make-up, and is not above such a fate." Thus he remains . . .

Again, the monk compares his body to a corpse such as one might see thrown aside in a charnel ground, a skeleton with flesh and blood adhering and held together by sinews; or a skeleton without flesh but with blood adhering and held together by sinews; or a skeleton without flesh or blood but held together by sinews; or just bones scattered about in all directions – here a hand-bone, there a foot-bone, here a shin-bone, there a thigh-bone, here a hip-bone, there the spine, here the skull; and he reflects: "My body is of a similar nature, a similar make-up, and is not above such a fate." Thus he remains . . .

Again, the monk compares his body to a corpse such as one might see thrown aside in a charnel ground, bones whitened like seashells, or bones a year old in a heap, or bones decayed to dust; and he reflects: "My body is of a similar nature, a similar make-up, and is not above such a fate."

Thus he remains observing the body as body inwardly, or observing the body as body outwardly, or observing the body as body both inwardly and outwardly. He remains observing the arising of phenomena in the body, or the ceasing of phenomena in the body, or the arising and ceasing of phenomena in the body. Or he is mindful that the body exists, just to the extent necessary for knowledge and awareness. And he remains detached, grasping at nothing in the world. This is how the monk remains observing the body as body.

2. Feelings[11]

And how does the monk remain observing feelings as feelings? In this case the monk, on experiencing a pleasant feeling, knows he is experiencing a pleasant feeling; on experiencing a painful feeling, he knows he is experiencing a painful feeling; and on experiencing a feeling that is neither pleasant nor painful, he knows he is experiencing a feeling that is neither pleasant nor painful. On experiencing a pleasant physical feeling, he knows he is experiencing a pleasant physical feeling; . . . a pleasant non-physical feeling; . . . a painful physical feeling; . . . a painful non-physical feeling; . . . a physical feeling that is neither pleasant nor painful; and on experiencing a non-physical feeling that is neither pleasant nor painful, he knows he is experiencing a non-physical feeling that is neither pleasant nor painful.

Thus he remains observing feelings as feelings inwardly, or . . . outwardly, or . . . both inwardly and outwardly. He remains observing the arising of phenomena in feelings, or the ceasing . . ., or the arising and ceasing . . . . Or he is mindful that feelings exist, just to the extent necessary for knowledge and awareness. And he remains detached, grasping at nothing in the world. This is how the monk remains observing feelings as feelings.

3. Mental States[12]

And how does the monk remain observing mental states as mental states? In this case the monk knows a desiring mind as a desiring mind; he knows a mind without desire as a mind without desire.

He knows a hating mind as a hating mind; he knows a mind without hate as a mind without hate.

He knows . . . a deluded mind; . . . an undeluded mind.

. . . a cramped mind; . . . a scattered mind.

. . . a mind grown great; . . . a mind not grown great.

. . . a surpassable mind; . . . an unsurpassable mind.

. . . a concentrated mind; . . . an unconcentrated mind.

He knows a liberated mind as a liberated mind; he knows an unliberated mind as an unliberated mind.

Thus he remains observing mental states as mental states inwardly, or . . . outwardly, or . . . both inwardly and outwardly. He remains observing the arising of phenomena in mental states, or the ceasing . . ., or the arising and ceasing . . . . Or he is mindful that mental states exist, just to the extent necessary for knowledge and awareness.

And he remains detached, grasping at nothing in the world. This is how the monk remains observing mental states as mental states.

4. Mental Objects[13]

And how does the monk remain observing mental objects as mental objects?

(a) The Five Hindrances: In this case the monk remains observing mental objects as mental objects in terms of the five hindrances. And how does the monk remain observing mental objects as mental objects in terms of the five hindrances? If sensual desire is present within him, he knows that sensual desire is present within him; and if sensual desire is not present within him, he knows that sensual desire is not present within him. He knows how sensual desire that was not present comes to arise within him; and he knows how sensual desire that has arisen within him is eliminated; and he knows how sensual desire that has been eliminated will not arise again in the future.

If ill-will . . . slackness and drowsiness . . . distraction and worry . . . doubt is present within him, he knows that doubt is present within him; and if doubt is not present within him, he knows that doubt is not present within him. He knows how doubt that was not present comes to arise within him; and he knows how doubt that has arisen within him is eliminated; and he knows how doubt that has been eliminated will not arise again in the future.

Thus he remains observing mental objects as mental objects inwardly, or . . . outwardly, or . . . both inwardly and outwardly. He remains observing the arising of phenomena in mental objects, or the ceasing . . ., or the arising and ceasing . . . . Or he is mindful that mental objects exist, just to the extent necessary for knowledge and awareness. And he remains detached, grasping at nothing in the world. This is how the monk remains observing mental objects as mental objects in terms of the five hindrances.

(b) The Five Aggregates: Again, the monk remains observing mental objects as mental objects in terms of the five clinging aggregates. And how does the monk remain observing mental objects as mental objects in terms of the five clinging aggregates? In this case the monk reflects: Such is the body, such is the arising of the body, such is the passing away of the body; such is feeling . . .; such is perception . . .; such are the mental activities . . .; such is consciousness, such is the arising of consciousness, such is the passing away of consciousness.

Thus he remains observing mental objects as mental objects inwardly, or . . . outwardly, or . . . both inwardly and outwardly . . . in terms of the five clinging aggregates.

(c) The Six Sense-Bases: Again, the monk remains observing mental objects as mental objects in terms of the six internal and external sense-bases. And how . . .? In this case the monk knows the eye, and he knows visual objects, and he knows whatever fetter arises dependent on the two, and he knows how a fetter that had not arisen comes to arise, and he knows how a fetter that has arisen is eliminated, and he knows how a fetter that has been eliminated will not arise in the future. He knows the ear, and he knows sounds, . . . He knows the nose, and he knows odours, . . . He knows the tongue, and he knows tastes, . . . He knows the body, and he knows tactile objects, . . . He knows the mind,[14] and he knows mental objects, and he knows whatever fetter arises dependent on the two, and he knows how a fetter that had not arisen comes to arise, and he knows how a fetter that has arisen is eliminated, and he knows how a fetter that has been eliminated will not arise in the future.

Thus he remains observing mental objects as mental objects inwardly, or . . . outwardly, or . . . both inwardly and outwardly . . . in terms of the six internal and external sense-bases.

(d) The Seven Factors of Enlightenment: Again, the monk remains observing mental objects as mental objects in terms of the seven factors of enlightenment. And how . . .? In this case, if mindfulness is present within him, he knows that mindfulness is present within him; and if mindfulness is not present within him, he knows that mindfulness is not present within him; and he knows how mindfulness that was not present comes to arise within him; and he knows how mindfulness that has arisen within him comes to full development.

If investigation of the Dharma[15] . . . energy . . . joy . . . tranquillity . . . concentration . . . equanimity is present within him, he knows that equanimity is present within him; and if equanimity is not present within him, he knows that equanimity is not present within him; and he knows how equanimity that was not present comes to arise within him; and he knows how equanimity that has arisen within him comes to full development.

Thus he remains observing mental objects as mental objects inwardly, or . . . outwardly, or . . . both inwardly and outwardly . . . in terms of the seven factors of enlightenment.

(e) The Four Noble Truths: Again, the monk remains observing mental objects as mental objects in terms of the four noble truths. And how does the monk remain observing mental objects as mental objects in terms of the four noble truths? In this case the monk knows as it really is: This is suffering; he knows as it really is: This is the arising of suffering; he knows as it really is: This is cessation of suffering; he knows as it really is: This is the way of practice leading to the cessation of suffering.

Thus he remains observing mental objects as mental objects inwardly, or . . . outwardly, or . . . both inwardly and outwardly. He remains observing the arising of phenomena in mental objects, or the ceasing . . ., or the arising and ceasing of phenomena in mental objects. Or he is mindful that mental objects exist, just to the extent necessary for knowledge and awareness. And he remains detached, grasping at nothing in the world. This is how the monk remains observing mental objects as mental objects in terms of the four noble truths.

Anyone who cultivates these four foundations of mindfulness for seven years may expect one or the other of two results: either enlightenment here and now or, if there is some residue, the state of the non-returner.[16] Let alone seven years, anyone who cultivates these four foundations of mindfulness for six years . . . five years . . . four years . . . three years . . . two years . . . one year . . . seven months . . . one month . . . one week may expect one or the other of two results: either enlightenment here and now or, if there is some residue, the state of the non-returner.

Mindfulness of Breathing

From Ānāpāna-sati Sutta

Mindfulness of breathing, monks, if cultivated and much practised, is of great benefit, of great advantage. Mindfulness of breathing, if cultivated and much practised, brings to perfection the four foundations of mindfulness; the four foundations of mindfulness, if cultivated and much practised, bring to perfection the seven factors of enlightenment; the seven factors of enlightenment, if cultivated and much practised, bring to perfection liberation through insight.

And how is mindfulness of breathing cultivated? In this case a monk, having gone into the forest, or to the base of a tree, or to a deserted place, sits down with legs crossed and body erect, and establishes mindfulness in the present.

First Tetrad

Mindfully he breathes in; mindfully he breathes out.

1 When breathing in a long breath, he knows he is breathing in a long breath; and when breathing out a long breath, he knows he is breathing out a long breath.
2 When breathing in a short breath, he knows he is breathing in a short breath; and when breathing out a short breath, he knows he is breathing out a short breath.
3 He practises experiencing the whole body while breathing in; . . . while breathing out.
4 He practises calming the bodily activities while breathing in; . . . while breathing out.

Second Tetrad

5 He practises experiencing joy[17] while breathing in; . . . while breathing out.
6 He practises experiencing pleasure while breathing in; . . . while breathing out.
7 He practises experiencing the mental activities while breathing in; . . . while breathing out.
8 He practises calming the mental activities while breathing in; . . . while breathing out.

Third Tetrad

9 He practises experiencing the mind[18] while breathing in; . . . while breathing out.
10 He practises gladdening the mind while breathing in; . . . while breathing out.
11 He practises concentrating the mind while breathing in; . . . while breathing out.
12 He practises liberating the mind while breathing in; . . . while breathing out.

Fourth Tetrad

13 He practises observing impermanence while breathing in; . . . while breathing out.
14 He practises observing fading away[19] while breathing in; . . . while breathing out.
15 He practises observing cessation while breathing in; . . . while breathing out.
16 He practises observing relinquishment while breathing in; he practises observing relinquishment while breathing out.

The Four Foundations of Mindfulness

And how does mindfulness of breathing, if cultivated and much practised, bring to perfection the four foundations of mindfulness?

At any time that the monk, when breathing in or out a long or a short breath, knows he is breathing in or out a long or a short breath; and at any time that he practises experiencing the whole body or calming the bodily activities, while breathing in or while breathing out – at such a time he is observing the body as body, resolute, aware and mindful, having put aside worldly desire and sadness; because, I say, in- and out-breathing is one of the activities of the body.

At any time that the monk practises experiencing joy, or experiencing pleasure, or experiencing the mental activities, or calming the mental activities, while breathing in or while breathing out – at such a time he is observing feelings as feelings, resolute, aware and mindful, having put aside worldly desire and sadness; because, I say, full attention to in- and out-breathing is one of the feelings.

At any time that the monk practises experiencing the mind, or gladdening the mind, or concentrating the mind, or liberating the mind, while breathing in or while breathing out – at such a time he is observing mental states as mental states, resolute, aware and mindful, having put aside worldly desire and sadness; because, I say, without mindfulness and awareness one cannot cultivate mindfulness of in- and out-breathing.

At any time that the monk practises observing impermanence, or fading away, or cessation, or relinquishment, while breathing in or while breathing out – at such a time he is observing mental objects as mental objects, resolute, aware and mindful, having put aside worldly desire and sadness; because, I say, having seen with insight the giving up of desire and sadness, he becomes one who looks on with perfect equanimity.

In this way mindfulness of breathing, if cultivated and much practised, brings to perfection the four foundations of mindfulness.[20]

Reading 7

The Jhānas

From Sallekha Sutta

Detached from sense-desires, detached from unwholesome states, a monk enters and remains in the first jhāna (level of concentration), in which there is applied and sustained thinking, together with joy and pleasure born of detachment . . . .

And through the subsiding of applied and sustained thinking, with the gaining of inner stillness and oneness of mind, he enters and remains in the second jhāna, which is without applied and sustained thinking, and in which there are joy and pleasure born of concentration . . . .

And through the fading away of joy, he remains equanimous, mindful and aware, and he experiences in his body the pleasure of which the noble ones say: "equanimous, mindful, and dwelling in pleasure," and thus he enters and remains in the third jhāna . . . .

And through the giving up of pleasure and pain, and through the previous disappearance of happiness and sadness, he enters and remains in the fourth jhāna, which is without pleasure and pain, and in which there is pure equanimity and mindfulness . . . .

And, through the complete transcending of material perceptions, through the disappearance of contact-perceptions, through non-attention to variety-perceptions, aware that space is endless, he enters and remains in the realm of endless space . . . .

And through the complete transcending of the realm of endless space, aware that consciousness is endless, he enters and remains in the realm of endless consciousness . . . .

And through the complete transcending of the realm of endless consciousness, aware that nothing exists, he enters and remains in the realm of nothingness . . . .

And through the complete transcending of the realm of nothingness, he enters and remains in the realm of neither perception nor non-perception.[21]

The Meditator's Progress

From Sāmañña-phala Sutta

Now, there appears in the world an accomplished one, an arahant, a fully-enlightened being, . . . a blessed one, a buddha. He is one who has, through his own super-knowledge, fully realised this world . . . and he proclaims it. He teaches, in both spirit and letter, the Dharma, which is excellent in its beginning, middle, and end; and he sets forth the fully perfected, pure, holy life.

This Dharma is heard by a householder, or a householder's son, or a person born into some family or other. On hearing it that person comes to have faith in the Buddha. And having gained faith, he reflects: "The household life is a narrow, dusty way; the homeless life is free as the air. It is not easy for one living as a householder to lead the holy life, perfect and pure like a polished conch-shell. What if I were to shave off my hair and beard, put on yellow robes, and go forth from the household life into the homeless life?" Then, after some time, he gives up his property, great or small, leaves his circle of relatives, great or small, shaves off his hair and beard, puts on yellow robes, and goes forth from the household life into the homeless life.

Having gone forth in this way, he lives according to the monastic rules. He maintains right behaviour, seeing danger in the slightest transgression, observing and practising the rules he has adopted concerning activities of body and speech. He lives a wholesome and pure life: he is equipped with morality, his sense doors are guarded, he is equipped with mindfulness and awareness, and he is contented.

How is that monk equipped with morality? Giving up killing, he lives abstaining from killing, renouncing the club and the sword, scrupulous and compassionate, concerned for the welfare of all living beings. This is part of his morality. Abstaining from taking of what has not been given, . . . abstaining from unchastity, . . . [and so on, through a long list of moral restraints].

Then the monk, being thus equipped with morality, perceives no danger from any quarter, such is his moral restraint. He is just like a duly anointed warrior king who has conquered his enemies and consequently perceives no danger from any quarter. In the same way the monk, being thus equipped with morality, perceives no danger from any quarter, such is his moral restraint. Equipped with this noble morality, he experiences pure happiness in himself. This is how he becomes equipped with morality.

How does he guard the sense-doors? On seeing a visible object with the eye, he does not grasp at that object's major features nor at its secondary characteristics. If he were to leave the eye-faculty unguarded, then evil, unwholesome states such as desire and sadness would overwhelm him; he therefore practises guarding the eye-faculty, maintaining and cultivating restraint of the eye-faculty. On hearing a sound with the ear, . . . on smelling an odour with the nose, . . . on tasting a flavour with the tongue, . . . on sensing a tactile object with the body, . . . on becoming conscious of an image with the mind, he does not grasp at its major features nor at its secondary characteristics, . . . maintaining and cultivating restraint of the mind-faculty. Equipped with this noble sense restraint, he experiences pure happiness in himself. This is how he guards the sense doors.

How does he become equipped with mindfulness and awareness?[22] He acts with awareness in going back and forth, in looking ahead or behind, in bending and stretching, in wearing his robes and carrying his bowl, in eating and drinking, in chewing and swallowing, in defecating and urinating, in walking, standing, and sitting, in going to sleep and waking up, in speaking and keeping silent – always he acts with awareness. This is how he is equipped with mindfulness and awareness.

How is he contented? He is satisfied with his robes to protect his body and with almsfood to satisfy his stomach, and wherever he goes he takes them with him. Just like a bird flying here and there burdened by nothing but its wings, so the monk is satisfied . . . This is how he is contented.

Then, equipped with this noble morality, with this noble restraint of the senses, with this noble mindfulness and awareness, with this noble contentment, he selects an isolated dwelling place: in the forest, at the base of a tree, in a mountain cave or ravine, a charnel ground, a jungle thicket, or on a heap of straw in the open. Then, having eaten after returning from the alms round, he sits down with legs crossed and body erect, and establishes mindfulness in the present. Putting aside worldly desire, he remains with his mind free of desire, and purifies his mind of it. Putting aside ill-will and hatred, he remains with his mind free of hatred; and by cultivating compassion and benevolence for all living beings he purifies his mind of ill-will and hatred. Putting aside slackness and drowsiness, he remains with his mind free of slackness and drowsiness; and by developing light-perception and mindfulness and awareness, he purifies his mind of slackness and drowsiness. Putting aside distraction and worry, he remains undistracted, and with the mind inwardly calm, he purifies his mind of distraction and worry. Putting aside doubt, he remains with doubt left behind; and free of uncertainty as to what things are wholesome, he purifies his mind of doubt.

And once he has put aside these five hindrances, gladness arises in him. From gladness comes joy; with joy in his mind, his body becomes tranquil; with his body tranquil, he feels pleasure; and feeling pleasure, his mind becomes concentrated.

Detached from sense-desires, detached from unwholesome states, he enters and remains in the first jhāna, in which there is applied and sustained thinking, together with joy and pleasure born of detachment. And he suffuses his body with that detachment-born joy and pleasure; he soaks, fills, and permeates it, so that there is no spot in his entire frame that is not touched by that detachment-born joy and pleasure.

It is just like a skilled bath attendant or his apprentice, kneading soap-powder together with water in a basin, and forming from them one lathery mass, with the water so mixed into the soap that none of it escapes. In the same way the monk suffuses his body . . . so that there is no spot in his entire frame that is not touched by that detachment-born joy and pleasure.

And through the subsiding of applied and sustained thinking, with the gaining of inner stillness and oneness of mind, he enters and remains in the second jhāna, which is without applied and sustained thinking, and in which there are joy and pleasure born of concentration. And he suffuses his body . . . so that there is no spot in his entire frame that is not touched by that concentration-born joy and pleasure.

It is just like a deep pool fed by a spring beneath, which has no inflow from north, south, east, or west, and into which the rain-god sends down no seasonal showers; and the spring beneath suffuses the pool with cool water; it soaks, fills, and permeates it, so that there is no spot in the entire pool that is not touched by that cool spring water. In the same way the monk suffuses his body . . . so that there is no spot in his entire frame that is not touched by that concentration-born joy and pleasure.

And through the fading away of joy, he remains equanimous, mindful and aware, and he experiences in his body the pleasure of which the noble ones say: "equanimous, mindful, and remaining in pleasure," and thus he enters and remains in the third jhāna. And he suffuses his body . . . so that there is no spot in his entire frame that is not touched by that pleasure that is free of joy.

It is just like a pond with lotuses, blue, red, or white, which are born in the water, growing in the water, never removed from the water, and fed from the water's depths, so that they are suffused with the cool water . . . In the same way the monk suffuses his body . . . so that there is no spot in his entire frame that is not touched by that pleasure that is free of joy.

And, through giving up pleasure and pain, and through the previous disappearance of happiness and sadness, he enters and remains in the fourth jhāna, which is without pleasure and pain, and in which there is pure equanimity and mindfulness. And he sits suffusing his body . . . so that there is no spot in his entire frame that is not touched by that mental purity and clarity.

It is just like a man sitting wrapped from head to foot in a white robe, so that there is no part of his body that is not touched by that robe. In the same way the monk sits suffusing his body . . . so that there is no spot in his entire frame that is not touched by that mental purity and clarity.

With his mind thus concentrated, purified, clear, unblemished, free of impurities, supple, ready for work, firm, and imperturbable, he applies and directs his mind to knowledge and vision. And he knows: "This body of mine is physical, composed of the four elements, born of mother and father, sustained on rice and gruel, an impermanent thing, susceptible to injury, wear and tear, breaking up, and destruction; and this consciousness of mine is bound to it and dependent upon it."

It is just like a gem, a beryl, pure, excellent, with eight facets, well cut, clear, transparent, flawless, perfect in every respect, which is strung on a string coloured blue, yellow, red, white, or orange. A man with good eyes, taking it in his hand, would know: "This is a gem, . . . strung on a string . . . " In the same way, the monk, with his mind thus concentrated, . . . imperturbable, applies and directs his mind to knowledge and vision. And he knows: "This body of mine is physical, . . . and this consciousness of mine is bound to it and dependent upon it."

And with his mind thus concentrated, . . . imperturbable, he applies and directs his mind to the producing of a mind-made body. Out of this body he produces another body, having form, mind-made, complete in all its limbs and parts.

It is just like a man drawing out a reed from its sheath; that man would know: "This is the reed, this is the sheath. The reed and the sheath are different things. The reed has been drawn from the sheath." Again, it is like a man drawing a sword from its scabbard . . . . Again, it is like a man drawing a snake from its slough . . . . In the same way the monk, with his mind thus concentrated, . . . imperturbable, applies and directs his mind to the producing of a mind-made body . . . complete in all its limbs and parts.

And with his mind thus concentrated, . . . imperturbable, he applies and directs his mind to the supernormal powers. He manifests the various powers: being one, he becomes many, or being many, he becomes one; he becomes visible or invisible; he passes unhindered through walls, ramparts, and mountains as if passing through air; he dives into the ground and emerges from it as if it were water; he walks on water without sinking, as if on dry land; sitting cross-legged, he flies through the air like a bird on the wing; he touches and strokes with his hand the sun and moon, mighty and powerful though they are; and he even reaches with his body as far as the Brahma realm.

It is just like a skilful potter or his apprentice, who can produce from well-prepared clay whatever kind of bowl he chooses; or like a skilful ivory-carver or his apprentice, who can produce from well-prepared ivory whatever kind of ivory object he chooses; or like a skilful goldsmith or his apprentice, who can produce from well-prepared gold whatever kind of gold article he chooses. In the same way the monk with his mind thus concentrated, . . . imperturbable, applies and directs his mind to the supernormal powers . . .

And with his mind thus concentrated, . . . imperturbable, he applies and directs his mind to the divine ear. With the divine ear, which is pure and superhuman, he hears sounds both divine and human, whether far or near.

It is just like a man going along a highway who hears the sound of a large drum, a small drum, a conch trumpet, cymbals, or a kettle-drum; and he knows: "That is a large drum, . . . a kettle-drum." In the same way the monk, with his mind thus concentrated, . . ., imperturbable, applies and directs his mind to the divine ear . . . .

And with his mind thus concentrated, . . . imperturbable, he applies and directs his mind to the knowledge that penetrates minds.

With his own mind he knows and penetrates the minds of other beings, other persons.[23]

He knows a desiring mind as a desiring mind; he knows a mind without desire as a mind without desire.

He knows a hating mind as a hating mind; he knows a mind without hate as a mind without hate.

He knows . . . a deluded mind; . . . an undeluded mind.

. . . a cramped mind; . . . a scattered mind.

. . . a mind grown great; . . . a mind not grown great.

. . . a surpassable mind; . . . an unsurpassable mind.

. . . a concentrated mind; . . . an unconcentrated mind.

He knows a liberated mind as a liberated mind; he knows an unliberated mind as an unliberated mind.

It is just like a woman, or a man, or a lad, young and fond of their appearance, examining their face reflected in a brightly polished mirror, or in clear water in a vessel: if there was a blemish on their face, they would know it. In the same way the monk, with his mind thus concentrated, . . . imperturbable, applies and directs his mind to the knowledge that penetrates minds . . . .

And with his mind thus concentrated, . . . imperturbable, he applies and directs his mind to the knowledge consisting in recollection of former existences.[24] He recollects various former existences, thus: one birth, two births, three . . . four . . . five . . . ten . . . twenty . . . thirty . . . forty . . . fifty . . . a hundred . . . a thousand . . . a hundred thousand births, and many an eon of integration and many an eon of disintegration and many an eon of integration-and-disintegration, knowing: "I had such and such a name, I was of such and such a clan and of such and such a caste, and I ate such and such food. I had such and such pleasant and painful experiences, and my life ended in such and such a way. Passing away there, I arose in another state where I had such and such a name, . . . and my life ended in such and such a way. Passing away there, I arose here." Thus he recollects many former existences in all their modes and details.

It is just like a man going from his own village to another, from that to yet another, and from there returning to his home village. He would know: "I went from my own village to that other one, where I stood or sat in such and such a way, spoke or remained silent in such and such a way; and from that village I went to another, where I stood or sat in such and such a way, spoke or remained silent in such and such a way; and from there I have just returned here to my own village." In the same way the monk with his mind concentrated, . . .

imperturbable, applies and directs his mind to the knowledge consisting in recollection of former existences . . . .

And with his mind thus concentrated, . . . imperturbable, he applies and directs his mind to the knowledge of the passing away and arising of beings. With the divine eye, which is pure and superhuman, he sees beings as they pass away and as they arise. He perceives that beings are lowly or excellent, beautiful or ugly, well off or badly off, according to the consequences of their deeds; and he reflects: "Indeed, these beings who had wrong conduct of body, speech, and mind, who scoffed at the noble ones, who held wrong views and performed actions based on wrong views – they, after the breaking up of the body, after death, have arisen in a sorrowful state, a bad destiny, the abyss, hell. But these other beings who had right conduct of body, speech, and mind, who did not scoff at the noble ones, who held right views and performed actions based on right views – they, after the breaking up of the body, after death, have arisen in a good state, a heavenly realm." Thus, with the divine eye, which is pure and superhuman, he sees beings as they pass away and as they arise. He perceives that beings are lowly or excellent, beautiful or ugly, well off or badly off, according to the consequences of their deeds.

It is just like a man with good eyes standing in a tall building at a crossroads, who can watch the people entering or leaving the houses, walking in the street, or sitting in the middle of the crossroads; he would know: "These people are entering or leaving . . . . " In the same way a monk with his mind thus concentrated, . . . imperturbable, applies and directs his mind to the knowledge of the passing away and arising of beings . . . .

And with his mind thus concentrated, . . . imperturbable, he applies and directs his mind to the knowledge that destroys the influences.[25] He knows as it really is: "This is suffering, this is the arising of suffering, this is the cessation of suffering, this is the path leading to the cessation of suffering." He knows as it really is: "These are the influences, this is the arising of the influences, this is the cessation of the influences, this is the path leading to the cessation of the influences." Knowing thus, seeing thus, his mind is freed from the influence of desire . . . from the influence of becoming . . . from the influence of ignorance. In freedom the knowledge arises: "I am freed"; and he knows: "Destroyed is birth, lived is the holy life, done is what was to be done, there is no more of being thus and thus."

It is just like a man with good eyes standing on the shore of a clear, transparent mountain lake, and able to see the clams and shells, the gravel and pebbles, and the shoals of fish both moving and at rest; he would know: "In this clear, transparent mountain lake there are clams and shells . . . " In the same way the monk, with mind concentrated, purified, clear, unblemished, free of impurities, supple, ready for work, firm, and imperturbable, applies and directs his mind to the knowledge that destroys the influences, . . . and he knows: "Destroyed is birth, lived is the holy life, done is what was to be done, there is no more of being thus and thus."[26]

Section II

Classical Masters

INTRODUCTION

This section presents extracts from the writings of six classical authorities on meditation. They represent a wide range of Buddhist schools: Theravāda, Mādhyamika, Tiantai, Sōtō Zen, Rinzai Zen, and Gelugpa.

The first, *Concentration on the Earth Disk* (Reading 9), is by the great fifth-century commentator Buddhaghosa. Born in India a thousand years after the Buddha's time, Buddhaghosa spent much of his life in Sri Lanka. There he wrote his *Path of Purification* (*Visuddhimagga*), a systematic exposition of the entire Buddhist path of practice as understood in the Theravāda. In the section reproduced here Buddhaghosa describes a concentration technique based on gazing at a specially prepared disk or *kasiṇa*. Such disks are rarely used at the present day; however, the principal meditative stages described by Buddhaghosa are familiar to competent practitioners of most concentration techniques.

The author/compiler of the next item, *Self-Protection through Mindfulness* (Reading 10), is Śāntideva, an eighth-century Indian master. Śāntideva belonged to the Mādhyamika, a Mahāyāna school that is usually identified more with philosophical argumentation than with meditation. However, in his *Compendium of Training* (*Śikṣā-samuccaya*), from which this extract is taken, he says much about meditation. Here he is discussing the practice of mindfulness, explaining it with the aid of quotations from earlier Mahāyāna texts. Śāntideva's account of the four foundations of mindfulness differs slightly from that given in the Pali texts, particularly as regards mindfulness of the body and of dharmas.

Zhiyi (or Chih-I), the author of *Calm and Insight* (Reading 11), was a founding father of the Tiantai school of Buddhism in sixth-century China. His was a syncretic teaching, which brought together elements from all the major schools of his day. Consequently his writings cover a wide range of practices, including devotion, symbolic ritual, and – as in the present extract – meditation for calm and insight (*samatha* and *vipassanā*). The extract is from his manual entitled *Introduction to Calm and Insight*. It explains how these two aspects of the practice may be applied separately or in combination, and in two different situations: while seated in formal meditation and while engaged in everyday activities.

The next two items represent the two major schools within the Zen tradition: Sōtō and Rinzai. Both are brief, in true Zen style. The first, *Seated Meditation* (Reading 12), is by Dōgen, the thirteenth-century Japanese monk who learned Sōtō practice in China and then introduced it into his homeland. The section quoted is from the earliest and most authentic version of his *Fukan Zazen Gi* (*Teachings for the Promotion of Seated Meditation*). It comprises a set of instructions for the practice of *zazen*, seated meditation. Initially straight-forward and explicit, the instructions become increasingly obscure and meagre as they move from concentration to insight.

The other major Zen sect, Rinzai, is well known for its emphasis on the *kōan*, a type of cryptic riddle that serves as meditation object. An early and still widely used collection of kōans is *Mumonkan* (*The Gateless Gateway*) compiled in the thirteenth century by the Chinese monk Mumon (Wumen). It contains forty-eight kōans, each accompanied by Mumon's no less cryptic comment and verse. *Some Zen Kōans* (Reading 13) presents four representative examples.

Tibet, where Buddhism first became established in the seventh century, is widely thought of as the heartland of Buddhist meditative practice. *Fastening the Mind* (Reading 14) is representative of one of the major Tibetan meditative traditions, that of the Gelugpa. It is by the great master Tsongkhapa, who flourished in the late fourteenth and early fifteenth centuries. Tsongkhapa studied and practised in all the existing Tibetan schools of Buddhism before founding his new, reformed school, the Gelugpa. One of his most significant writings is his *Lamrim Chenmo*, or *Great Book on the Stages of the Path*. This is a long, detailed, and sometimes difficult exposition of the path to enlightenment according to his reformed understanding. The section reproduced here deals with the fundamental meditative practice of concentration, or "fastening the mind."

Of the practices described in these six extracts some, such as kasiṇa gazing and the kōan, are not at all well documented in the suttas/sūtras, which purportedly record the Buddha's original teaching. The appearance of such practices in these later works can be interpreted in various ways. It may be that these practices were indeed taught by the Buddha, but were passed on only orally, from teacher to disciple, in a special transmission outside the scriptures. Or it may be that such practices are simply later developments introduced by innovative teachers in response to specific needs. The latter possibility does not necessarily diminish the value of such practices as means to the two major goals of Buddhist meditation: mental stillness or samatha, and liberating insight or vipassanā.

Reading 9

Concentration on the Earth Disk

Buddhaghosa

A monk who has thus severed the lesser impediments, should, after having returned from the alms round, eaten his meal, and shaken off the drowsiness due to the meal, sit down comfortably in a secluded place and apprehend the sign of earth, whether artificial or natural.

He should sit on a well-covered chair with legs one span and four fingers high, placed two and a half cubits from the disk.[27] For if he sits further away than that, he will not see the disk clearly; and if he sits closer he will see the defects in the disk. If he sits on a higher seat, he will have to bend his neck to look at the disk; and if he sits on a lower one, his knees will ache.

Having seated himself in the manner described, he should reflect on the dangers inherent in sense desires, for example thinking: "Sense desires give no satisfaction." In this way he should arouse in himself a longing to escape from sense desires, to practise the renunciation which is the way out of all suffering. He should then arouse joy and happiness by recollecting the virtues of Buddha, Dharma, and Sangha; then respect by reflecting: "Now this is the way of renunciation followed by all buddhas, silent buddhas, and their noble disciples"; and then enthusiasm by reflecting: "Through this practice I shall surely come to taste the bliss of emancipation." After that he should, with his eyes partly open, apprehend and develop the sign.[28]

If he opens his eyes too wide, they will become fatigued and the disk will be too clearly visible, which will prevent the sign becoming apparent to him. If he does not open them wide enough, the disk will not be sufficiently clear and his mind will become drowsy, which will also prevent the sign from becoming apparent to him. So he should keep his eyes partly open and, as if looking at his face in a mirror, apprehend and develop the sign.

The Acquired Sign

The colour of the disk should not be considered; nor should its characteristics be attended to. While not entirely ignoring the colour, the meditator should fix his mind principally on the concept of earth, recognizing the colour as a secondary property of the physical entity. That concept can be called by any name for earth that one likes . . . . The most obvious name is "earth" itself; so the concept can be developed by repeating, "earth, earth."

The meditator should reflect on the disk now with the eyes open, now with them shut. And he should go on developing it in this way a hundred times, a thousand times, and more, until the acquired sign (*uggaha-nimitta*) arises. The acquired sign is said to have arisen when, through practising in this way, he is able to see the disk just as clearly with his eyes shut as with them open. Once the acquired sign has arisen, he should move from the original meditation place to his quarters and continue his sitting there.

The Counterpart Sign

As he continues to develop the acquired sign, eventually the hindrances are suppressed, the defilements subside, the mind attains access concentration (*upacāra-samādhi*), and the counterpart sign (*paṭibhāga-nimitta*) arises.

The counterpart sign differs from the earlier acquired sign in the following way. In the acquired sign any defect in the disk is visible. The counterpart sign, however, appears a hundred times, a thousand times more pure, seeming to emerge from the acquired sign like a circular mirror being drawn from its case, or like a well-polished mother-of-pearl dish, or like the full moon emerging from behind a cloud, or like cranes against a rain cloud. The counterpart sign has no outward appearance or location, otherwise it would be visible to the eye, gross, susceptible of comprehension, and possessed of the three characteristics.[29] But it is not like that; for it is merely an appearance, born of perception in one who has attained concentration. With its arising the hindrances are quite suppressed, the defilements subside, and the mind attains access concentration.

Two Kinds of Concentration

Here concentration is of two kinds: access concentration (*upacāra-samādhi*) and fixed concentration (*appanā-samādhi*). The mind becomes concentrated in two degrees: at the level of access and at the level of attainment. It achieves concentration at the level of access by abandoning the hindrances, and at the level of attainment by manifesting the jhāna factors.[30] These two kinds of concentration differ in the following way. In access concentration the jhāna factors are not strong; and because they are not strong, the mind in access concentration sometimes is focused on the sign as object and sometimes lapses into the stream of becoming (bhavanga).[31] It is just like a young child who, when lifted up and stood on its feet, repeatedly falls down again. In fixed concentration, however, the factors are strong; and because they are strong, the mind in fixed concentration, having once cut off the stream of becoming, can maintain itself for a whole night and day, with a continuum of wholesome impulsions (javana).[32] It is just like a strong man who, rising from his seat, can remain standing for a whole day.

Protecting the Sign

The arising of the counterpart sign, which comes together with access concentration, is very difficult to achieve. So if the meditator is able to attain fixed concentration in the same sitting by prolonging the sign, that is excellent. If not, then he must protect the sign diligently as if it were the fetus of a great monarch.

So guard the sign, nor count the cost,
And what is gained will not be lost.
Who fails to have this guard maintained
Will lose each time what he has gained.[33]

For one who practises in this way, assiduously nurturing the sign, it will not be long before fixed concentration is achieved.

Ten Skills in Fixed Concentration

However, should this practice not produce the result, then the meditator should develop ten kinds of skill in fixed concentration, as follows:

1 making the physical basis clean,
2 maintaining balanced faculties,
3 developing skill regarding the sign,
4 exerting the mind when it should be exerted,
5 restraining the mind when it should be restrained,

6 encouraging the mind when it should be encouraged,
7 viewing the mind with equanimity when it should be viewed with
  equanimity,
8 avoiding unconcentrated people,
9 associating with concentrated people,
10 dedication to the practice.

Mechanism of Fixed Concentration

While he is thus directing his mind to the sign, he realizes that fixed concentration is about to be attained. Then, through the constant repeating of "earth, earth," there arises mind-door adverting, having that same earth disk as its object and cutting off the stream of becoming. After that come either four or five impulsions having the same object. The last of them is an impulsion of the material (*rūpa*) sphere; the others are of the sense (*kāma*) sphere, but with stronger than normal applied thought, sustained thought, joy, pleasure, and mental one-pointedness.[34]

The names [of the first four, or three, impulsions] are: "preliminary" (*parikamma*), because it is preliminary to fixed concentration; "access" (*upacāra*) because it is near to fixed concentration, or takes place in its vicinity; "conformity" (*anuloma*) because it conforms to what precedes the "preliminary" and to the fixed concentration that will follow; and "change-of-lineage" (*gotrabhū*) for the last of them because it transcends the inferior lineage and brings about the exalted lineage. So, to state it in full, the names are *either*: (1) preliminary, (2) access, (3) conformity, (4) change-of-lineage, (5) fixed concentration; *or*: (1) access, (2) conformity, (3) change-of-lineage, (4) fixed concentration. Thus fixed concentration is either the fourth or the fifth stage, according as insight is rapid or sluggish. Thereafter the impulsions cease and the stream of becoming resumes.

The First Jhāna

At this point, "detached from sense-desires, detached from unwholesome states, he enters and remains in the first jhāna, in which there is applied and sustained thought (*vitakka-vicāra*) together with joy (*pīti*) and pleasure (*sukha*) born of detachment." And so he attains the first jhāna, which has eliminated five factors,[35] is endowed with five factors, is excellent in three ways, possesses ten characteristics, and is based on the earth disk.

With respect to the first jhāna, the meditator should acquire five kinds of mastery: mastery in adverting, attaining, determining, emerging, and reviewing. Mastery in adverting means that he adverts to the first jhāna wherever, whenever, and for however long, he wishes; and he has no difficulty in adverting to it. Mastery in attaining means that he attains the first jhāna wherever, . . . and he has no difficulty in attaining it. And mastery in determining, emerging, and reviewing are to be similarly understood.

The meaning of this is explained as follows. When he emerges from the first jhāna, there is first adverting to applied thought (*vitakka*), cutting off the stream of becoming; and immediately following that adverting, there arise either four or five impulsions having that applied thought as object; and then there are two arisings of the stream of becoming. Next comes adverting with sustained thought (*vicāra*) as object, followed by impulsions in the manner just described. When he is able to direct his mind uninterruptedly in this way to all five jhāna factors, then mastery in adverting has been achieved. This mastery was perfected in the Blessed One's Twin Miracle. Others have attained it on occasion. There is no quicker mastery in adverting than this.

Mastery in attaining is exemplified in the ability of the venerable Mahā-Moggallāna to enter jhāna quickly, as when he tamed the serpent king, Nandopananda.

Mastery in determining is the ability to determine the duration of the jhāna, e.g. for exactly a finger-snap or exactly ten finger-snaps.

Mastery in emerging is the corresponding ability to emerge from jhāna promptly.

Mastery in reviewing has already been mentioned under mastery in adverting, for the reviewing impulsions are those that arise immediately following the adverting impulsions mentioned there.

When he has once achieved these five kinds of mastery, then on emerging from the now familiar first jhāna he is able to see faults in it. He realizes that the attainment is threatened by the proximity of the hindrances, and that its factors are weakened by the grossness of applied and sustained thought (*vitakka-vicāra*). He should then reflect that the second jhāna is more calm, and, giving up his attachment to the first jhāna, he should set about attaining the second.

The Second Jhāna

When he emerges from the first jhāna, and reviews its jhāna factors with mindfulness and awareness, applied and sustained thought appear gross to him while joy, pleasure, and mental one-pointedness (*pīti, sukha, cittekaggatā*) appear calm. Then he repeatedly brings to mind the same sign, "earth, earth," in order to eliminate the gross factors and develop the calm factors, and he realizes that the second jhāna is about to be attained. Then there arises mind-door adverting having that same earth disk as its object and cutting off the stream of becoming. After that come either four or five impulsions having the same object. The last of them is an impulsion of the material sphere belonging to the second jhāna; the others are of the sense sphere, as already stated.

And at this point, "through the subsiding of applied and sustained thought, with the gaining of inner stillness and oneness of mind, he enters and remains in the second jhāna, which is without applied and sustained thought, and in which there are joy and pleasure born of concentration." And so he attains the second jhāna, which has eliminated two factors, is endowed with three factors, is excellent in three ways, possesses ten characteristics, and is based on the earth disk.

Once this has been attained in this way, and he has achieved mastery in the five ways already described, then on emerging from the now familiar second jhāna he is able to see faults in it. He realizes that the attainment is threatened by the proximity of applied and sustained thought, and that its factors are weakened by the grossness of joy (*pīti*) . . . . He should then reflect that the third jhāna is more calm, and, giving up his attachment to the second jhāna, he should set about attaining the third.

The Third Jhāna

When he emerges from the second jhāna, and reviews its jhāna factors with mindfulness and awareness, joy appears gross to him while pleasure and mental one-pointedness appear calm. Then he repeatedly brings to mind the same sign, "earth, earth," in order to eliminate the gross factors and develop the calm factors, and he realizes that the third jhāna is about to be attained. Then there arises mind-door adverting having that same earth disk as its object and cutting off the stream of becoming. After that come either four or five impulsions having the same object. The last of them is an impulsion of the material sphere belonging to the third jhāna; the others are as already stated.

And at this point, "through the fading away of joy, he remains equanimous, mindful and aware, and he experiences in his body the pleasure of which the Noble Ones say: 'equanimous, mindful, and dwelling in pleasure,' and thus he enters and remains in the third jhāna." And so he attains the third jhāna, which has eliminated one factor, is endowed with two factors, is excellent in three ways, possesses ten characteristics, and is based on the earth disk.

Once this has been attained in this way, and he has achieved mastery in the five ways already described, then on emerging from the now familiar third jhāna he is able to see faults in it. He realizes that the attainment is threatened by the proximity of joy, and that its factors are weakened by the grossness of pleasure (*sukha*) . . . . He should then reflect that the fourth jhāna is more calm, and, giving up his attachment to the third jhāna, he should set about attaining the fourth.

The Fourth Jhāna

When he emerges from the third jhāna, and reviews its jhāna factors with mindfulness and awareness, pleasure appears gross to him while neutral feeling and mental one-pointedness appear calm. Then he repeatedly brings to mind the same sign, "earth, earth," in order to eliminate the gross factors and develop the calm factors, and he realizes that the fourth jhāna is about to be attained. Then there arises mind-door adverting having that same earth disk as its object and cutting off the stream of becoming. After that come either four or five impulsions having the same object. The last of them is an impulsion of the material sphere belonging to the fourth jhāna; the others are as already stated.

But there is this difference: because pleasant feeling does not stand in the causal relation of repetition to neutral feeling, which is to arise in the fourth jhāna, these impulsions are associated with neutral feeling; and consequently pleasure disappears simply owing to that association.

And at this point, "through giving up pleasure and pain, and through the previous disappearance of happiness and sadness, he enters and remains in the fourth jhāna, which is without pleasure and pain, and in which there is pure equanimity and mindfulness." And so he attains the fourth jhāna, which has eliminated one factor, is endowed with two factors, is excellent in three ways, possesses ten characteristics, and is based on the earth disk.

Reading 10

Self-Protection through Mindfulness

Śāntideva

There are these twelve applications of mindfulness that lead to avoidance of wasteful effort:

1 Mindfulness that respects the law of karma by observing the Buddha's injunctions and not transgressing.
2 Mindfulness of the body when it is motionless.
3 Mindfulness of the essential nature of the body from moment to moment when it is engaged in activity.
4 Mindfulness in making bodily movements in the event of disturbances likely to evoke joy, fear, and so on.
5 Mindfulness in observing the four postures (walking, standing, sitting, and reclining).
6 Mindfulness which, from time to time, checks the appropriateness of the postures to guard against inappropriate posture.
7 Mindfulness when speaking, so as to restrain excessive or unseemly movements of hands, feet, and head, or of facial expression, caused by pleasure, pride, excitement, or partiality.
8 Mindfulness in speaking, so that one uses an appropriately moderate tone of voice, not speaking too loudly lest one fall into the fault of rudeness.
9 Mindfulness when with uneducated people, so that one's ideas remain acceptable and intelligible to them.
10 Mindfulness which keeps that wild elephant, the mind, firmly tethered to the post of inner calm.
11 Mindfulness which notes the condition of the mind from moment to moment.
12 Mindfulness which, in the midst of the crowd, maintains the above aims, even at the expense of other activities.

By such deployment of mindfulness one will succeed in avoiding wasteful effort. It is said: "Mindfulness becomes keen through dedication." Here "dedication" means making mindfulness one's primary task. It is the opposite of careless inattention.

Again, it is said: "Dedication and zeal arise from knowing the importance of inner stillness." What is this "stillness" (śama)? It is the calm (śamatha) that is described in the Akṣayamati Sūtra thus:

> What is meant by imperturbable calm? It is calming the mind, calming the body, guarding the sense faculties so that they do not distract one. It is freedom from conceit, from unrestraint, restlessness, and fickleness. It is gentleness, guardedness, plia-bility, seemly behaviour, mental collectedness. It is avoidance of crowds and delight in solitude, physical and mental seclusion. It is a preference for forest-dwelling, fewness of wants, and attention to the postures. It is knowing the right time, the right occasion, the right amount, and keeping liberation in view. It is being easy for lay people to support, being content with little, and so on.

And what is "the importance of inner stillness"? It is its capacity to yield insight into the true nature of things; for the Buddha said: "Whoever is concentrated sees the true nature of things."

One should know that "the importance of inner stillness" lies in being able to attain, for oneself and for others, liberation from endless suffering, such as rebirth in purgatory; and being able to attain, for oneself and others, supreme happiness, both worldly and supramundane; and being able to attain the Beyond. One should therefore cultivate an ardent longing for inner stillness. Just as a person locked in a burning house longs for cool water, so one should long for inner stillness and dedicate oneself to the practice. In this way mindfulness will be constantly present, and through this constant mindfulness one will avoid all wasteful effort. In one who avoids wasteful effort, lowly and unprofitable states will not arise.

Therefore, he who wishes to protect himself should begin at the foundation, which is mindfulness, and maintain that mindfulness constantly present.

In the Ratnamegha Sūtra it is stated:

> All things originate in the mind. When the mind is truly known, all things are known.
> The mind is the source of all action, both skilful and unskilful.
> The mind leads the world; yet it does not know itself.
> The mind is like a whirling fire-brand, like a heaving wave, like a

blazing forest fire, like a mighty flood. If one observes closely, dwelling with mindfulness well directed to the mind, one will not be mastered by the mind, but will attain mastery over the mind. And when the mind is mastered, all things are mastered.

Avoidance of Distraction

When there is loss of awareness and lack of mindfulness, the mind becomes unstable, because it is always being distracted from the goal. But if, with mindfulness and awareness, involvement in outward activity can be avoided, then the mind can maintain one-pointed attention as long as it wishes.

The Four Foundations of Mindfulness

With the mind rendered pliant, one should undertake the practice of the four foundations of mindfulness.

1. The Body

In the *Dharmasangīti Sūtra* mindfulness of the body is explained as observation of the body's impurities, thus:

> And again, the practitioner directs mindfulness to the body thus: This body is merely a collection of feet, toes, legs, chest, loins, abdomen, navel, spine, heart, ribs, hands, arms, shoulders, neck, jaws, forehead, head, and skull. It has been built up by life-producing karma and is the abode of a myriad sundry defilements, desires, and fancies. It comprises also many other components: hair, nails, teeth, . . . Thus he observes the body . . . Again, this body did not come from the past, nor will it continue into the future. It has no existence in past or future, except in our false suppositions. It contains no doer and no perceiver. In its beginning, middle, and end it has no root anywhere. It has no master, no owner; and it owns nothing. Using extraneous, conventional names we call it our body, our frame, our possession, abode, carcase; but this body is devoid of substance. Born of the mother's blood and the father's semen, it is by nature impure, putrid, and evil-smelling. It is subject to disturbance by the thieves of greed, hatred, delusion, fear, and despair. It is always liable to decline and collapse, to breaking up, dissolution, and crumbling away. And it is prey to a myriad different diseases.

2. Feelings

It is said in the *Ratnacūḍa Sūtra*:

When the practitioner develops mindfulness of feelings as feelings, he conceives a great compassion for those beings who are attached to the happiness of feelings. And he trains himself to realize: "Happiness is freedom from feelings." He therefore practises mindfulness of feelings as feelings, in order that all beings may become detached from feelings. He braces himself to achieve the cessation of feelings in all beings; he does not strive for the cessation of feelings just for his own sake.

Whatever feelings there are in him are pervaded by a profound compassion. When experiencing a pleasant feeling, he conceives a profound compassion for all beings who are inclined to desire, and he himself gives up any inclination to desire. When experiencing an unpleasant feeling, he conceives a profound compassion for all beings who are inclined to hatred, and he himself gives up any inclination to hatred. When experiencing a neutral feeling, he conceives a profound compassion for all beings who are inclined to delusion, and he himself gives up any inclination to delusion.

He is not attracted to pleasant feeling, but strives to eradicate such attraction. He is not repelled by unpleasant feeling, but strives to eradicate repulsion. He is not subject to ignorance in neutral feeling, but strives to eradicate ignorance.

Whatever feeling he experiences, he recognizes it as transient, as unsatisfactory, as devoid of self. He recognizes pleasant feeling as transient and unpleasant feeling as a thorn, and toward neutral feeling he remains indifferent. Thus, the pleasant is transient, the unpleasant is suffering, and the neutral is devoid of self.

3. Mental States[36]

It is said in the *Ratnacūḍa Sūtra*:

He examines his mental states thus: Is there present the mental state of desire, or hatred, or delusion? Is this state in the past, the future, or the present? What is past has ceased, the future is not yet come, and the present mental state cannot endure. Mental states are within, not outside, nor between the two. Mental states are formless, invisible, intangible, inconceivable, unstable, without abode. Mental states are like a baited hook, having a pleasant appearance, but causing pain. They are like bluebottle flies, taking for pure what is impure. Mental states are like an enemy who causes great distress. They are like a vampire that sucks one's energy and is always seeking a weak point to gain access. Mental states are like a thief, stealing all one's good inclinations.

4. Mindfulness of Mental Objects (dharmas)

It is said in the *Ratnacūḍa Sūtra*:

A practitioner observing mental objects as mental objects perceives thus: Only mental objects arise in a process of arising; only mental objects cease in a process of ceasing. And there is not in them any substance, any being, soul, creature, man, person, personality, any human being that is born, grows old, passes away, and is reborn. It is in the very nature of mental objects that they arise if the conditions for their arising exist, and do not arise if those conditions do not exist. As they are produced, so they arise, whether good, bad, or neutral. No "producer" creates them, and yet mental objects do not arise without their corresponding causes.

The same sūtra says: "Even when the mental objects are of little consequence, the practitioner continues to observe them, never losing the fully aware and enlightened state."

Calm and Insight

Zhiyi

Calm and insight[37] can be practised in two ways: while seated in formal meditation, and while engaged in karmic activities and confronting the world.

Practising Calm and Insight While Seated

Although one can practise in any of the four postures,[38] the seated posture is the best for practitioners of the path. The practice of calm and insight while seated will therefore now be discussed and explained. It has five different objectives: to control the coarse, disturbed mind of the beginner; to treat the ailments of a sinking mind or a floating mind; to suit the occasion; to adjust the concentated, refined mind; and to balance concentration and wisdom. These are now discussed in turn.

1. To control the coarse, disturbed mind of the beginner. When the practitioner first sits in meditation, his mind is coarse and disturbed. He should therefore practise calm to get rid of that condition; and if the practice of calm does not achieve it, he should practise insight. This is what is meant by "practising calm and insight to control the coarse, disturbed mind of the beginner." It will now be explained under the two practices of calm and insight.

First, the practice of calm, which is of three kinds:

(a) Calming by fastening (the mind) on some object; that is to say, fastening the mind on to such points as the tip of the nose or the navel. This prevents the mind from straying. As the sūtra says, "Fasten the mind and do not let it have its way, and it will be like a caged monkey."

(b) Calming by controlling the mind; that is to say, controlling the mind whenever it begins to move, thus preventing it from wandering. As the sūtra says, "The mind is master of the five senses; therefore you should calm the mind."

Both of these kinds of practice have to do with the physical; they need not be distinguished from each other.

(c) Calming by realizing the truth; that is to say, knowing that all states (dharmas) that arise in the thinking mind are born of causes and conditions and are devoid of selfhood. Knowing this, the mind does not grasp at them, and when the mind does not grasp at them, deluded ideas are extinguished. Hence it is called calming . . . .

For a beginning practitioner stilling the mind is not easy. Forcing it to be still may result in insanity. As in learning archery, one hits the mark only after long practice.

Second, the practice of insight, which is of two kinds:

(a) Insight as a means to control. Examples are: contemplation of the impurities (of the body) in order to overcome desire; contemplation of loving-kindness in order to overcome hatred; analysis into the (four) elements in order to overcome attachment to self; and counting of the breaths in order to overcome excessive thinking. These practices are all of a type.

(b) Right insight, which sees all states as devoid of reality and as born of causes and conditions. The causes and conditions are without self-nature; *that* is the reality. Having once realized that all it contemplates is empty, the mind that has the ability to see this naturally ceases to arise. This principle is often discussed in the texts. Please attend to it. As the verse in the sūtra says, "All states are transient, constantly arising in thoughts. One who has perceived their emptiness, has no further thoughts of them."

2. *To treat the ailments of a sinking mind or a floating mind*: While the practitioner is seated in meditation, his mind may at times become dull, blocked, forgetful, slack, inattentive, or drowsy. At such times he should practise insight to awaken it. If, however, while he is in seated meditation, his mind is floating, drifting, restless, anxious, and uneasy, then he should practise calm to still it. This is, in brief, the practice of calm and insight to treat the ailments of a sinking mind or a floating mind. But one has to know which is the right medicine

for which ailment, and use it appropriately. One must not use the wrong one.

3. To suit the occasion: If the practitioner, when seated in meditation, practises insight in order to treat a sinking mind, but the mind does not become clear and sharp, then he should try practising calm to still it. If, when it becomes still, he feels that body and mind are at ease and quiet, then he should know that calm is appropriate, and should use calm to quieten the mind. On the other hand, if when seated in meditation, he practises calm in order to treat a floating mind, but the mind does not become still and sharp, then he should try practising insight. If, when there is insight, he feels that the mind is clear, quiet, and stable, then he should know that insight is appropriate, and should use insight to quieten the mind. This is, in brief, the practice of calm and insight to suit the occasion. But one has to judge the occasion rightly and practise accordingly, so that the mind becomes stable and the defilements are eliminated; then one realizes all gateways to the Dharma.

4. To adjust the concentrated, refined mind: As mentioned, the practitioner has already used calm and insight to control the coarse, disturbed mind. After the mental disturbances have been eliminated, he attains the concentrated state. Because of the fineness of the concentrated mind, he feels his body to be empty and still, and experiences joy and happiness. It may happen that he takes advantage of this refined state of mind to grasp at false views. If he does not know that concentration of mind is for the purpose of eliminating hollow falsehoods, he is sure to become attached to those views, and if such attachment arises he will cling to them as true. If, however, he knows these hollow falsehoods to be untrue, then the twin defilements of desire and false view will not arise. This is the practice of calm.

If, in spite of practising calm, the mind still clings to desire and false view, creating karma endlessly, then he should practise insight, contemplating the concentrated, refined mind. If he fails to find the concentrated, refined mind, he will not grasp at false view concerning concentration; and if he does not grasp at false view concerning concentration, then the defilements of desire and false view, and all karma, will be eliminated. This is the practice of insight.

This is, in brief, the practice of calm and insight to adjust the concentrated, refined mind. The distinction between the methods of calm and insight is as above, but with this difference that here the concern is to eliminate the subtle defect of false view concerning concentration.

5. *To balance concentration and wisdom:* The practitioner, while seated in meditation, may enter dhyāna (concentration) as a result of practising either calm or insight. And it may be that although he has attained concentration, he has no wisdom. This is dull dhyāna; it cannot cut through the fetters (which bind one in samsara). Or he may attain just a small degree of wisdom, being unable to generate true wisdom, cut through all the fetters, and realize all Dharma-gateways. At such a time he should resolve the problem by practising insight, so as to bring concentration and wisdom into balance. He will then be able to cut through the fetters and realize all gateways to the Dharma.

On the other hand, the practitioner while seated in meditation may, through practising insight, have a mind that is clear and enlightened; but though he has bright, discriminating wisdom, he has little concentration. His mind will then be unstable and scattered, like a candle in a windy place, which is not able to illuminate objects. He is therefore not able to escape from birth and death. At such a time he should again practise calm. By practising calm, his mind becomes concentrated and, like a candle in a closed room, is able to penetrate the darkness, and illuminate objects. This is, in brief, the practice of calm and insight to balance concentration and wisdom.

If the practitioner, sitting in formal meditation with body erect, is able in this manner to correctly apply these five ways of practising calm and insight, then he will not fail in his purpose. Know that such a person is practising well the Buddha's teaching, and that practising it well, he will by no means live his life in vain.

Practising Calm and Insight while Engaged in Karmic Activities and while Confronting the World.

Formal sitting with body erect is the very best way of entering the path. However, one has this tiresome body and is obliged to become involved in karmic activities. If the practitioner yields to circumstances and confronts the world without practising calm or insight, then his practice will be only intermittent, and he will continue to make karma. How, then, can he quickly come to conform to the Buddha's teaching? If he can at all times continuously practise the skills of concentration and wisdom, then he will certainly be able to penetrate to the Buddha's teaching in its entirety.

What is meant by "practising calm and insight while engaged in karmic activities"? Karmic activities are these six: walking, standing, sitting, reclining, doing, and speaking. What is meant by "practising calm and insight while confronting the world"? The world comprises these six: visible forms confronted by the eye, sounds confronted by the ear, odours by the nose, tastes by the tongue, tactile objects by the body, and mental images confronted by the mind. If the practitioner cultivates calm and insight while involved in these twelve, then that is what is meant by practising calm and insight while engaged in karmic activities and while confronting the world.

1. Walking. When walking, the practitioner should reflect thus: Why do I now wish to walk? Is it because of the power of defilements, for the sake of evil, mindless things? If so, then I should not be walking. If, however, it is not because of defilements, but for the sake of things that are good, beneficial, and in accordance with Dharma, then I should be walking.

How does one practise calm while walking? If, while walking, the practitioner comprehends that it is because of his walking that all his defilements and all his good and evil states exist, and if he fully comprehends that his state of mind when walking, along with all the states involved in the walking, are insubstantial, then deluded ideas will cease. This is the practice of calm.

And how does one practise insight while walking? The practitioner should reflect thus: It is because the mind moves the body that there is forward movement, which is called walking. It is because of this walking that there exist all defilements and good and evil states. He should therefore introspectively examine his mind when walking, not seeing just the outward manifestation. He should comprehend that the walker and all states involved in the walking, are ultimately empty. This is the practice of insight.

2. Standing. When standing still, the practitioner should reflect thus: Why do I now wish to stand still? Is it because of the power of defilements, for the sake of evil, mindless things? If so, then I should not be standing still. If, however, it is not because of defilements, but for the sake of things that are good, beneficial, and in accordance with Dharma, then I should be standing still.

How does one practise calm while standing still? If, while standing, the practitioner comprehends . . .

And how does one practise insight while standing? The practitioner should reflect thus: It is because the mind establishes the body in one place that there is what is called standing. It is because of this standing . . .

3. Sitting: When seated, the practitioner should reflect thus: Why do I now wish to sit? . . .

How does one practise calm while seated? If, while seated the practitioner comprehends . . .

And how does one practise insight while sitting? The practitioner should reflect thus: It is because the mind has the idea of crossing the legs and settling the body . . .

4. Reclining: When lying down, the practitioner should reflect thus: Why do I now wish to lie down? . . .

How does one practise calm while reclining? If, when lying down to rest, the practitioner comprehends . . .

And how does one practise insight while reclining? The practitioner should reflect thus: It is because I am weary that I am dull and give rein to the six passions . . .

5. Doing: When doing anything, the practitioner should reflect thus: Why do I now wish to do this? . . .

What is meant by practising calm while doing? If, when doing anything, the practitioner comprehends . . .

And what is meant by practising insight while doing? The practitioner should reflect thus: It is because the mind moves the body, making the hands do all sorts of things, . . .

6. Speaking: When speaking, the practitioner should reflect thus: Why do I now wish to speak? If I am speaking in accordance with defilements, for the sake of saying evil, mindless things, then I should not be speaking. If, however, it is for the sake of good and beneficial things, then I should be speaking.

How does one practise calm while speaking? If, when speaking, the practitioner comprehends that it is because of this speaking that all his defilements and good and evil states exist, and if he comprehends that the defilements and good and evil states involved in the speaking mind and in the act of speaking are all insubstantial, then his deluded ideas will cease. This is the practice of calm.

And how does one practise insight while speaking? The practitioner should reflect thus: It is because the mind is motivated to cause the breath to move, striking against the throat, lips, tongue, teeth, and palate, that sound comes out, producing speech. It is because of this speech that there exist all good and evil states. He introspectively examines his mind when speaking, not seeing just the outward manifestation. He should comprehend that the one who is speaking, and all states involved in the speaking, are ultimately empty. This is the practice of insight.

The above six methods of practising calm and insight are to be applied as the occasion demands. Each one of them includes the five objectives spoken of earlier.

Next, the practice of calm and insight in connection with the six sense doors.

1. *When the eye sees visible forms*: Practising calm, the practitioner recognizes that the seeing of a form is like the reflection of the moon in water: it is unstable and unreal. When he sees a pleasant form, he does not respond with desire and liking; when he sees an unpleasant form he does not respond with hatred and dislike; and when he sees a form that is neither pleasant nor unpleasant, he does not respond with delusion and confused thoughts.

And how does one practise insight when the eye sees visible forms? The practitioner should reflect thus: When something is seen, it is by nature empty. Why is this? In the clear space between the sense organ and the physical object there is neither the seen nor any discrimination. It is through the coming together of causes and conditions that there arises visual consciousness, followed by intellect, and hence the ability to discern all sorts of forms. And it is because of this that there exist all the defilements and good and evil states. So he should introspectively examine the mind that knows forms, not seeing just the outward manifestation. He should know that the seeing and all associated states are ultimately empty. This is the practice of insight.

2. *When the ear hears sounds*: Practising calm, the practitioner when hearing a sound, knows it as an auditory phenomenon. When he hears a pleasant sound, . . .

And how does one practise insight when the ear hears sounds? The practitioner should reflect thus: When something is heard, it is by nature empty and without essence; but from the coming together of the sense organ and the physical object there arises auditory consciousness, . . .

3. *When the nose smells odours*: Practising calm, the practitioner when smelling an odour, knows it as unreal, like a flame. When he smells a pleasant odour, . . .

And how does one practise insight when the nose smells odours? The practitioner should reflect thus: My present smelling of this odour is a deception, unreal. Why is that? From the coming together of the sense organ and the physical object there arises olfactory consciousness, . . .

4. *When the tongue tastes flavours*: Practising calm, the practitioner when tasting a flavour, knows it as like something in a dream or a fantasy. When he tastes a pleasant flavour, . . .

And how does one practise insight when the tongue tastes flavours? The practitioner should reflect thus: My present tasting of this flavour is truly without substance. Why is that? Because the six flavours,[39] inner and outer, are by nature not distinct. It is from the coming together of the tongue [and the object] there arises taste consciousness, . . .

5. *When the body perceives tactile sensations*: Practising calm, the practitioner when perceiving a tactile sensation, knows it as like a shadow, a fantasy, something unreal. When he perceives a pleasant tactile sensation, he does not respond with liking; when he perceives an unpleasant tactile sensation he does not respond with dislike; and when he perceives a tactile sensation that is neither pleasant nor unpleasant, he does not respond with thoughts that discriminate. This is the practice of calm.

And how does one practise insight when the body perceives tactile sensations? The practitioner should reflect thus: Light, heavy, cold, warm, rough, smooth – such are called tactile sensations; the head, the trunk, and the four limbs are called the body. The tactile sensations are by nature hollow and false. It is from the coming together of causes and conditions that there arises tactile consciousness, followed by intellect, memory, and thinking, which discriminate the phenomenon as painful, pleasant, and so on. Hence it is called perceiving tactile sensations. So he introspectively examines the mind that perceives tactile sensation, not seeing just the outward manifestation. He should know that the perceiving of tactile sensation and all associated states are ultimately empty. This is the practice of insight.

6. *When the mind knows mental images*: In this case the practice of calm and insight is as explained above for the beginner's seated meditation.

These practices of calm and insight based on the six sense organs are to be applied as occasion demands. Each one of them involves the five objectives discussed earlier. As those objectives have already been broadly distinguished, they will not be discussed again here.

If the practitioner is able to practise calm and insight in all these situations – walking, standing, sitting, reclining, seeing, hearing, feeling, knowing, and so on – then he is is truly a follower of the Mahāyāna path.

Seated Meditation

Dōgen

For the practice of Zen, a quiet room is required. Practise moderation in eating and drinking. Detach yourself from all involvements and leave off all affairs. Do not think in terms of good and bad; do not involve yourself with right and wrong. Stop the movements of consciousness; stop the reflections of memory, thought, and consideration.

For your seat, spread a thick sitting mat and place a cushion on it. Sit in either the full lotus or the half lotus posture. For the full lotus posture, first place the right foot on the left thigh, then the left foot on the right thigh. For the half lotus posture, just let the left foot rest on the right thigh.

Loosen your robes and girdle, and arrange them neatly. Next, place your right hand [palm upwards] on your left foot, and your left hand on your right palm. Rest the tips of the thumbs together. Then straighten your body and sit upright. Do not tilt to left or right, forward or backward.

Ears and shoulders should be in line, as should nose and navel. Rest the tongue against the hard palate, and keep the lips and the teeth closed. The eyes must always remain open.

Having adjusted your posture, you should then regulate your breathing. If a thought arises, be aware of it; and having become aware of it, let it pass. After long practice you will forget about outside objects, and will naturally become one-pointed. This is the art of seated meditation (*zazen*), the Dharma-gateway to great peace and joy.

Once you master this, the body will naturally become light and at ease, the mind will become alert and sharp, and right view will become distinct. The taste of Dharma will sustain your mind; calm, purity, and joy will prevail; and your every-day life will flow on naturally. Once you attain insight, you will be [in your natural element] like a dragon getting to water or like a tiger reaching the mountains. Know that at that time right view is present, and delusion and agitation have ceased.

In getting up from the meditation seat, move the body slowly and gently, avoiding gross or sudden movements. Constantly guard and maintain the power of collectedness. By constant observation, you will make the break-through into the state without remainder. You will let go of self, which was the obstacle. That is the consummation of the path. Truly, this unique entry to enlightenment is the highest, the ultimate. First attaining full understanding and then turning it into half enlightenment – that is found only in this teaching. Smiling when a flower is held up [as Mahākāśynpa did], attaining the essence when bowing [as Huige did] – these are examples of the attainment of the great liberation through the power of this teaching. How else could practitioners like them have attained the highest wisdom?

Reading 13

Some Zen Kōans

Mumon

1. Jōshū's "Wash Your Bowl"

A monk said to Jōshū, "I have just entered this monastery. Please teach me."

"Have you eaten your rice porridge?" asked Jōshū.

"Yes, I have," replied the monk.

"Then you had better wash your bowl," said Jōshū.

With this the monk gained insight.

Mumon's comment:

When he opens his mouth, Jōshū shows his gall bladder. He displays his heart and liver. I wonder if this monk really did hear the truth. I hope he did not mistake the bell for a jar.

Mumon's verse:

Endeavouring to interpret clearly,
You retard your attainment.
Don't you know that flame is fire?
Your rice has long been cooked.

2. Nansen's "Ordinary Mind is the Way"

Jōshū asked Nansen, "What is the Way?"

"Ordinary mind is the Way," Nansen replied.

"Shall I try to seek after it?" Jōshū asked.

"If you try for it, you will become separated from it," responded Nansen.

"How can I know the Way unless I try for it?" persisted Jōshū.

Nansen said, "The Way is not a matter of knowing or not knowing. Knowing is delusion; not knowing is confusion. When you have really reached the true Way beyond doubt, you will find it as vast and boundless as outer space. How can it be talked about on the level of right and wrong?"

With these words, Jōshū came to a sudden realization.

Mumon's comment:

Nansen dissolved and melted away before Jōshū's questions, and could not offer a plausible explanation. Even though Jōshū comes to a realization, he must delve into it for another thirty years before he can fully understand it.

Mumon's verse:

The spring flowers, the autumn moon;
Summer breezes, winter snow.
If useless things do not clutter your mind,
You have the best days of your life.

3. Proceed on from the Top of the Pole

Sekisō Oshō asked, "How can you proceed on further from the top of a hundred-foot pole?"

Another eminent teacher of old said, "You, who sit on the top of a hundred-foot pole, although you have entered the Way you are not yet genuine. Proceed on from the top of the pole, and you will show your whole body in the ten directions."

Mumon's comment:

If you go on further and turn your body about, no place is left where you are not the master. But even so, tell me, how will you go on further from the top of a hundred-foot pole? Eh?

Mumon's verse:

He darkens the third eye of insight
And clings to the first mark on the scale.
Even though he may sacrifice his life,
He is only a blind man leading the blind.

4. Jōshū's "Mu"

A monk asked Jōshū, "Has a dog the Buddha Nature?"

Jōshū answered, "Mu."

Mumon's comment:

In order to master Zen, you must pass the barrier of the patriarchs. To attain this subtle realization, you must completely cut off the way of thinking. If you do not pass the barrier, and do not cut off the way of thinking, then you will be like a ghost clinging to the bushes and weeds.

Now, I want to ask you, what is the barrier of the patriarchs? Why, it is this single word "Mu."[40] That is the front gate to Zen. Therefore it is called the "Mumonkan[41] of Zen." If you pass through it, you will not only see Jōshū face to face, but you will also go hand in hand with the successive patriarchs, entangling your eyebrows with theirs, seeing with the same eyes, hearing with the same ears. Isn't that a delightful prospect? Wouldn't you like to pass this barrier?

Arouse your entire body with its three hundred and sixty bones and joints and its eighty-four thousand pores of the skin; summon up a spirit of great doubt and concentrate on this word "Mu." Carry it continuously day and night. Do not form a nihilistic conception of vacancy, or a relative conception of "has" or "has not." It will be just as if you swallow a red-hot iron ball, which you cannot spit out even if you try. All the illusory ideas and delusive thoughts accumulated up to the present will be exterminated, and when the time comes, internal and external will be spontaneously united. You will know this, but for yourself only, like a dumb man who has had a dream. Then all of a sudden an explosive conversion will occur, and you will astonish the heavens and shake the earth.

It will be as if you snatch away the great sword of the valiant general Kan'u and hold it in your hand. When you meet the Buddha, you kill him; when you meet the patriarchs, you kill them. On the brink of life and death, you command perfect freedom; among the sixfold worlds and four modes of existence, you enjoy a merry and playful samādhi.

Now, I want to ask you again, "How will you carry it out?" Employ every ounce of your energy to work on this "Mu." If you hold on without interruption, behold: a single spark, and the holy candle is lit!

Mumon's verse:

The dog, the buddha nature,
The pronouncement, perfect and final.
Before you say it has or has not,
You are a dead man on the spot.

Fastening the Mind

Tsongkhapa

This has three parts:

1 Settling the technique without fault;
2 Clearing away the technique with fault;
3 Teaching the measure of watches.

1. Settling the Technique without Fault

Here, the samādhi to be accomplished has two distinguishing features, as follows: it has the strength of the vivid part consisting in exceeding vividness of mind; and it has the non-predicating fixation part consisting in fixation on the meditative object as a single area. Some persons add "pleasure" as a third (distinguishing feature), and others add also "clarity" as a fourth. However, "clarity" is included in the first distinguishing feature, so there is no need to refer to it separately. Again, the rapture and pleasure that are the euphoria of feeling arise in the fruit of the samādhi to be accomplished on this occasion; but they do not arise as concomitants of the samādhi comprised by the threshold of the first meditation,[42] and pleasure of body and pleasure of mind do not arise as concomitants of the samādhi of the fourth meditation stated to be the best foundation for accomplishing the merits of the three vehicles. Consequently, that (i.e. pleasure) is not counted here. Moreover, the great strength of the vivid part is not in the samādhi comprised by the formless plane(s), according to the *Sūtrālaṃkāra* text, "likewise meditation apart from the formless realm . . . " That is to say, aside from the bodhisattvas who have attained power, the bodhisattvas accomplish their merits by taking recourse to the samādhi(s) comprised by the meditation planes. Consequently, there is no fault in expounding the vivid-part kind of distinguishing feature.

The issuance of that sort of strength of the vivid part is interrupted by fading, and the non-discursive thought consisting of a single area (of mind) is interrupted by scattering. Hence fading and scattering are the reason that becomes the chief obstacle for accomplishing the aspects of samādhi. Therefore, the one who has well determined the subtle and crude forms of fading and scattering, and having determined them does not know any ways to protect the samādhi defeated by these two, would have no possibility of calming – we need not speak of discerning! Therefore, the wise who aim at samādhi should become skilled in that method. Now, fading and scattering are the condition hostile to the accomplishment of calming. The determination of that hostile condition and the actual method of defeating that (condition) are explained later on. Here I shall set forth the method of generating the samādhi which is the favourable condition for the accomplishment of calming.

Samādhi is the fixation of mind in a single area on a meditative object; furthermore, one must dwell continuously on the meditative object.

Again, whatever be the basic meditative object of the mind, there are two requirements: (1) a means so as not to be distracted from that (meditative object); (2) a knowledge of the true state of affairs (viz.:) distraction or non-distraction, the threat of distraction or the non-threat of distraction. The former is mindfulness and the latter is awareness. The *Commentary on the Sūtrālaṃkāra* states: "Mindfulness and awareness are the fastener, since the former prevents straying from the meditative object of the mind and since the latter recognizes the straying."

When the meditative object slips away through failure of mindfulness, the meditative object is lost immediately after the straying (of mind). Hence mindfulness is the basis for the non-slipping-away of the meditative object. Regarding the method by which mindfulness fastens mind to the meditative object, upon distinct recall of the foundation of the meditative object as previously discussed, in case too low a level (of distinct recall) occurs, the one who recognizes that (state of affairs) generates a force of grasping pattern held in succession and raises the mind aloft, thus again fixing (the mind) without investigation on whatever be (the meditative object). Mindfulness has three distinguishing features, which are alluded to in this passage of the *Samuccaya*: "What is mindfulness? The non-slipping-away of the mind in regard to the familiar entity; the agent of non-distraction."

(a) The distinguishing feature consisting of the domain of

meditative object means "the familiar entity," because mindfulness does not arise in regard to a domain that was previously unfamiliar. In the present context, it is the arising of the foundation of meditative object previously ascertained.

(b) The distinguishing feature consisting of the aspect of grasping pattern means "the non-slipping-away of mind," i.e., the non-slipping-away of that domain from the mind. In the present context, it is the non-slipping-away of the foundation of meditative object. The method of non-slipping-away is taught by the gurus as the idea, "The foundation of meditative object is like this," which can be a question by another person or a personal involvement in discursive thought – and it says nothing about the sheer capacity of mindfulness. Rather, the mind is tied to the meditative object, has uninterrupted mindfulness of it, and does not stray away in even the slightest measure; for no sooner does it stray, than mindfulness is lost. Hence, one finishes settling the mind, as previously (explained), on the foundation of meditative object, and arouses the idea, "(I am) tied to the meditative object in this manner." Thereupon, again without discursive thought, the force of that discrimination protects without interruption: this is the essential point of the method of taking recourse to mindfulness.

(c) The distinguishing feature consisting of the agent and action means the activity of non-distraction of the mind away from the meditative object.

The discipline tying mind in that way to the meditative object is expressed by the simile of training an elephant; for example, a wild elephant is tied with many massive cords to a trunk or post. However the elephant [may] stamp as he has learned to do, he is indeed unable to do anything (about it), and being more and more enmeshed with the sharp hooks, is defeated and subdued ("broken in"). The mind is like the untrained elephant. When it is bound with the cord of mindfulness to the firm post of the previously discussed meditative object, [even] if it is unwilling to remain there, it is gradually brought under control, goaded by the hook of awareness. The *Madhyamakahṛdaya* tells it this way:

Having bound with the cord of mindfulness
To the firm post of meditative object,
The elephant of mind going astray –
It is gradually brought under control by the hook of insight.

Also, the *Bhāvanākrama II* states: "With the cords of mindfulness and awareness, one should bind the elephant of mind to that trunk of meditative object." Although in the former work awareness is compared to a hook, and in the latter work it is compared to a cord, that is not a contradiction. Mindfulness is the thing that continuously binds the mind to the meditative object; however, awareness also in due course fastens the mind to the meditative object. One takes recourse to the recognition through awareness of the actual fact of fading and scattering or of the threat of fading and scattering in order to settle on the basic meditative object without falling into the power of those (faults); and because, as was previously quoted, the teacher Vasubandhu has declared that both mindfulness and awareness are the fastener to the meditative object.

It is said that samādhi is accomplished by recourse to mindfulness, and it is said that mindfulness, like a cord, ties the mind continuously to the meditative object in concreteness. Therefore, the chief guardian method for the accomplishment of samādhi is the guardian method consisting of mindfulness. Furthermore, mindfulness owns the grasping pattern which has the aspect of certainty. Hence, when one is protecting the samādhi and is without the firm grasping pattern of conclusive awareness, even the appearance of the vivid part constituting clarity of mind is a sudden shock to the fixation (of mind); and when there is no issuance of the vivid part issuing with the strength of conclusive awareness, it (i.e., the appearance of the vivid part) does not originate along with the power of mindfulness; and for that reason it only occurs with protection of the samādhi when not obstructed by subtle fading.

One should be mindful of this precept: "Without settling on some other foundation of meditative object, such as the body of a deity, one guards only the non-discursive thought of the mind; thus, one should settle the mind without any discursive thought whatever on any sensory domain." Then he must not allow the mind to issue forth (to another sensory domain), or to stray away (from the meditative object); and that non-straying means the same as the mindfulness that does not allow the meditative object to slip away. That kind of contemplation, without transgressing the method of protecting mindfulness, also must depend on the mindfulness evincing the force of conclusive awareness.

2. Clearing away the Technique with Fault

One should clear away this certain wayward reflection: "Granted that there is practically no fault of fading when one settles (his mind) with no discursive thought in the manner previously explained, namely, by enhancing the casting of awareness, which restricts; but then there is much scattering (of thought) and one notices that he is unable to prolong the (mind's) fixation part, so the loftiness of the clear vision is again lowered. When one notices that the fixation part is quickly produced by relaxation of the restriction, his great precept is this means (*upāya*)." When they reach the conclusion from this train of thought, they loudly proclaim, "The best relaxation is the best cultivation."

That position makes no distinction between the production of fading and the production of cultivation. Indeed, a faultless samādhi requires the possession of two distinguished features as previously explained, but the firmness of the mind's fixation part without discursive thought does not by itself suffice. If it were that way, then (one might as well say) when drowsiness muddies the mind, there is fading; and when that (drowsiness) is absent, there is the vivid part consisting in the clarity of mind, wherefore the samādhi is faultless. This position does not distinguish between torpor and fading; consequently, I shall explain these two (states) extensively further on.

It means that either one has the vivid part through engaging in the strong clear vision of intense restriction (of the mind) and finds it difficult, by reason of the preponderance of scattering, to gain the fixation part; or else one has the fixation part through guarding with much relaxation, and, by reason of the preponderance of fading, has no vividness which evinces the strength (of the clear vision). Because it is very difficult to decide on the balance of firmness and relaxation that does not go on to either excessive restriction or excessive relaxation, it is difficult to generate the samādhi free from fading or scattering. Following the profound purport, the teacher Candragomin states:

> When one takes recourse to endeavour, scattering ensues;
> When one avoids this, there is shrinking.
> Since it is difficult to achieve equipoise as their balance,
> What should my turbulent mind do?

"Taking recourse to endeavour" is excessive restriction; when one engages in this, scattering ensues. If, in avoiding this restriction, there is excessive relaxation, there arises the retreat of the mind's inward stability. Consequently, the mind's dwelling in equal parts free from fading and scattering is the meaning of the passage "it is difficult to achieve. equipoise as their balance." That is the case, moreover, because Buddhaśānti writes in his commentary on that verse: "'Endeavour' means here proceeding with enclosure with a venture in the virtuous category"; and, "When he avoids this endeavour, i.e., gives up effort after noticing the fault that threatens to be a scattering, he shrinks within the mind."

The *Deśanāstava* also mentions:

When one engages with zeal, scattering ensues.
When one relaxes (from) this, there is shrinking.
Since it is difficult to achieve success as their balance point,
What should my turbulent mind do?

And its commentary explains it clearly:

When there is effort, proceeding with enclosure, by reason of the great zeal the mind is assailed by the occurrence of scattering and distraction; so as a result of effort one does not achieve fixation of the mind.

Now, the work pointed out that it is difficult to achieve success as the balance point free from the two extremes of fading and scattering, or to achieve the samādhi of equipoise as their balance. Since there would be no occasion for difficulty if relaxation sufficed; and since the work said that fading arises as a consequence of this (relaxation), it is clear that such a method does not manage to accomplish samādhi. Āryāsanga lays down that it is not enough to have the vivid part with only the mind's clarity when it is over-relaxed, but that one must have the restriction part with the grasping pattern: "Among these, the mental orientation proceeding with enclosure belongs to him who settles and rightly settles (the mind)."[43] He thus refers to the first two thoughts among the nine means of mind fixation. The *Bhāvanākrama I* also says: "He clears away fading and again should grasp more firmly precisely that meditative object." Besides, the *Bhāvanākrama II* says: "Thereupon, having removed fading, with his mind he sees very clearly the meditative object, whatever it be. That is what he should do." When that text speaks of seeing very clearly with the mind, it does not refer to just the vividness of the sensory domain but also refers to the exceedingly vivid and firm grasping pattern of discrimination.

This technique of relying on mindfulness is of highest importance. If one does not know this, then no matter how much he cultivates the tokens of protection, he remains with numerous faults, such as coursing in great forgetfulness and coursing in dullness of the insight, which supernally investigates the natures (*dharma*); and when his samādhi is firm, it causes vanity. At the time when the mind is tied to the meditative object by mindfulness in the way previously explained, is it proper to arouse the discursive thought which supervises whether or not the meditative object is well grasped? This should be done, because the *Bhāvanākrama II* states:

> After one has settled his mind in that way on whatever desired meditative object, he should settle his mind continually pursuant to just that (meditative object). When he has settled (his mind) upon that (meditative object) he should investigate his mind this way: he should examine it, thinking, "Is (my) mind well held to the meditative object; or is there fading; or is there a distraction due to the arising (in the mind) of an external sensory domain?"

Now, there is no such consideration when one abandons samādhi. And when one abides in samādhi, one may or may not be abiding in the basic meditation object as previously established; in the case when one is not abiding in it, one manages only to notice the passing into either fading or scattering. When one is settled in the samādhi, he should supervise at intervals that are neither too short nor too long. When one does it with merely no exhaustion of the strength and force of the previous discrimination, it is necessary to proceed for a long time in possession of that strength by continuous arousal of that discrimination, and necessary quickly to recognize fading and scattering. Accordingly, one protects by being just mindful, at intervals, of the previous meditative object; and because a great power of mindfulness is necessary as a basis for proceeding in continuity, there is the protective method of mindfulness. The *Śrāvakabhūmi* states:

> Among those, what is a single area of mind? He said: The stream of consciousness with mindfulness again and again, with matching meditative object, accompanied with continuity, irreproachable pleasure – is called samādhi, as well as a single area of virtuous mind. What is one mindful of again and again? He said: Whatever doctrines are upheld and heard, and whatever precepts and instructions are obtained from the gurus. When one has made that the ruler and faces toward the sign of the equipoised plane, one makes mindfulness conform, fastens it, yoked continuously, to that meditative object.

Furthermore, the *Madhyānta-vibhāga-ṭīkā* states: "'Mindfulness' means the non-slipping-away of the meditative object; 'meditative object' means the precept-entity, the mental recitation, to be fixed in the mind." Thus, taking recourse to mindfulness is so as to destroy the forgetfulness involved in straying from the meditative object. The non-slipping-away of the meditative object involving the destruction of that (forgetfulness) is recitation of the meditative object by the mind: again and again one orients the mind to the meditative object. For example, if one fears that he will forget something he knows, it will be hard to forget it if he again and again recalls it in his mind.

Hence mindfulness, at intervals, of the meditative object requires having the power of mindfulness; and supervision through holding the meditative object successively without the mind's straying away is the means of proceeding by having the power of awareness that fully recognizes fading and scattering. So one should realize that it is very difficult to generate the possession of the power of mindfulness and of awareness if one is opposed (to those two requirements), thinking, "Such as that is also discursive thought."

3. Teaching the Measure of Watches

Now, in regard to that tying of mind to the meditative object by mindfulness, is there or is there not a definite measure of watches, that could be termed "settling for so long an interval"? All the preceding gurus of the diverse lineages of Tibet said one must perform many brief watches. The reason given by some is that if one has the cultivation for short watches in good divisions, then he tastes the cultivation even during the in-between times, while if he has a lengthy watch he becomes tired. Others maintained that if one has a lengthy watch, it is easy to fall into the dominion of fading and scattering, as a consequence of which it is difficult to produce the faultless samādhi. The measure of watches is not set forth clearly in such great texts as the *Śrāvakabhūmi*. However, the *Bhāvanākrama III* states: "One should engage (in meditation) in that order for as long as one is able, whether for twenty-four minutes, one and one-half hours, or three hours."[44] That remark is made in the phase of watch measure for the time when one cultivates discerning and has already produced calming; however, it is obviously the same from the outset in the phase of producing calming; so one should act accordingly.

Furthermore, if, as previously explained, one practises at intervals with discursive thought the protective method of mindfulness and awareness, consisting in mindfulness of the meditative object and the view which supervises, no fault arises, whether the watch be brief or lengthy. However, generally the beginner observes too long a watch. Then, if he strays through the slipping-away (of the meditative object), his mind may have fading or scattering even for a long time, and unless he is acquainted (with such signs) he has no speedy determination (of what is happening). On the other hand, even if mindfulness does not slip away, it is easy for him to fall under the control of fading or scattering, and he has no speedy determination of the occurrences of fading and scattering. Of these two (possibilities), the former constitutes an interruption in the possession of the power of mindfulness; and the latter represents an interruption in the possession of the power of awareness. So it is very difficult (for that beginner) to break off the fading or scattering.

In particular, the non-determination of the occurrence of fading or scattering when one strays after the meditative object slips away, is much worse than the non-determination of the occurrence of fading or scattering when one does not forget the meditative object. Hence, it is of great importance to have the protective method for mindfulness, as previously discussed, that constitutes the opponent which impedes the failure of mindfulness when one is straying. It is necessary to have a brief watch if one has small force of awareness amounting to much forgetfulness in the event of straying and amounting to non-determination promptly of fading and scattering. There is no fault in having either a brief or a long watch if one is able to recognize promptly the fading or scattering and if it is hard for the slipping-away to occur. Following the deep purport, [that *Bhāva-nākrama* passage] expresses no certainty of the watch length, the twenty-four minute period, and so on. In short, it is necessary to accord with the capacity of one's own discrimination; therefore (that passage) stated, "as long as one is able."

Moreover, if no adventitious impediment to body or mind occurs, one is equipoised. And if it occurs, one gives up the cultivation while performing industriously, and immediately thereupon has a cultivation which dispels the interruption of elements. That is the deep purport of the wise, so one should understand as an ancillary to the cultivation that one should do it that way no matter what the length of the watch.

Section III

Contemporary Masters

INTRODUCTION

This section introduces the teachings of nine meditation masters of the modern era, representing a variety of traditions.

We begin with an overview of several Theravādan meditation techniques. *A Spectrum of Meditative Practices* (Reading 15), is a collection of extracts from the book *All About Buddhism* by Australian bhikkhu, Shrāvasti Dhammika. The author lived in Sri Lanka for many years before moving to Singapore in 1985, where he served until recently as spiritual adviser to several Buddhist groups. In this selection he explains mindfulness of breathing (*ānāpāna-sati*), the recollections (*anussati*), loving-kindness meditation (*mettā-bhāvanā*), the stages of concentration (*jhāna*), and the four foundations of mindfulness (*satipaṭṭhāna*).

The next item, *Observing Your Mind* (Reading 16), presents some key teachings of Achaan Chah, as collected by Jack Kornfield and Paul Breiter in their book, *A Still Forest Pool.* Until his death in 1992, Achaan Chah was abbot of Wat Pa Phong, a forest monastery in northeast Thailand. He was well known for his simple, direct teachings on mindfulness and insight meditation. In the selection presented here, the Achaan (teacher) gives practical advice on how to observe and investigate the mind, how to practise walking meditation, how to develop concentration, and how to persevere with one's practice.

The author of *Insight by the Nature Method* (Reading 17) is another recently deceased Thai monk, Buddhadasa. This well known meditator, scholar, and social critic spent much of his life at Suan Mok, the forest monastery he founded in southern Thailand. In this short section from his book, *Handbook for Humankind*, Buddhadasa advocates the development of insight based on naturally occurring concentration. He contrasts this with the formal, strictly systematized practice taught by many meditation masters. Despite his comments on formal meditation practice and deep concentration, Buddhadasa was an authority on mindfulness of breathing, and that technique continues to be taught to the many meditators who visit Suan Mok.

Insight through Mindfulness (Reading 18) is from a talk given by the prominent Burmese meditation master, Mahasi Sayadaw (U Sobhana Mahathera, died 1982). The talk was recorded as the Sayadaw was instructing a group of practitioners at the beginning of a meditation course in Yangkon in 1951. Thereafter it was played back repeatedly at successive meditation courses, as a clear and straightforward presentation of his particular meditative technique. Mahasi emphasizes continuous mental labelling of all bodily and mental sensations and movements, usually practised in an intensive retreat setting. His style of practice, often called Burmese *satipaṭṭhāna*, has gained wide acceptance, and is now taught in numerous meditation centres around the world.

The Meditative Mind (Reading 19) comes from Dhiravamsa's book, *The Way of Non-attachment*, which is a refreshingly dynamic presentation of the practice of insight meditation. Born in Thailand in 1935, Dhiravamsa trained as a monk and soon became one of the most creative representatives of Theravāda Buddhism in the West. He founded a meditation centre at Hindhead in Surrey, England, and from 1969 spent several months each year in the United States and Canada conducting meditation workshops and retreats. He has since returned to lay life, but continues in his role of meditation master. In this item he describes the truly meditative mind – clearly aware, fresh, and deeply enquiring; and he tells how we can cultivate this state in our daily life.

Watching Thoughts and Emotions (Reading 20) is a direct transcript of instructions given to a group of meditators, and of the discussion that followed. The teacher is Godwin Samararatne, a widely respected exponent of insight meditation, who divides his time between his own centre in Sri Lanka and various other centres around the world. The technique is basically mindfulness. Most vipassanā practices focus on the body and the feelings, the first and second of the traditional four bases of mindfulness. Here, however, the principal objects of the meditator's attention are thoughts and emotions, respectively the fourth and third of the four bases of mindfulness. Thoughts and emotions are often suppressed by meditators rather than observed. The practice of watching them with moment-to-moment awareness is rightly advocated here as an advanced form of insight meditation. The meditation instructions, which cover only a couple of pages in the transcript, actually extended over about twenty minutes. The reader should understand a pause of about one minute following each paragraph.

The next item, *Zen Mind* (Reading 21), is from *Zen Mind, Beginner's Mind*, a collection of informal talks on Zen practice by Shunryu Suzuki. Suzuki Roshi (died 1971) was a direct spiritual descendant of the thirteenth-century master Dōgen (Reading 12). On a teaching visit to the United States in 1958 he encountered such interest in Zen that he stayed on. After becoming a permanent resident, he founded the Zen Mountain Centre, the first Zen training monastery outside Asia. In this extract Shunryu Suzuki offers guidance in *zazen* (seated meditation), and points out some pitfalls. Some of his kōan-like statements – for example, "When a frog becomes a frog, Zen becomes Zen" – are no doubt meant to be grasped with "Zen mind" rather than with the intellect.

The first of our two modern representatives of Tibetan tradition is Sangye Khadro (Kathleen McDonald). *Some Tibetan Practices* (Reading 22) is extracted from her book *How to Meditate*. The author received her lower ordination at Kopan Monastery, Nepal, in 1974 and her higher ordination at Hsi Lai Temple in Los Angeles in 1988. She has taught in Europe, America, Australia, and most recently in Singapore. Here she describes and explains some characteristically Tibetan techniques: analytical meditation on emptiness, visualization, meditation on compassion, and the development of inner heat. Though she does not say it explicitly here, Sangye Khadro emphasizes the need for proper guidance in meditation, and recommends that readers seek a competent teacher before attempting any of these practices.

The selections brought together as *Meditation in Tantra* (Reading 23) are from the book *Introduction to Tantra* by Tibetan lama Thubten Yeshe. Born near Lhasa in 1935, Lama Yeshe entered the great Sera monastery at the age of six and studied Buddhist philosophy and meditation for the next eighteen years. He continued his studies after fleeing to India, and by the 1970s had begun taking Western students. In 1971 he established the Foundation for the Preservation of the Mahayana Tradition, now a world-wide organization. He died in 1984. In the selections reproduced here, Lama Yeshe begins by explaining the true nature of the mind, using the metaphor of clear sky (mind) and passing clouds (thoughts). He then describes how to realize this true nature through the practice of tantric meditation.

The nine readings in this section represent a precious collection of teachings by modern masters on the practical and experiential aspects of meditation. Though far from being exhaustive, they provide an adequate overview of the variety of methods and approaches available. The aspiring meditator may draw on them when attempting to make an informed decision about which type of practice to undertake. And the practitioner who is already committed to some particular technique or style of meditation will certainly benefit from recognizing the variety of alternative practices currently available, and noting how they agree or differ in respect of goals, methods, and perspectives.

It is perhaps artificial to distinguish "contemporary masters" (Section III) from "classical masters" (Section II), because the two groups form a continuum. The continuity of the present with the past is evident in cases like that of the contemporary master Shunryu Suzuki (Reading 21) and his direct spiritual forefather, the twelfth-century master Dōgen (Reading 12). It is widely considered that the continuity extends back beyond the classical masters to the Buddha himself (Section I). However, that is less certain, particularly as regards the detailed content of the teachings. How faithfully the teachings of later masters reflect those of the Buddha is a difficult question, one that is unlikely to be answered until meditation in all its aspects is much better understood than it is at present.

Reading 15

A Spectrum of Meditative Practices

Dhammika Bhikkhu

1. Mindfulness of Breathing

The most basic Buddhist meditation is mindfulness of breathing (*ānāpāna-sati*). This simple but effective technique induces relaxation, develops mental discipline, and leads to concentration. Describing its advantages, the Buddha says:

> This intent concentration on in-and-out breathing, if cultivated and developed, is something peaceful and excellent, something perfect in itself, and a pleasant way of living also. Not only that, it dispels evil, unskilled thoughts that have arisen and makes them vanish in a moment. It is just as when, in the last month of the hot season, the dust and dirt fly up and suddenly a great rain lays it and makes it settle in a moment.[45]

Sitting in a comfortable position and closing the eyes, attention is focused on the in-and-out movement of the breath. Counting the breaths from one to thirty will help prevent the attention from straying. Another thing that will help is trying to keep the body still. But when the attention does stray – either to external distractions like noises, or to internal distractions like thoughts, daydreams, memories, or bodily irritations or discomfort – we should patiently and gently return to counting. It is this continual bringing the attention back that will guarantee success.

How long should we meditate for? To start with, we should practise mindfulness of breathing for fifteen minutes at least once a day, extending the time by five minutes each week until we reach forty-five minutes. Then we should meditate for forty-five minutes each day until we get to the stage where even though the attention may stray, we are able to notice its wanderings quickly and return it to the breath with a minimum of effort.

Because we have probably never before attempted to discipline the mind, and because its habit patterns are probably well established, we are bound to encounter difficulties and obstacles, at least in the beginning. The most obvious of these will be thoughts that stubbornly pull our attention away from the breath. The Buddha suggests five ways of dealing with such thoughts: displacement, consideration of their disadvantages, paradoxical intention, non-interference, and suppression.[46]

At times, apparently unusual things can happen during meditation that might distract us by giving rise to anxiety or curiosity. While being straight, the body might feel as if it is leaning to one side, the hands or some other part of the body might feel as if they have disappeared, there might be unusual sensations on the body, or a brilliant light might appear in the mind. These and other phenomena that may happen to us are only tricks the mind conjures up in order to distract us; all of them are harmless, and all of them will simply disappear if they are ignored. Another thing that sometimes happens, particularly if our meditation is going well, and which can give rise to anxiety, is that the breath becomes so shallow that it can no longer be perceived. When we realize that the breath seems to have stopped, we might be startled. However, we only need to remind ourselves that the breath has not stopped and indeed cannot stop, and that it has only become soft and shallow because the body, being very relaxed, needs only a little oxygen. Another common problem meditators have is numbness or discomfort in the legs. As the discomfort is usually only mild and will soon disappear as our legs become used to being bent, it is best to simply ignore the discomfort. However, if the discomfort continues or intensifies into pain, it might be good to experiment with a different posture. What must be understood, though, is that any posture will be uncomfortable for a while, and if we keep on moving or adjusting our legs for every little irritation, the discomfort will certainly continue. When it becomes easier to keep attention on the breath, counting can be dropped and one can focus attention on the movement of the breath.

2. The Recollections

Once we are practising mindfulness of breathing regularly and have got to the stage where our attention is more and more fixed on the breath, we are ready to add the practice of the recollections (*anussati*) to our meditation. There are several recollection meditations taught by the Buddha, the most important being recollections on Buddha, Dhamma, and Sangha, on virtue, generosity, and spiritual friends, on death, and on peace. Recollection is practised by directing our thoughts towards a particular subject and then carefully pondering upon it. The Buddha says: "Whatever one ponders on and thinks about often, the mind gets a leaning in that way."[47] And this is certainly true. Any type of thought that is prominent in our mind will have an influence upon our personality and behaviour. To consciously and intentionally think positive thoughts will, in time, encourage such thoughts to arise quite naturally, and from that will spring deeds associated with such thoughts.

When we practise the *pūjā*, we do the recollection on the Buddha, Dhamma, and Sangha at the same time. The recollection on the Buddha can also be done by reading devotional literature that evokes thoughts similar to those expressed in the *Kamalañjali*:

You were kind to the cruel, fair to the unjust, good to the evil, benevolent to the harmful, and you acted in ways no one has ever done before. O Victor, Compassionate One, Just, Abode of Virtues, Righteous One, who lives solely for the welfare of others, truly it is in you that my heart finds delight.

Although you lived in the turmoils of existence, you always maintained your noble conduct, and by remaining equanimous in the midst of excitement, you fulfilled the perfections; so whenever I remember you day or night, in dreams, at any time, O Victor, O Wise One, it is in this that my heart finds delight.

You gave things difficult to give, did what was hard to do and forgave those who did great wrong, O Matchless Treasure-house of Compassion; and when, O Sage, I reflect on your spotless virtues, whether by day, night, or at any time, it is then that my heart finds great delight.

Truly did you practise the most difficult form of moral conduct and tame those who were obstinate; likewise, with a merciful heart did you extend kindness even to the most hard-hearted; therefore, O Sage, whenever I reflect on your spotless virtues, whether by day, night, or at any time, my heart finds delight.[48]

Until we can do it independently, it might be useful to quietly and slowly read the recollections below to help guide our thoughts.[49]

The Recollection on Generosity

Have I this day begrudged sharing the great abundance I enjoy? Engrossed in what is mine, without a thought for others, have I enjoyed what is mine alone? Without meanness or greed, have I delighted in giving? I here and now before the Buddha resolve always to be one who gives and shares.

I will give, but never what is harmful, even when asked.
I will give, not just to those I like, but to strangers and even to the hostile.
I will give, being mindful of the needs of others, not waiting to be asked.
I will give humbly, without desire for recognition.
I will give and I will also let others give to me.
I will give, not letting second thoughts taint my generosity.
I will give, knowing that generosity helps develop renunciation.

May my generosity transform the mean and pacify the hostile.
May my generosity befriend the newcomer and comfort the unhappy.
May my generosity dissolve all greed and clinging and help in the freeing of the heart.

Concerning the next recollection, the Buddha says: "You should recollect spiritual friends like this: 'It is indeed a gain for me. Indeed, it is good for me that I have beautiful friends, compassionate, desiring my welfare, and who encourage and teach me.'"[50] The recollection on spiritual friends encourages us to think about our relationships with others and what we can do in order to become more friendly and loving.

The Recollection on Friendship

Have I this day failed to act as a close friend to those who I have met? Have I, through body, speech, or mind, been hostile, indifferent, or rude to any other being? Have I sought to take advantage of others, not looking upon them as if they were grandparents, parents, brothers, or sisters? I here and now before the Buddha resolve to be as our Lord himself, a true friend to all the world.

As a friend, I will help the troubled, counsel the misguided, and comfort the lonely.

As a friend, I will never misuse another's confidence in me to mislead or to deceive.

As a friend, I will abandon neither evil-doer nor fool, for if I do who shall be their guide?

As a friend, I will ignore ingratitude and mistrust and continue to offer my friendship.

As a friend delighting always in concord, I will speak of others' good deeds and be silent about their faults.

As a friend, I will long remember good done to me and soon forget the bad.

May my friendliness win me the friendship of others.

May my friendliness protect me from hostility, anger, and aggression.

May my friendliness grow into love and compassion and help in the freeing of the heart.

The recollection on death, which consists in thinking of our own mortality, can be most useful in encouraging us to live properly and not fear death when it does approach us.

The Recollection on Death

I sit now before the Buddha and contemplate that he and all who knew him are now dead. Since his great demise, countless beings have come, bided their time, and gone. The names and deeds of but a few are remembered. Their many pains, their joys, their victories and defeats, like themselves are now but shadows. And so it will be with all who I know. Passing time will turn the calamities I worry about, the possibilities I fear, and the pleasures I chase after into mere shadows. Therefore, I will contemplate the reality of my own death that I may understand what is of true value in life.

Because death may soon come, I will repay all debts, forgive all transgressions and be at odds with none.

Because death may soon come, I will squander no time brooding on past mistakes, but use each day as if it were my last.

Because death may soon come, I will purify my mind rather than pamper the body.

Because death may soon come, and separation from those I love, I will develop detached compassion rather than possessiveness and clinging.

Because death may soon come, I will use each day fully, not wasting it on fruitless pursuits and vain longings.

May I be prepared when death finally comes.
May I be fearless as life ebbs away.
May my detachment help in the freeing of the heart.

The purpose of the recollection on peace is to encourage us to live in harmony with others and to promote peace and non-contention whenever we can. It also reminds us that lasting peace can only be experienced through the attaining of Nirvāṇa.

The Recollection on Peace

I sit now before the Buddha and contemplate that by seeing the aggregates as empty, he attained great peace. It is his unmoved stillness and sorrowless compassion that shall be my inspiration. Those who are angry at injustice, impatient for change, despairing at tragedy, elated today and depressed tomorrow, are soon exhausted. But those whose minds are always still and who abide in peace are abundant in energy. They, like the Buddha, are islands of peace in a sea of turmoil and a refuge to all beings.

Therefore I will seek peace and quiet, avoiding always the loud, the noisy, and those who wish to argue.
I will strive to restore harmony to those who are at odds.
I will speak without abuse or harshness, gentle always, with words sweet and true.
I will strive to be conciliatory and yielding, never being a source of conflict for others.

May all who live in turmoil find the peace they long for.
May my heart be free from the agitation of the defilements.
May my abiding in peace help in the freeing of the heart.

How long should recollection meditation be done for? This depends upon how we feel at any particular time. At times, quiet contemplation and reflection for five or ten minutes might be enough, and at other times, it might be useful to do it for twenty or thirty minutes. Another important thing to remember is that although it is good to do one of the recollections each day after finishing a period of mindfulness of breathing, the recollections can be done at any time. The Buddha says the recollections "should be developed as you walk, as you stand, as you sit, and as you lie, as you conduct your business, and as you dwell in your home crowded with children."[51]

3. The Meditation on Love

The next meditation practice we will examine is the meditation on love (*mettā-bhāvanā*). The purpose of this meditation is to dispel ill-will and to strengthen that most important of qualities, love (*mettā*).

Love is a strong feeling of warmth and affection towards another which expresses itself in trying to please the one who is loved. Love is one of the four qualities which together are called the four sublime states (*brahma-vihāra*), the others being compassion (*karuṇā*), sympathetic joy (*muditā*), and equanimity (*upekkhā*). Compassion is a feeling of pity which arises when we see beings suffer.

Balancing compassion is sympathetic joy, which is a rejoicing in the happiness or success of others. Equanimity is a state of mind free from any strong feelings, either for or against anyone. It is emotional balance or equipoise.

The four sublime states – love, compassion, sympathetic joy, equanimity – can be seen in several different ways: as four related but separate qualities or as different aspects of love. They can be seen as the different ways love can be expressed according to the situation, just as light produces diverse colours as it is reflected through the different facets of the same diamond. Thus love, in the sense of affection and warmth, is the sensitive Buddhist's response to the open and friendly person, compassion to those in distress, sympathetic joy to those who are happy, and equanimity to hostile or unpleasant people.

Everyone feels love towards at least some people – parents, children, spouse, or friends. But at the same time, this love for someone can co-exist with jealousy, possessiveness and the desire to dominate or control. Likewise, it is possible to have love towards some, while hating or being indifferent towards others. The higher and more refined love is free from negative defilements and is pervasive, that is, it is felt equally towards all beings – animals as much as humans – the friendly and the hostile, the virtuous and the immoral. All other virtues and good deeds are secondary to having a loving heart.

How is the meditation on love practised? If, during or after completing our daily period of mindfulness of breathing, the mind feels particularly light, peaceful, or happy, this is the best time to do the practice. Remaining in the usual meditation posture, we first think of ourselves, become aware of the happiness or peace that we are feeling, and then wish ourselves well. This can be done by saying to ourselves words like this: "May I be well and happy. May I be free from distress and worry. May my mind be free from ill-will. May my heart be filled with love. May I be well and happy. May I be well and happy." Having done this, we then proceed to think of a person we love, a neutral person, and then a person we dislike, one after the other, wishing each of them well as we do so, in words similar to those above. Having done this, we then wish all beings well: "May all beings be well and happy. May all be free from distress and worry. May their minds be free from ill-will. May their hearts be filled with love. May all beings be well and happy. May they all be well and happy." The meditation on love should be done in an unhurried way, taking altogether perhaps ten or fifteen minutes.

Sometimes while practising the meditation on love, we think of a disliked person and wish them well while in fact really feeling no love towards them at all. Isn't this, some people ask, merely pretence? No, it is not. Although we may, at present, feel no good-will towards that person, the recognition of our negative feelings and the desire to wish to transform them into positive feelings is important. In time, hatred will change into equanimity and from that into friendliness and concern.

When, through the practice of the meditation on love, we learn to shrug off insults rather than get angry, to forgive rather than plot revenge, and to be kind rather than rude, officious or uncaring, our interactions with others become considerably more enjoyable and our life becomes generally more happy.

What we have discussed above is what might be called the development of love through passive means, but equally important is the development of love through active means. This refers to enhancing and strengthening our love by acting in a more loving way. The *Cariyāpiṭaka* commentary expresses this idea well when it says: "One should think: 'I cannot provide for the welfare and happiness of others merely by wishing it. Let me make an effort to accomplish it.'"[52]

To put aside our own interests or desires for the sake of others is to act with love. To be helpful to someone who might have hurt us in the past is to act with love. To give up our free time in order to spend it helping those in need is to act with love. Such behaviour is necessary for purifying the mind. Done with selflessness and pure intentions, such acts are as much a part of the meditation on love as is sitting quietly with legs crossed.

4. The Jhānas

When all the steps we have previously discussed are practised regularly, and for longer periods of time, and when conditions are right, a state of mind called jhāna is attained. The word *jhāna* means "to ponder" or "to meditate," and the Buddha describes four levels of this state, each more pure and refined than the preceding one. It was these states of mind that the Buddha developed just prior to his enlightenment and which led to his enlightenment, and in the *Dhammapada*, he underlines the importance of the jhānas when he says: "No jhāna, no wisdom; no wisdom, no jhāna. But one who has both jhāna and wisdom, he truly is close to nirvana."[53]

The Buddha describes the first jhāna like this: "Detached from sense pleasures and unskilled states of mind, one enters and abides in the first jhāna, which has logical and wandering thought present, and is filled with a joy and happiness that is born of detachment."[54]

We will have a careful look at the first jhāna so that it can be recognised when it is attained. Logical thought (*vitakka*, from *takka* meaning "logic") refers to conscious and directed thinking, usually used in problem solving. Wandering thought (*vicāra*, from *carati* meaning "to move" or "to wander") refers to the scattered and unconnected thoughts that make up so much of the ordinary mind: "Logical thought is like the hand that grips firmly, and wandering thought is like the hand that rubs; as when one grips a tarnished metal dish firmly with one hand, and with the other hand rubs it with powder, oil, and a fibre pad."[55]

In the first jhāna, the mind is much quieter than usual, and although there is some logical and wandering thought, none of the five hindrances are present. Attention is settled on the breath with a minimum amount of effort and there is a general feeling of joy (*pīti*) and happiness (*sukha*). This positive feeling is born of detachment (*viveka-ja*), that is, it is a result of being detached or free from the five hindrances, if only temporarily. The joy might come like a sudden flash, in waves, or it might make the whole body feel light, but more usually it will be a subtle pervasive feeling coming suddenly and fading gradually.[56]

In the beginning, the first jhāna will only remain for perhaps a few moments, but even so, it may give rise to a very strong desire to maintain it, and also to re-experience it again during the next meditation sitting. This desire can only create agitation and tension, which will make the mind fall back to its ordinary state or cause us to spend the next meditation sitting dissatisfied and frustrated. When the first jhāna is attained, it should be enjoyed and experienced fully, and when it starts to subside, as it must, it should be allowed to go like a good friend who has paid a visit, whose company has been enjoyed, and who now has to leave. The meditator's task is now to continue regular practice so that he or she does not just enter the jhanic state momentarily and from time to time, but comes to abide in it for extended periods. Even though the first jhāna is the lowest and least refined of the four jhānas, its attainment has an extremely positive effect on the mind, which in turn brings about many important and wholesome changes in the personality.

Once the first jhāna has been attained, it is not long before attention becomes one-pointed (*ekodibhāva*) and fixed on the movement of the breath, thoughts stop completely (*avitakka avicāra*), an inner tranquillity is experienced, and the mind is fully concentrated. This state is called the second jhāna and is described by the Buddha like this: "By the stopping of logical and wandering thoughts, by gaining inner tranquillity and one-pointedness of mind, one enters and abides in the second *jhāna*, which is without logical and wandering thought, and is filled with a joy and happiness born of concentration."[57]

Joy and happiness are still present in the second jhāna, but now they are said to be born of concentration (*samādhi-ja*); that is, rather than being a reaction to sense stimulation, which is what ordinary happiness is, this positive feeling is due to *not* reacting to sense stimulation. With the attainment of the second jhāna, perfect concentration has been developed.

5. Mindfulness

We are made up of five aggregates, all of which are impermanent, unsatisfactory, and without self-nature; and when we see this as it really is, a profound change takes place in us. We are able to live without craving, and in peace and joy. But no amount of theorizing or conceptual understanding will bring about this change. If we wish to see things as they really are, we must look at them carefully. Normally we react to every experience we have with like or dislike, by comparing and judging, and of course by identifying with each experience, and considering it to be "mine." In short, we are involved in our experience and to that extent, we do not see it as it really is. Mindfulness allows us to "step out of" our experience, as it were, and observe it with a detached alert awareness. To do this is to get an entirely different and more accurate insight into things, and our detached, non-involved attitude means we can respond to our experiences in the most appropriate way rather than reacting impulsively and mindlessly as we usually do.

The Buddha taught four foundations of mindfulness (*satipaṭ-ṭhāna*), four things on which we should develop our mindfulness or direct our mindfulness towards, and not surprisingly, they correspond approximately to the five aggregates. They are mindfulness of body, of feeling (*vedanā*), of mind (*citta*), and of mental objects (*dhammas*).[58]

Mindfulness of the body means to be aware of the movements, tensions, comings and goings of the body. Mindfulness of feelings means to be aware of the different sensations that arise on the body, and to simply observe them in a detached manner. Mindfulness of mind is to be aware of the quality of the mind at any one time, whether it has many thoughts or few, what emotions are present, whether it is agitated or not, and so on. Mindfulness of mental objects is to be aware of the contents of the thoughts in the mind, to actually listen to what they are saying rather than react to them.

How is mindfulness meditation practised? As before, one sits in a comfortable posture, with the eyes closed and the hands nestled in the lap, and then practises mindfulness of breathing for a while, perhaps for ten minutes. Then one selects one of the four foundations of mindfulness, mindfulness of mental objects being the best to start with. Having less thoughts than usual, one merely watches them as they arise, persist for some time, and then disappear, without reacting to them in any way. The Buddha describes the practice like this: "Seen, thoughts arise; seen, they persist; seen, they pass away."[59] One should become what the Buddha calls "a detached onlooker of the mind."[60] When there are no thoughts to observe, one should simply watch the gentle in-and-out movement of the breath. If extremely passionate thoughts arise, and it is impossible not to get involved in them, it is best to return to doing mindfulness of breathing for a while. The practice should be done for at least an hour per day.

At this stage, more and more attention should be given to maintaining mindfulness in daily life. This can be done by selecting a particular activity, and resolving to be as mindful as possible while doing it. One could choose putting on one's clothes in the morning, preparing meals, or eating, bathing, walking from one place to another, and so on. If one selects eating, for example, instead of reading, talking, daydreaming, or thinking about what has to be done after the meal is finished, one would give oneself fully to the task at hand. One would move the body and chew and taste the food consciously and knowingly. It is not necessary to do all this unnaturally slowly, although it might require that one's actions be just a little slower than usual. Nor does it mean that one must have a blank expression on the face. Some people mistakenly think that a good Buddhist should never smile, and should try to look as serious as possible. But if mindfulness meditation is done properly, as the Buddha says, "your features will be serene" and "your complexion will be bright and radiant."

Reading 16

Observing your Mind

Achaan Chah

Begin practice by sitting up straight and paying attention. You can sit on the floor; you can sit in a chair. At first, you need not fix your attention on much. Simply be mindful of in-and-out breathing. If you find it helpful, you can also repeat "Buddho," "Dharmo," or "Sangho" as a mantra while you watch the breath going in and out. In this awareness of breathing, you must not force. If you try to control your breathing, that is not yet correct. It may seem that the breathing is too short, too long, too gentle, too heavy. You may feel that you are not passing the breath properly, or you may not feel well. Just let it be, let it settle by itself. Eventually the breath will enter and exit freely. When you are aware of and firmly established in this entry and exit, that is correct breathing.

When you become distracted, stop and refocus your attention. At first, when you are focusing it, your mind wants it to be a certain way. But do not control it or worry about it. Just notice it and let it be. Keep at it. Samādhi will grow by itself. As you go on practising in this way, sometimes the breath will stop, but here again, do not fear. Only your perception of the breath has stopped; the subtle factors continue. When the time is right, the breath will come back on its own as before.

If you can make your mind tranquil like this, wherever you find yourself – on a chair, in a car, on a boat – you will be able to fix your attention and enter into a calm state immediately. Wherever you are, you will be able to sit for meditation.

Having reached this point, you know something of the Path, but you must also contemplate sense objects. Turn your tranquil mind toward sights, sounds, smells, tastes, touches, thoughts, mental objects, mental factors. Whatever arises, investigate it. Notice whether you like it or not, whether it pleases or displeases you, but do not get involved with it. This liking and disliking are just reactions to the world of appearances – you must see a deeper level. Then, whether something initially seems good or bad, you will see that it is really only impermanent, unsatisfactory, and empty. File everything that arises into those three categories – good, bad, evil, wonderful, whatever it is, put it there. This is the way of vipassanā, by which all things are calmed.

Before long, knowledge and insight into impermanence, unsatisfactoriness, and emptiness will arise. This is the beginning of true wisdom, the heart of meditation, which leads to liberation. Follow your experience. See it. Strive continuously. Know the truth. Learn to give up, to get rid, to attain peace.

When sitting in meditation, you may have strange experiences or visions such as seeing lights, angels, or buddhas. When you see such things, you should observe yourself first to find out what state the mind is in. Do not forget the basic point. Pay attention. Do not wish for visions to arise or not to arise. If you go running after such experiences, you may end up babbling senselessly because the mind has fled the stable. When such things do come, contemplate them. When you have contemplated them, do not be deluded by them. You should consider that they are not yourself; they too are impermanent, unsatisfactory, and not self. Though they have come about, do not take them seriously. If they do not go away, re-establish your mindfulness, fix your attention on your breathing, and take at least three long inhalations and exhalations – then you can cut them off. Whatever arises, keep re-establishing your attention. Do not take anything as yourself – everything is only a vision or a construction of the mind, a deception that causes you to like, grasp, or fear. When you see such constructions, do not get involved. All unusual experiences and visions are of value to the wise person but harmful to the unwise. Keep practising until you are not stirred by them.

If you can trust your mind in this way, there is no problem. If it wants to be glad, you just know that this gladness is uncertain, unstable. Do not fear your visions or other experiences in practice; just learn to work with them. In this way, defilements can be used to train the mind, and you come to know the natural state of the mind, free from extremes, clear, unattached.

As I see it, the mind is like a single point, the centre of the universe, and mental states are like visitors who come to stay at this point for short or long periods of time. Get to know these visitors well. Become familiar with the vivid pictures they paint, the alluring stories they tell, to entice you to follow them. But do not give up your seat – it is the only chair around. If you continue to occupy it unceasingly, greeting each guest as it comes, firmly establishing yourself in awareness, transforming your mind into the one who knows, the one who is awake, the visitors will eventually stop coming back. If you give them real attention, how many times can these visitors return? Speak with them here, and you will know every one of them well. Then your mind will at last be at peace.

Some Hints on Practising

As you practise, various images and visions may arise. You see an attractive form, hear a sound that stirs you – such an image must be observed too. This kind of vipassanā image can have even more energy than one that may arise from simple concentration. Whatever arises, just watch.

Someone recently asked me, "As we meditate and various things arise in my mind, should we investigate them or just note them coming and going?" If you see someone passing by whom you do not know, you may wonder, "Who is that? Where is he going? What is he up to?" But if you know the person, it is enough just to notice him pass by.

Desire in practice can be friend or foe. At first, it spurs us to come and practise; we want to change things, to understand, to end suffering. But to be always desiring something that has not yet arisen, to want things to be other than they are, just causes more suffering.

Someone asked, "Should we just eat when hungry, sleep when tired, as the Zen masters suggest, or should we experiment by going against the grain at times? And if so, how much?" Of course, one should experiment, but no one else can say how much. All of this is to be known within oneself. At first, in our practice, we are like children learning to write the alphabet. The letters come out bent and sloppy, time and again – the only thing to do is to keep at it. And if we do not live life like this, what else is there for us to do?

A good practice is to ask yourself very sincerely, "Why was I born?" Ask yourself this question three times a day, in the morning, in the afternoon, and at night. Ask every day.

The Buddha told his disciple Ananda to see impermanence, to see death with every breath. We must know death; we must die in order to live. What does this mean? To die is to come to the end of all our doubts, all our questions, and just be here with the present reality. You can never die tomorrow, you must die now. Can you do it? Ah, how still, the peace of no more questions!

Real effort is a matter of the mind, not of the body. Different methods of concentration are like ways of earning a living – the most important thing is that you feed yourself, not how you manage to get the food. Actually, when the mind is freed from desires, concentration arises naturally, no matter what activity you are engaged in.

Drugs can bring about meaningful experiences, but the one who takes a drug has not made causes for such effects. He has just temporarily altered nature, like injecting a monkey with hormones that send him shooting up a tree to pick coconuts. Such experiences may be true but not good, or good but not true, whereas Dharma is always both good and true.

Sometimes we want to force the mind to be quiet, and this effort just makes it all the more disturbed. Then we stop pushing and some concentration arises. But in the state of calm and quiet, we begin to wonder, "What's going on? What's happening now?" and we are agitated again.

The day before the first monastic council, one of the Buddha's disciples went to tell Ananda, "Tomorrow is the Sangha Council. Others who attend are fully enlightened." Since Ananda was at this time still incompletely enlightened, he determined to practise strenuously all through the night, seeking full awakening. But in the end, he just made himself tired. He was not making any progress for all his efforts, so he decided to let go and rest a bit. As soon as his head hit the pillow, he became enlightened. In the end, we must learn to let go every last desire, even the desire for enlightenment. Only then can we be free.

Contemplate Everything

As you proceed with your practice, you must be willing to carefully examine every experience, every sense door. For example, practise with a sense object such as a sound. Listen. Your hearing is one thing, the sound is another. You are aware, and that is all there is to it. There is no one, nothing else. Learn to pay careful attention. Rely on nature in this way, and contemplate to find the truth. You will see how things separate themselves. When the mind does not grasp or take a vested interest, does not get caught up, things become clear.

When the ear hears, observe the mind. Does it get caught up and make a story out of the sound? Is it disturbed? You can know this, stay with it, be aware. At times you may want to escape from the sound, but that is not the way out. You must escape through awareness.

Sometimes we like the Dharma, sometimes we do not; but the problem is never the Dharma's. We cannot expect to have tranquillity as soon as we start to practise. We should let the mind think, let it do as it will, just watch it and not react to it. Then, as things contact the senses, we should practise equanimity. See all sense impressions as the same. See how they come and go. Keep the mind in the present. Do not think about what has passed; do not think, "Tomorrow I'm going to do it." If we see the true characteristics of things in the present moment, at all times, then *everything* is Dharma revealing itself.

Train the heart until it is firm, until it lays down all experiences. Then things will come and you will perceive them without becoming attached. You do not have to force the mind and sense objects apart. As you practise, they separate by themselves, showing the simple elements of body and mind.

As you learn about sights, sounds, smells, and tastes according to the truth, you will see that they all have a common nature – impermanent, unsatisfactory, and empty of self. Whenever you hear a sound, it registers in your mind as this common nature. Having heard is the same as not having heard. Mindfulness is constantly with you, protecting the heart. If your heart can reach this state wherever you go, there will be a growing understanding within you, which is called investigation, one of the seven factors of enlightenment. It revolves, it spins, it converses with itself, it solves, it detaches from feelings, perceptions, thoughts, consciousness. Nothing can come near it. It has its own work to do. This awareness is an automatic aspect of the mind that already exists and that you discover when you train in the beginning stages of practice.

Whatever you see, whatever you do, notice everything. Do not put the meditation aside for a rest. Some people think they can stop as soon as they come out of a period of formal practice. Having stopped practice, they stop being attentive, stop contemplating. Do not do it that way. Whatever you see, you should contemplate. If you see good people or bad people, rich people or poor people, watch. When you see old people or small children, youngsters or adults, contemplate all of it. This is the heart of our practice.

In contemplating to seek the Dharma, you should observe the characteristics, the cause and effect, the play of all the objects of your senses, big and small, white and black, good and evil. If there is thinking, simply contemplate it as thinking. All these things are impermanent, unsatisfactory, and empty of self, so do not cling to them. Awareness is their graveyard; dump them all here. Then, seeing the impermanence and emptiness of all things, you can put an end to suffering. Keep contemplating and examining this life.

Notice what happens when something good comes to you. Are you glad? You should contemplate that gladness. Perhaps you use something for a while and then start to dislike it, wanting to give or sell it to someone else. If no one comes to buy it, you may even try to throw it away. Why are we like this? Our life is impermanent, constantly subject to change. You must look at its true characteristics. Once you completely understand just one of these incidents, you will understand them all. They are all of the same nature.

Perhaps you do not like a particular sight or sound. Make note of that – later, you may like it, you may become pleased with what formerly displeased you. Such things do happen. When you realize clearly that all such things are impermanent, unsatisfactory, and not self, you will dump them all and attachment will not arise. When you see that all the various things that come to you are the same, there will be only Dharma arising.

Once having entered this stream and tasted liberation, you will not return, you will have gone beyond wrongdoing and wrong understanding. The mind, the heart, will have turned, will have entered the stream, and it will not be able to fall back into suffering again. How could it fall? It has given up unskilful actions because it sees the danger in them and cannot again be made to do wrong in body or speech. It has entered the Way fully, knows its duties, knows its work, knows the Path, knows its own nature. It lets go of what needs to be let go of, and keeps letting go without doubting.

All that I have said up to now has merely been words. When people come to see me, I have to say something. But it is best not to speak about these matters too much. Better to begin practice without delay. I am like a good friend inviting you to go somewhere. Do not hesitate; just get going. You won't regret it.

Walking Meditation

Work with the walking meditation every day. To begin, clasp the hands in front of you, maintaining a very slight tension that compels the mind to be attentive. Walk at a normal pace from one end of the path to the other, knowing yourself all the way. Stop and return. If the mind wanders, stand still and bring it back. If the mind still wanders, fix attention on the breath. Keep coming back. Mindfulness thus developed is useful at all times.

Change positions when physically tired, but not as soon as you feel an impulse to change. First, know why you want to change – is it physical fatigue, mental restlessness, or laziness? Notice the sufferings of the body. Learn to watch openly and carefully. Effort in practice is a matter of the mind, not the body. It means constantly being aware of what goes on in the mind without following like and dislike as they arise. Sitting or walking all night is not in itself energetic effort if one is not aware in this way.

As you walk from one predetermined point to another, fix the eyes about two yards in front of you and fix the attention on the actual feeling of the body, or repeat the mantra "Buddho." Do not fear things that arise in the mind; question them, know them. The truth is more than thoughts and feelings, so do not believe and get caught by them. See the whole process arising and ceasing. This understanding gives rise to wisdom.

When consciousness arises, we should have awareness of it at the same time, like a light bulb and its light. If you are not alert, the hindrances will catch hold of the mind – only concentration can cut through them. Just as the presence of a thief prevents negligence with our possessions, so the reminder of the hindrances should prevent negligence in our concentration.

Learning Concentration

In our practice, we think that noises, cars, voices, sights, are distractions that come and bother us when we want to be quiet. But who is bothering whom? Actually, we are the ones who go and bother them. The car, the sound, is just following its own nature. We bother things through some false idea that they are outside us and cling to the ideal of remaining quiet, undisturbed.

Learn to see that it is not things that bother us, that we go out to bother them. See the world as a mirror. It is all a reflection of mind. When you know this, you can grow in every moment, and every experience reveals truth and brings understanding.

Normally, the untrained mind is full of worries and anxieties, so when a bit of tranquillity arises from practising meditation, you easily become attached to it, mistaking states of tranquillity for the end of meditation. Sometimes you may even think you have put an end to lust or greed or hatred, only to be overwhelmed by them later on. Actually, it is worse to be caught in calmness than to be stuck in agitation, because at least you will want to escape from agitation, whereas you are content to remain in calmness and not go any further.

When extraordinarily blissful, clear states arise from insight meditation practice, do not cling to them. Although this tranquillity has a sweet taste, it too must be seen as impermanent, unsatisfactory, and empty. Absorption is not what the Buddha found essential in meditation. Practise without thought of attaining absorption or any special state. Just know whether the mind is calm or not and, if so, whether a little or a lot. In this way it will develop on its own.

Nevertheless, concentration must be firmly established for wisdom to arise. To concentrate the mind is like turning on the switch, and wisdom is the resulting light. Without the switch, there is no light, but we should not waste our time playing with the switch. Likewise, concentration is the empty bowl and wisdom the food that fills it and makes the meal.

Do not be attached to the object of meditation such as a mantra. Know its purpose. If you succeed in concentrating your mind using the mantra "Buddho," let the mantra go. It is a mistake to think that to stop repeating "Buddho" would be laziness. "Buddho" means "the one who knows." If you become one who knows, why repeat the word?

Stick to it

Endurance and moderation are the foundation, the beginning of our practice. To start we simply follow the practice and the schedule set up by ourselves or in a retreat or monastery. To train an animal, we have to restrain it; likewise, we need to restrict ourselves. An animal which is difficult to train should be given little food. Here we have the ascetic practices to limit ourselves in regard to food, robes, and living quarters, to bring us down to bare essentials, to cut away infatuation.

These practices are the basis for concentration. Constant mindfulness in all postures and activities will make the mind calm and clear. But this calm is not the end point of practice. Tranquil states give the mind a temporary rest, as eating will temporarily remove hunger, but that is not all there is to life. You must use the calmed mind to see things in a new light, the light of wisdom. When the heart becomes firm in this wisdom, you will not adhere to worldly standards of good and bad, and will not be swayed by external conditions. With wisdom, dung can be used for fertilizer; all our experiences become sources of insight. Normally we want praise and dislike criticism, but with a clear mind we see them as equally empty. Thus, we can let go of all these things and find peace.

Do not worry about how long it will take to get results; just do it. Practise endurance. If your legs hurt, tell yourself, "I have no legs." If your head aches, think, "I do not have a head." If you get sleepy when sitting at night, think, "It is daytime." During meditation using mindfulness of breathing, if you have uncomfortable feelings in the chest, take a few long, deep breaths. If the mind wanders, just hold your breath and let the mind go where it will; it will not go far.

You can change postures after an appropriate time, but do not be a slave to your restlessness or feelings of discomfort. Sometimes it is good just to sit on them. You feel hot, your legs are painful, you are unable to concentrate – just tell it all to die. The feelings will get more and more intense and then hit a breaking point, after which you will be calm and cool. But the next day your mind will not want to do it again. Training yourself requires constant effort. By practising over a long period of time, you will learn when to push, and when to relax; you will learn to separate physical fatigue from laziness.

Do not worry about enlightenment. When growing a tree, you plant it, water it, fertilize it, keep the bugs away; and if these things are done properly, the tree will naturally grow. How quickly it grows, however, is something you cannot control.

At first, endurance and persistence are necessary, but after a time, faith and certainty arise. Then you see the value of practice and want to do it; you want to avoid socializing and be by yourself in quiet places; you seek extra time just to practise and to study yourself.

Just do the practice, beginning with the basic steps: being honest and clean and being aware of whatever you do. All the rest will follow.

Insight by the Nature Method

Buddhadasa Bhikkhu

Now we shall see how concentration can come about, naturally on the one hand, and as a result of systematic practice on the other. The end result is identical in the two cases: the mind is concentrated and fit to be used for carrying out close introspection. One thing must be noticed, however. The intensity of concentration that comes about naturally is usually sufficient and appropriate for introspection and insight, whereas the concentration resulting from systematic training is usually excessive, more than can be made use of. Furthermore, misguided satisfaction with that highly developed concentration may result. While the mind is fully concentrated it is likely to experience such a satisfying kind of bliss and well-being that the meditator may become attached to it or imagine it to be the fruit of the path. Naturally occurring concentration which is sufficient and suitable for use in introspection is harmless, having none of the disadvantages inherent in concentration developed by means of intensive training.

In the Tipiṭaka there are numerous references to people attaining naturally all stages of path and fruit.[61] This generally came about in the presence of the Buddha himself but also happened later with other teachers. These people did not go into the forest and sit, assiduously practising concentration on certain objects in the way described in later manuals. No systematic effort was involved when arahantship was attained by the first five disciples of the Buddha on hearing the Discourse on Non-selfhood, or by the one thousand hermits on hearing the Fire Sermon. In these cases keen, penetrating insight came about quite naturally. These examples clearly show that natural concentration is liable to develop of its own accord while one is attempting to understand clearly some question; and that the resulting insight, as long as it is firmly established, is sure to be quite intense and stable. It happens naturally, automatically, in just the same way that the mind becomes concentrated the moment we set about doing arithmetic. The same happens when firing a gun. When we take aim the mind automatically becomes concentrated and steady.

Normally we completely overlook this naturally occurring concentration because it does not appear the least bit magical, miraculous, or awe-inspiring. But through the power of just such concentration, most of us could actually attain liberation. We could attain the path, the fruit, nirvana, and arahantship, just by means of natural concentration. It is something most of us either already have or can readily develop. We ought to do everything we can to cultivate it, to make it function perfectly and yield the appropriate results. That is just what most of those people did who succeeded in attaining enlightenment without knowing anything of modern concentration techniques.

Now let us look at the nature of the stages of inner awareness leading to full insight into the world, that is, into the five aggregates (*khandhas*). The first stage is joy (*pīti*), mental happiness, or spiritual well-being. Doing good in some way, even giving alms, considered the most basic form of merit-making, can be a source of joy. Higher up, at the level of morality, completely blameless conduct by way of word and deed brings an increase in joy. We also discover that joy of a definite kind is associated with the lower stages of concentration.

This joy or rapture has in itself the power to induce tranquillity. Normally the mind is quite unrestrained, continually falling slave to all sorts of thoughts and feelings associated with enticing things outside. It is normally restless, not calm. But as spiritual joy becomes established, calm and steadiness are bound to increase in proportion. When steadiness has been perfected, the result is full concentration. The mind becomes tranquil, steady, flexible, manageable, and at ease. It is then ready to be used for any chosen purpose, in particular for the elimination of the defilements.

It is not a case of the mind's being rendered silent, hard, and rocklike. Nothing like that happens at all. The body feels normal, but the mind is especially calm and suitable for use in reflection and introspection. It is perfectly clear, cool, still, and restrained. This is quite unlike sitting in deep concentration. A deeply concentrated mind is in no position to investigate anything. It cannot practise introspection at all; it is in a state of unawareness and is of no use for insight. *Deep concentration is a major obstacle to insight practice.* To practise introspection one must first return to the shallower levels of concentration; then one can make use of the power the mind has acquired. Insight so developed is natural insight, the same sort as was gained by some individuals while sitting listening to the Buddha expounding the Dharma. It is conducive to reflection and introspection of the right kind, the kind that brings understanding, and it involves neither ceremonial procedures nor miracles.

This does not mean, however, that insight will arise instantaneously. One cannot be an arahant straight off. The first stage in insight may come about at any time, depending once again on the intensity of the concentration. It may happen that what arises is not true insight because one has been practising incorrectly or is enveloped in too many false views. If insight develops in only small measure, it may convert a person into an *ariya* at the lowest stage. Or, if it is not sufficient to do that, it will at least make him or her a high-minded individual, an ordinary person of good qualities. If conditions are right and good qualities have been properly and adequately established, it is possible to become an *arahant*, a fully enlightened being.

The expression "insight into the true nature of things" refers to realizing transience (*anicca*), unsatisfactoriness or suffering (*dukkha*), and non-selfhood (*anattā*). It means seeing that nothing is worth getting, that no object whatsoever should be grasped at and clung to as being a self or as belonging to a self, as being good or bad, attractive or repulsive. Liking or disliking anything, even an idea or a memory, is clinging. To say that nothing is worth getting or being is the same as saying that nothing is worth clinging to. "Getting" refers to setting one's heart on property, position, wealth, or any attractive object. "Being" refers to the awareness of one's status as husband, wife, rich man, poor man, winner, loser, or even the awareness of being oneself. If one can completely give up clinging to the idea of being oneself, then being oneself will no longer be subject to suffering.

If we were to give up trying to get or to be anything, how could we continue to exist? The words "getting" and "being" as used here refer to getting and being based on mental defilements, craving, the idea of "worth getting," "worth being," so that the mind does get and be in real earnest. These factors lead to depression, anxiety, and distress, or at least to a heavy burden on the mind from beginning to end. Knowing this truth, we shall be constantly on the alert, keeping watch over the mind to see that it does not fall slave to getting and being through the influence of grasping and clinging.

The world and all things have the property of impermanence, of worthlessness, and of not belonging to anyone.

A skeptic may ask: "If nothing at all is worth getting or being, does it follow that nobody ought to do any work or build up wealth, position, and property?" Anyone who comprehends this subject can see that a person equipped with right knowledge and understanding is actually in a far better position to carry out any task than one subject to strong desires and lacking in understanding. Very briefly, in becoming involved in things, we must do so mindfully, and our actions must not be motivated by craving.

The Buddha and all the other arahants were completely free of desire; yet they succeeded in doing many things far more useful than what any of us are capable of. If we look at accounts of how the Buddha spent his day, we find that he slept for only four hours and spent the rest of the time working. We spend more than four hours a day just amusing ourselves. If the defilements responsible for the desire to be and get things had been completely eliminated, what was the force that motivated the Buddha and all arahants to act? They were motivated by discrimination coupled with loving-kindness (*mettā*). Even actions based on natural bodily wants, such as receiving and eating alms food, were motivated by discrimination. They were free of defilements, free of all desire to keep on living in order to be this or to get that. They had the ability to discriminate between what was worthwhile and what was not; this was the motivating force in all they did. If they found food, well and good. If not, it made no difference. When they were suffering with fever, they knew how to treat it and did so as well as possible on the basis of this knowledge. If the fever was quite overpowering, they recalled that to die is natural. Whether they lived or died was of no significance to them. The two were of equal value in their eyes.

If one is to be completely free of suffering, this is the best attitude to have. There is no need for a self as master of the body. Discrimination alone enables the body to carry on by its natural power. The example of the Buddha shows that the power of pure discrimination and pure goodwill alone is sufficient to keep an arahant living in the world and, what is more, doing far more good to others than people who are still subject to craving. People with defilements are likely to do only what benefits themselves, since they act out of selfishness. By contrast, the deeds of enlightened beings are entirely self-less and so are perfectly pure.

To come to know the true nature of things is the objective of every Buddhist. It is the means by which we can liberate ourselves. Regardless of whether we are hoping for worldly benefits, wealth, position, and fame; or for benefits in the next world such as heaven;

or for the supramundane benefit, the path, the fruit, and nirvana; whatever we are hoping for, the only way to achieve it is by means of right knowledge and insight. In the texts it is said that we become purified through insight and not by any other means. Our path to freedom lies in gaining the insight, the clear vision, which sees that in all things there neither is nor has ever been anything at all worth grasping at or clinging to, worth getting or being, worth risking life and limb for. We *have* things and we *are* things only in terms of worldly, relative truth.

In worldly language we say we are this or that, just because in any society it is expedient to recognize by names and occupations. But we must not believe that we really *are* this or that, as is assumed at the level of relative truth. To do so is to behave like crickets, which, when their faces become covered with dirt, become disoriented and muddled and proceed to bite one another until they die. We humans, when our faces become covered in dirt, when we are subject to all sorts of delusions, become so bewildered and disoriented that we do things no human being would ever do under ordinary circumstances – killing, for instance. So let us not go blindly clinging to relative truths; rather, let us be aware that they are just relative truths, essential for society but nothing more. We have to be aware of what this body-and-mind really is, what its true nature is. In particular we have to be aware of its impermanence, unsatisfactoriness, and non-selfhood, and make sure we always remain independent of it.

As for the wealth and position that we cannot do without, let us regard these too as relative truths, so that we can break free from the existing custom of saying, "This belongs to So-and-so" or "That belongs to Such-and-such." The law watches over ownership rights for us; there is no need for us to cling to the idea of "mine." We ought to possess things purely and simply for the sake of convenience and ease, not so they can be master over our minds.

When we have really come to perceive clearly that nothing is worth getting or being, disenchantment (*nibbidā*) develops in proportion to the intensity of the insight. This is a sign that the clinging has become less firm and is starting to give way. It is a sign that we have been slaves for so long that the idea of trying to escape has at last occurred to us. This is the onset of disenchantment and disillusionment, when one becomes fed up with one's own stupidity in grasping and clinging to things, believing things to be worth having and being. As soon as disenchantment has set in, there is bound to come about a natural, automatic process of disentangle-ment (*virāga*), as if a rope with which one had been tightly bound were being untied, or a rinsing out, as when the dye that had been firmly fixed in a piece of cloth is removed by soaking it in the appropriate substances. This process, whereby clinging gives way to a breaking free or a dissolving out from the world or from the objects of that clinging, was called by the Buddha emancipation (*vimutti*). This stage is most important. Though not the final stage, it is an essential step toward complete liberation. When one has broken free to this extent, complete liberation from suffering is assured.

Once broken free from slavery, one need never again be a slave to the world. One becomes pure and uncontaminated where previously one was defiled in every way. To be enslaved to things is to be defiled in body, speech, and mind. To break free from slavery to the delightful tastes of the world is to achieve a condition of purity and never be defiled again. This purity (*visuddhi*), once it has been attained, will give rise to a genuine calm and coolness free from all turbulence, strife, and torment. This state of freedom from oppression and turbulence was called by the Buddha simply Peace (*sānti*), that is, stillness, coolness in all situations. It is virtually the same thing as nirvana.

The word "nirvana" (*nibbāna*) has been translated as "absence of any instrument of torture." Taken another way, it means "extinction without remainder." So the word "nirvana" has two very important meanings: first, absence of any source of torment and burning, freedom from all forms of bondage and constraint; and second, extinction, with no fuel for the further arising of suffering. The combination of these meanings indicates a condition of complete freedom from suffering. The word "nirvana" also has several other useful meanings. It can be taken to mean the extinction of suffering, or the complete elimination of defilements, or the state of coolness, or the condition that is the cessation of all suffering, all defilements, and all karmic activity. The word "nirvana" is used by various sects, but often in quite different senses. For instance, one group takes it to mean simply calm and coolness, because they identify nirvana with deep concentration. Other groups even consider nirvana to be total absorption in sensuality.

The Buddha defined nirvana as simply that condition of freedom from bondage, torment, and suffering which results from seeing the true nature of the worldly condition of all things, and so being able to give up clinging to them. It is essential, then, that we recognize the great value of insight into the true nature of things, and that we endeavour to cultivate this insight by one means or another. Using one method we simply encourage it to come about of its own accord, naturally, by developing, day and night, the joy that results from mental purity, until the qualities we have described gradually evolve. The other method consists in developing mental power by following an organized system of concentration and insight practice. This latter technique is appropriate for people with a certain kind of disposition who may make rapid progress with it if conditions are right. But we can practise the development of insight by the nature method in all circumstances and at all times. We do it just by making our own way of daily living so pure and honest that there arise in succession spiritual joy, calm, insight into the true nature of things, disenchantment, disentanglement, escape, purification from defilements, and finally peace, nirvana.

Insight through Mindfulness

Mahasi Sayadaw

With every breath there occurs in the abdomen a rising-falling movement. A beginner should start with the exercise of noting this movement. This rising-falling movement is easy to observe because it is coarse and therefore more suitable for the beginner.

When contemplating rising and falling, the disciple should keep his mind on the abdomen. He will then come to know the upward movement or expansion of the abdomen on breathing in, and the downward movement or contraction on breathing out. A mental note should be made as "rising" for the upward movement and "falling" for the downward movement. If these movements are not clearly noticed by simply fixing the mind on them, one or both hands should be placed on the abdomen.

The disciple should not try to change the manner of his natural breathing. He should neither attempt slow breathing by the retention of his breath, nor quick breathing or deep breathing. If he does change the natural flow of his breathing, he will soon tire himself. He must therefore keep to the natural rate of his breathing and proceed with the contemplation of rising and falling.

On the occurrence of the upward movement of the abdomen, the mental note of "rising" should be made, and on the downward movement of the abdomen, the mental note of "falling" should be made. The mental noting of these terms should not be vocalized. In vipassanā meditation, it is more important to know the object than to know it by term or name. It is therefore necessary for the disciple to make every effort to be mindful of the movement of rising from its beginning to its end and that of falling from its beginning to its end, as if these movements were actually seen with the eyes. As soon as rising occurs, there should be the knowing mind close to the movement, as in the case of a stone hitting a wall. The movement of rising as it occurs and the mind knowing it must come together on every occasion. Similarly, the movement of falling as it occurs and the mind knowing it must come together on every occasion.

When there is no other conspicuous object, the disciple should carry on the exercise of noting these two movements as "rising, falling, rising, falling, rising, falling." While thus occupied with this exercise, there may be occasions when the mind wanders about. When concentration is weak, it is very difficult to control the mind. Though it is directed to the movements of rising and falling, the mind will not stay with them but will wander to other places. This wandering mind should not be let alone. It should be noted as "wandering, wandering, wandering" as soon as it is noticed that it is wandering. On noting once or twice the mind usually stops wandering; then the exercise of noting "rising, falling" should be continued. When it is again found that the mind has reached a place, it should be noted as "reaching, reaching, reaching." Then the exercise of noting "rising, falling" should be reverted to as soon as these movements are clear.

On meeting with a person in the imagination, it should be noted as "meeting, meeting," after which the usual exercise should be reverted to. Sometimes the fact that it is mere imagination is discovered when one speaks with that imaginary person, and it should then be noted as "speaking, speaking." The real purpose is to note every mental activity as it occurs. For instance, it should be noted as "thinking" at the moment of thinking, and as "reflecting," "planning," "knowing," "attending," "rejoicing," "feeling lazy," "feeling happy," "disgusted," etc., as the case may be, on the occurrence of each activity. The contemplation of mental activities and noticing them is called *cittānupassanā*, contemplation of mind.

Because people have no practical knowledge in vipassanā meditation, they are generally not in a position to know the real state of the mind. This naturally leads them to the wrong view of holding mind to be "person," "self," "living entity." They usually believe that "imagination is *I*," "*I* am thinking," "*I* am planning," "*I* am knowing," and so forth. They hold that there exists a living entity or self which grows up from childhood to adulthood. In reality, such a living entity does not exist. What does exist is a continuous process of elements of mind which occur singly, one at a time, in succession. The practice of contemplation is therefore being carried out with the aim of discovering the true nature of this mind-body complex.

While one is proceeding with the usual exercise, one may feel that one wants to swallow saliva. It should be noted as "wanting," and on gathering saliva as "gathering," and on swallowing as "swallowing," in the serial order of occurrence. The reason for contemplation in this case is because there may be a persisting personal view as "wanting to swallow is I," "swallowing is also I." In reality, "wanting to swallow" is mentality and not "I," and "swallowing" is materiality and not "I." There exist only mentality and materiality at that moment. By means of contemplating in this manner, one will understand clearly the process of reality. So too, in the case of spitting, it should be noted as "wanting" when one wants to spit, as "bending" on bending the neck (which should be done slowly), as "looking, seeing" on looking, and as "spitting" on spitting. Afterwards, the usual exercise of noting "rising, falling" should be continued.

Because of sitting for a long time, there will arise in the body unpleasant feelings of being stiff, being hot and so forth. These sensations should be noted as they occur. The mind should be fixed on that spot and a note made as "stiff, stiff" on feeling stiff, as "hot, hot" on feeling hot, as "painful, painful" on feeling painful, as "prickly, prickly" on feeling prickly sensations, and as "tired, tired" on feeling tired. These unpleasant feelings are *dukkha-vedanā* and the contemplation of these feelings is *vedanānupassanā*, contemplation of feeling.

Owing to the absence of knowledge in respect of these feelings, there persists the wrong view of holding them as one's own personality or self, that is to say, "*I* am feeling stiff," "*I* am feeling painful," "*I* was feeling well formerly but *I* now feel uncomfortable," in the manner of a single self. In reality, unpleasant feelings arise owing to disagreeable impressions in the body. Like the light of an electric bulb, which can continue to burn on a continuous supply of energy, so it is in the case of feelings, which arise anew on every occasion of coming in contact with disagreeable impressions.

It is essential to understand these feelings clearly. At the beginning of noting as "stiff, stiff," "hot, hot," "painful, painful," one may feel that such disagreeable feelings grow stronger, and then one will notice that a [state of] mind wanting to change the posture arises. This mind should be noted as "wanting, wanting." Then a return should be made to the feeling and it should be noted as "stiff, stiff" or "hot, hot," and so forth. If one proceeds in this manner of contemplation with great patience, unpleasant feelings will pass away.

There is a saying that patience leads to nibbāna (nirvana). Evidently this saying is more applicable in the case of contemplation than in any other. Plenty of patience is needed in contemplation. If a yogi (meditator) cannot bear unpleasant feelings with patience, but frequently changes his posture during contemplation, he cannot expect to gain concentration. Without concentration there is no chance of acquiring insight knowledge (*vipassanā-ñāṇa*) and without insight knowledge the attainment of the path, fruition and nibbāna cannot be won.

Patience is of great importance in contemplation. Patience is needed mostly to bear unpleasant bodily feelings. There is hardly any case of outside disturbances where it is not necessary to exercise patience. This means the observance of "restraint by patience." The posture should not be immediately changed when unpleasant sensations arise, but contemplation should be continued by noting them as "stiff, stiff," "hot, hot," and so on. Such painful sensations are normal and will pass away. In the case of strong concentration, it will be found that great pains will pass away when they are noted with patience. On the fading away of suffering or pain, the usual exercise of noting "rising, falling" should be continued.

On the other hand, it may be found that pains or unpleasant feelings do not immediately pass away even when one notes them with great patience. In such a case, one has no alternative but to change posture. One must, of course, submit to superior forces. When concentration is not strong enough, strong pains will not pass away quickly. In these circumstances there will often arise a mind wanting to change posture, and this mind should be noted as "wanting, wanting." After this, one should note "lifting, lifting" on lifting the hand, and "moving, moving" on moving forward.

These bodily actions should be carried out slowly, and these slow movements should be followed up and noted as "lifting, lifting," "moving, moving," "touching, touching," in the successive order of the process. Again, on moving one should note "moving, moving," and on putting down, note "putting, putting." If, when this process of changing posture has been completed, there is nothing more to be noted, the usual exercise of noting "rising, falling" should be continued.

There should be no stop or break in between. The preceding act of noting and the one which follows should be contiguous. Similarly the preceding concentration and the one which follows should be contiguous, and the preceding act of knowing and the one which follows should be contiguous. In this way the gradual development by stages of mindfulness, concentration, and knowledge takes place, and depending on their full development, the final stage of path-knowledge is attained.

In the practice of vipassanā meditation, it is important to follow the example of a person who tries to make fire. To make a fire in the days before matches, a person had to constantly rub two sticks together without the slightest break in motion. As the sticks became hotter and hotter, more effort was needed, and the rubbing had to be carried out incessantly. Only when the fire had been produced was the person at liberty to take a rest. Similarly, a yogi should work hard so that there is no break between the preceding noting and the one which follows, and between the preceding concentration and the one which follows. He should revert to his usual exercise of noting "rising, falling" after he has noted "painful sensations."

While thus occupied with his usual exercise, he may again feel itching sensations somewhere in the body. He should then fix his mind on the spot and make a note as "itching, itching." Itching is an unpleasant sensation. As soon as it is felt, there arises a mind which wants to rub or scratch. This mind should be noted as "wanting, wanting," after which no rubbing or scratching must be done as yet, but a return should be made to the itching and a note made as "itching, itching." While one is occupied with contemplation in this manner, itching in most cases passes away and the usual exercise of noting "rising, falling" should then be reverted to.

If, on the other hand, it is found that itching does not pass away, but that it is necessary to rub or scratch, the contemplation of the successive stages should be carried out by noting the mind as "wanting, wanting." It should then be continued by noting "raising, raising" on raising the hand, "touching, touching" when the hand touches the spot, "rubbing, rubbing" or "scratching, scratching" when the hand rubs or scratches, "withdrawing, withdrawing" on withdrawing the hand, "touching, touching" when the hand touches the body, and then the usual contemplation of "rising, falling" should be continued. In every case of changing postures, contemplation of the successive stages should be carried out similarly and carefully.

While thus carefully proceeding with the contemplation, one may find that painful feelings or unpleasant sensations arise in the body of their own accord. Ordinarily, people change their posture as soon as they feel even the slightest unpleasant sensation of tiredness or heat without taking heed of these incidents. The change of posture is carried out quite heedlessly just while the seed of pain is beginning to grow. Thus painful feelings fail to take place in a distinctive manner. For this reason it is said that, as a rule, the postures hide painful feelings from view. People generally think that they are feeling well for days and nights on end. They think that painful feelings occur only at the time of an attack of a dangerous disease.

Reality is just the opposite of what people think. Let anyone try to see how long he can keep himself in a sitting posture without moving or changing it. One will find it uncomfortable after a short while, say five or ten minutes, and then one will begin to find it unbearable after fifteen or twenty minutes. One will then be compelled to move or change one's posture by either raising or lowering the head, by moving the hands or legs, or by swaying the body either forward or backward. Many movements usually take place during a short time, and the number would be very large if they were to be counted for the length of just one day. However, no one appears to be aware of this fact because no one takes any heed.

Such is the order in every case, while in the case of a yogi who is always mindful of his actions and who is proceeding with contemplation, body impressions in their own nature are distinctly noticed. They cannot help but reveal themselves fully in their own nature because he is watching until they come into full view.

Though a painful sensation arises, he keeps on noting it. He does not ordinarily attempt to change his posture or move. Then, on the arising of mind wanting to change, he at once makes a note of it as "wanting, wanting," and afterwards he returns again to the painful sensation and continues his noting of it. He changes his posture or moves only when he finds the painful feeling unbearable. In this case he also begins by noting the wanting mind and proceeds with noting carefully each stage in the process of moving. For this reason the postures can no longer hide painful sensations. Often a yogi finds painful sensations creeping from here and there or he may feel hot sensations, aching sensations, itching, or the whole body as a mass of painful sensations. In this way painful sensations are found to be predominant because the postures cannot cover them.

If he intends to change his posture from sitting to standing, he should first make a note of the intending mind as "intending, intending," and proceed with the arranging of the hands and legs in the successive stages by noting as "raising," "moving," "stretching," "touching," "pressing," and so forth. When the body sways forward, it should be noted as "swaying, swaying." In the course of standing up, there occurs in the body a feeling of lightness as well as the act of rising. Attention should be fixed on these factors and a note made as "rising, rising." The act of rising should be carried out slowly.

Other Exercises: Walking

It is to be emphasized that the act of pulling up the body to the standing posture should be carried out slowly. On coming to an erect position, a note should be made as "standing, standing." If one happens to look around, a note should be made as "looking, seeing," and on walking each step should be noted as "right step, left step" or "walking, walking." At each step, attention should be fixed on the sole of the foot as it moves from the point of lifting the leg to the point of placing it down.

While walking in quick steps or taking a long walk, a note on one section of each step as "right step, left step" or "walking, walking" will do. In the case of walking slowly, each step may be divided into three sections: lifting, moving forward, and placing down. In the beginning of the exercise, a note should be made of the two parts of each step, as "lifting" by fixing the attention on the upward movement of the foot from the beginning to the end, and as "placing" by fixing on the downward movement from the beginning to the end. Thus the exercise which starts with the first step by noting as "lifting, placing" now ends.

Normally, when the foot is put down and is being noted as "placing," the other leg begins lifting to begin the next step. This should not be allowed to happen. The next step should begin only after the first step has been completed, and noted as "lifting, placing" for the first step and "lifting, placing" for the second step. After two or three days this exercise will be easy, and then the yogi should carry out the exercise of noting each step in three sections as "lifting, moving, placing." For the present, a yogi should start the exercise by noting as "right step, left step," or "walking, walking" while walking quickly, and by noting as "lifting, placing" while walking slowly.

Sitting

While one is walking, one may feel the desire to sit down. One should then make a note as "wanting." If one then happens to look up, note it as "looking, seeing, looking, seeing"; on going to the seat as "lifting, placing"; on stopping as "stopping, stopping"; on turning as "turning, turning." When one feels a desire to sit, note it as "wanting, wanting." In the act of sitting there occur in the body heaviness and also a downward pull. Attention should be fixed on these factors and a note made as "sitting, sitting, sitting." After having sat down there will be movements of bringing the hands and legs into position. They should be noted as "moving," "bending," "stretching," and so forth. If there is nothing to do and if one is sitting quietly, one should then revert to the usual exercise of noting as "rising, falling."

Sleeping

Though it is late at night and time for sleep, it is not advisable to give up the contemplation and go to sleep. Anyone who has a keen interest in contemplation must be prepared to face the risk of spending many nights without sleep.

When one feels sleepy, one should make a note of it as "sleepy, sleepy"; when the eyelids are heavy as "heavy, heavy"; when the eyes are felt to be dazzled as "dazzled, dazzled." After contemplating in the manner indicated, one may be able to shake off sleepiness and feel fresh again. This feeling should be noted as "feeling fresh, feeling fresh," after which the usual exercise of noting "rising, falling" should be continued. However, in spite of this determination, one may feel unable to keep awake if one is very sleepy. In a lying posture, it is easier to fall asleep. A beginner should therefore try to keep mostly to the postures of sitting and walking.

When the night is advanced, however, a yogi may be compelled to lie down and proceed with the contemplation of rising and falling in this position. He may perhaps fall asleep. While one is asleep, it is not possible to carry on with the work of contemplation. It is an interval for a yogi to relax. An hour's sleep will give him an hour's relaxation, and if he continues to sleep for two, three, or four hours, he will be relaxed for that much longer, but it is not advisable for a yogi to sleep for more than four hours, which is ample for a normal sleep.

Waking

A yogi should begin his contemplation from the moment of awakening. To be fully occupied with intense contemplation throughout his waking hours is the routine of a yogi who works hard with true aspiration for the attainment of the path and fruit. If it is not possible to catch the moment of awakening, he should begin with the usual exercise of noting "rising, falling." If he first becomes aware of the fact of reflecting, he should begin his contemplation by noting "reflecting, reflecting" and then revert to the usual exercise of noting "rising, falling." If he first becomes aware of hearing a voice or some other sound, he should begin by noting "hearing, hearing" and then revert to the usual exercise. On awakening there may be bodily movement in turning to this side or that, moving the hands or legs, and so forth. These actions should be contemplated in successive order.

If he first becomes aware of the mental states leading to the various actions of body, he should begin his contemplation by noting the mind. If he first becomes aware of painful sensations, he should begin with noting these painful sensations and then proceed with the noting of bodily actions. If he remains quiet without moving, the usual exercise of noting "rising, falling" should be continued. If he intends to get up, he should note this as "intending, intending" and then proceed with the noting of all actions, in serial order, in bringing the hands and legs into position. One should note "raising, raising" on raising the body; "sitting, sitting" when the body is erect and in a sitting posture; and one should also note any other actions of bringing the legs and hands into position. If there is then nothing in particular to be noted, the usual exercise of noting "rising, falling" should be reverted to.

Thus far we have mentioned things relating to the objects of contemplation in connection with the four postures and changing from one posture to another. This is merely a description of the general outline of major objects of contemplation to be carried out in the course of practice. Yet, in the beginning of the practice it is difficult to follow up all of them in the course of contemplation. Many things will be omitted, but on gaining sufficient strength in concentration, it is easy to follow up, in the course of contemplation, not only those objects already enumerated but many, many more. With the gradual development of mindfulness and concentration, the pace of knowledge quickens, and thus many more objects can be perceived. It is necessary to work up to this high level.

Washing and Eating

Contemplation should be carried out in washing the face in the morning or when taking a bath. As it is necessary to act quickly in such instances owing to the nature of the action itself, contemplation should be carried out as far as these circumstances will allow. On stretching the hand to catch hold of the dipper, it should be noted as "stretching, stretching"; on catching hold of the dipper as "holding, holding"; on immersing the dipper as "dipping, dipping"; on bringing the dipper towards the body as "bringing, bringing"; on pouring the water over the body or on the face as "pouring, pouring"; on feeling cold as "cold, cold"; on rubbing as "rubbing, rubbing"' and so forth.

There are also many different bodily actions in changing or arranging one's clothing, in arranging the bed or bed-sheets, in opening the door, and so on. These actions should be contemplated in detail serially as much as possible.

At the time of taking a meal, contemplation should begin from the moment of looking at the table and noted as "looking, seeing, looking, seeing"; when stretching the hand to the plate as "stretching, stretching"; when the hand touches the food as "touching, hot, hot"; when gathering the food as "gathering, gathering"; when catching hold of the food as "catching, catching"; after lifting when the hand is being brought up as "bringing, bringing"; when the neck is being bent down as "bending, bending"; when the food is being placed in the mouth as "placing, placing"; when withdrawing the hand as "withdrawing, withdrawing"; when the hand touches the plate as "touching, touching"; when the neck is being straightened as "straightening, straightening"; when chewing the food as "chewing, chewing"; while tasting the food as "tasting, tasting"; when one likes the taste as "liking, liking"; when one finds it pleasant as "pleasant, pleasant"; when swallowing as "swallowing, swallowing."

This is an illustration of the routine of contemplation on partaking of each morsel of food till the meal is finished. In this case too it is difficult to follow up on all actions at the beginning of the practice. There will be many omissions. Yogis should not hesitate, however, but must try to follow up as much as they can. With the gradual advancement of the practice, it will be easier to note many more objects than are mentioned here.

Reading 19

The Meditative Mind

Dhiravamsa

It is important for anybody wishing to develop meditation to be free from the desire for experience. Experiences will arise, but meditation is the way of awareness of experience, remaining free and independent. If one is psychologically dependent upon experience, or upon method, one is not quite on the path of meditation. Techniques are helpful at the beginning, but they have to be transcended. Even the object of meditation must be transcended in the end, otherwise there is no opening up and no independence. Psychological dependence is important for us to notice and to be free from. Freedom is the only goal of meditation. As human beings who are not free we need things to help us at first. So we use a method, or an object upon which to meditate. This is because we have been trained in this way, but we have to understand that all these things are only the helping factors.

Meditation is a very simple thing, but people overlook this and create complications. Simplicity is not so easy to understand, because it is profound. We appreciate a simple life, but it is not so easy to lead. One must first know what it is, and then live it. It concerns inward simplicity, which involves aloneness and freedom from conditioning, living without influence.

We must ask ourselves whether we are inwardly free, or whether instead we are caught up in ideas, actions, feelings, experiences. Knowledge and mental attitudes become an authority within, and people are run by this internalized authority. Outwardly, we may say we are against authority, whether political, social, or personal, but we should look into ourselves and see whether we are not enslaved by a far more subtle authority. Meditation helps us to do this, so that we can see how we have become as we are and why we behave or react in a certain way. All our reactions, physical or mental, must be investigated carefully, in order to understand. This way of looking into oneself to observe what is going on and how one is conditioned, and of listening to oneself, helps one to look beyond one's own situations and manifestations. By looking beyond I mean seeing through superficial appearances towards something deeper, something underlying the situation. For example, when you are nervous of something, first of all look at the state of being frightened itself. Then you can observe your reactive process, and see how it arises, because you are attentive and deeply watching your reactions in relation to other people and the environment. When this reactive process is threatened, there arises a feeling of nervousness. If you can be objective towards this feeling, you can look at where it comes from. What is the underlying factor of fear? Things arise because of conditions, causes. By looking beyond what is actually happening we can see the source of it.

This raises the question of consciousness. How are we conscious of things in life? The question of how is most important. We may know what we are conscious of: people, buildings, flowers, or other things in our environment. But how? And how are we conscious of ourselves? How does it arise? This is something to be found out, and meditation is a process of discovery. Is it pure or impure? Is it conditioned by various influences, such as education, training, or life experiences?

We approach all things in life according to our conditioned consciousness, produced by our internal and external environment, and therefore we are sure to see things in a certain way, and differently from other people. Most of our behaviour will be a reaction by the old towards the new; the old conditioned consciousness towards the new moment. Our actions often do not feel our own, and we suffer from doubt and guilt, with ideas of right and wrong, and good and bad, according to what we have been taught. These belong to the old consciousness, to reaction instead of action in life. Unless one can clear away conditioning from the consciousness, it is not free to be aware. The mind is intrinsically pure, or luminous, but is continually defiled by the intrusion of the sense-impressions pouring into it. These accumulate, so that consciousness cannot be illuminating, and becomes dull and disturbed. It is not free, because it works according to the states that act upon it.

In order to renew your consciousness, the first thing to do is to look into it and into life, which is always new. Life is flowing and fluctuating all the time, and because of this consciousness can be renewed and can flow with it. If things become unchangeable, there is no opportunity for anyone to be renewed. One would be an old person for ever. But this is not so. The truth is that everything is changeable, for better or for worse, depending on the understanding. In order to renew consciousness, one has to be aware of all the activities, emotions, thoughts, and sensations one has. You may feel it is too much to do to be aware all the time. People make excuses for not being aware. They also take awareness as a task, a burden, but this is not right. What do we do when we are not aware? Are we thinking, imagining, entertaining ourselves with memories, fantasies, or daydreams? Which is more satisfying: the pursuit of mere pleasure, or the understanding of things as they are? One has to distinguish the essential from the inessential in life. But without awareness there can be no such understanding.

One does not have to read books in order to understand oneself, or to renew one's own consciousness. The only work to be done is to develop full attention towards ourselves, towards what is going on. We act, we feel, we think, we do many things in life, but there is a vital factor in all this which is essential: *clear awareness.*

Consciousness is not the same as awareness. I said that consciousness is conditioned, which makes us react towards life in accordance with this conditioning. But awareness is not conditioned by anything. It is purely objective perception without the interference of the subject, of the self, the ego. Consciousness is the ego-trip, but awareness is selfless – an objective process of seeing, hearing, experiencing, understanding. When one is aware, one does not care for concepts, one has no preconceived ideas before being aware. Otherwise it becomes the production of sense-perception and consciousness. That is why we cannot concentrate upon the truth, for it cannot be recognised. If something can be recognised, it means it has been known before; and the known is the old, not the new. The truth is ever new. What we speak of as the truth is not the truth. We may have many concepts and descriptions of truth, but they are not the truth – they are something about it. There is no act of recognition when one encounters the truth – only awareness of it, and awareness does not build up memory. It is perception which does that. Perception is like a mirage which appears real until you come close to it. Seeing a rope in the moonlight, you think it is a snake. First of all you have a perception and conception of a snake, and feel fear, but when you stop thinking and come closer to look at it, you can see that it is not a snake but a rope. Then there is great relief, because the mirage has disappeared. This is why in Buddhism we say that perception is a kind of distortion, and we cannot rely upon it at all times.

Consciousness cannot therefore be renewed by perception, but by awareness and understanding. It is not only perception that is perverted or distorted; thought is also a distortion. Thought distorts reality, and reality cannot be reached through thought. In the West particularly, the way of thinking is used in the attempt to understand truth. This is like scratching your foot when you have your shoe on. You do not scratch the skin, but only the shoe. The intellect can touch only the symbol of truth but not the truth itself. This is why we have so many difficulties in understanding the truth. But when we give up this approach it is much easier. Intellectual people find it very difficult to understand, because they try to reach truth in their own way. They want to reach the new, but carry with them the old consciousness, which causes a reflection of the old on the new, distorting the understanding and conditioning the consciousness still further, on a deeper level, by the perversion of thought.

But how can we live without thought? Perhaps you can try and see. It may be very wonderful, yet it does not mean that one cannot think. Thinking can be a useful instrument in life, if one is free in relation to it, then thinking can unify. At a certain level, one uses thought to deal with facts and situations, but in order to reach beyond mere knowledge one has to stop thinking and adopt a different way.

Do we have the power to purify or renew our consciousness, or does it have to be given by something outside? Surely man has the potentiality to renew his consciousness without relying upon any external force. This power is hidden by our conditions. In order to discover it, we have to free ourselves from all our conditionings. We have to be completely alone, in the sense of not being conditioned by anything in life. Then this power can gradually grow in us. It cannot be given but can be discovered by each one of us.

Meditation is the way to clear away the barriers against reality, the creative energy within us. We need to cultivate awareness of how we become, how we live from moment to moment. We don't need to look up to something external as an authority, even a guru. Cultivate your own guru, which is awareness, the best friend who will not deceive anyone, then you will learn to understand yourself, and will not go in a false direction. You can develop your creative potential, and awaken from sleep. If you are fully awake you can be free and happy in life. But if you remain asleep, dreams, illusion, and confusion will dominate you. Sleep is only for the purpose of letting the body and the mind rest, but they can rest in meditation too. Waking from sleep is awakening. Waking up from ignorance is enlightenment. Enlightened people are those who have constant awareness in life, who are free from psychological sleep, whatever they are doing. Everybody has the potentiality for this.

In seeking for the significance of meditation, I wonder if we are sufficiently interested in *doing* meditation, in experiencing it for ourselves. The tendency in the West is to require to be convinced of something before starting it. However, even if we become completely convinced intellectually, this may stay in the head and not enter the heart – so the practice is never achieved. We enjoy reading, talking, and hearing about meditation, but usually what these are concerned with is ideas about meditation, not meditation itself. True meditation has to be experienced and lived in life, otherwise it is not understood in reality.

So we have to start from ourselves. Meditation is a way of life; it has to be lived. Although it is not something which is limited to practice in a retreat, such practice is necessary for periods, and this is why meditation centres came into being. Meditation can be brought into our whole life, but we cannot apply this straight away. We have to be trained, we need someone who can guide us, who can give instruction. Even so, all the work has to be done by oneself. The instructor cannot reveal the truth to you, or achieve enlightenment for you; he is only a good friend who can help you when you do not understand how to proceed, or how to go through the difficulty you have, and he can encourage the meditator to persist with the work. This is the way of self-reliance and non-dependence. In order to tackle a problem, one must see *through* it by not being carried away by thought. Instead we have to be aware of the thought itself, of how it comes to be, and how each thought connects with other thoughts. The first category of understanding a thought is to understand what kind of thought it is. We all have thoughts; they cannot be banished. Even if a person appears quiet outwardly, he is inwardly reacting continually to what is going on. If we become aware of what kind of reaction this is, that is the first step. Then we have to watch how this reaction arises. Is the cause really external, something outside which provokes a reaction; or does it lie within your mind, conditioned by past experience, knowledge, background, upbringing? Thus a clear perception is not possible, and all events and stimuli are interpreted by the individual according to his conditioning.

If this awareness is unclouded, we can meditate while we are talking, listening, or in any activity, watching everything with bare attention and clarity of mind. To meditate is simply to be aware, without complication. If you ask "*Who* is aware?" or "What should one be aware of?" then the activity of awareness in the present moment is side-tracked. Simplicity is essential, and although at first it may be difficult, it becomes easier with practice. When we ask questions about meditation we are unconsciously attempting to avoid practice. This is yet another form of reaction.

To understand how a thought comes to be, we have to see the conditions which give rise to it. Why do we have a particular thought at all? When you can observe closely enough how each thought presents itself, you will see that there is no thinker apart from the thinking, and there is no thinking apart from the thought. One has to be aware objectively of things as they are, and then one will understand the connection of all thoughts. Deeper than that, one will see what is the ground for their connection, because things do not connect in a vacuum. To see the wholeness of what is really there requires total attention and awareness.

The most important thing in meditation is *freedom*. This is really the central point of meditation. Are we free, or are we constantly carried away by something else? Do we conform to what cannot be free? When we are liberated, we are free to move, to look, to smile, to talk, to live, without being dictated to. We shall have universal consciousness because the ego is not present. As long as you remain tied to the consciousness of yourself as an entity needing to possess things or people, a being who acts, who must have protection, pleasure, support, approval, or interest, then pure consciousness is limited and restricted. With the "I" consciousness there is judgment, personal pride, aggression, loss, boredom, and fear. If the root of these things is dissolved, positive elements will flow naturally without imposed laws of morality, or social regulations, and mental illness and disturbance will not arise. Humility, gentleness, tenderness, are all generated without effort when man is free.

We need not expect total freedom quickly, but a gradual release from the grip of ideas, especially the idea of self. The mind tends to think in terms of ends, or an end point, but the work of liberation is a process, continued steadily with patience, with glimpses throughout the path of a timeless, deathless liberation within life. In that freedom there is love yet independence, equanimity, and understanding. There is no "actor," but the flow of intuitive wisdom.

The Meditative Mind

In order to understand the meditative mind, it is important to listen with a meditative mind. If you listen with a critical, intellectual mind, full of knowledge and attitudes, you will not be able to understand what the meditative mind is. Be prepared from the start, as otherwise your usual form of listening will be an obstacle.

Do you know how to listen with a meditative mind? It is quite simple, if you just open your mind and listen to what is being said without rejection or acceptance. With an open mind, your listening will be receptive, and intuitive wisdom will flow. If you are listening with expectancy or in anticipation of what the speaker will say, you may be disappointed, and this produces a problem which hinders the mind from true listening. The mind becomes frustrated and distracted, thinking about something else, which is why it is essential to keep the mind wide open and wide awake. Then it can embrace everything it comes across, without losing itself or becoming disturbed, and eventually the whole universe can be encompassed by such a mind.

The closed mind cannot listen because it is basically afraid, and any explanation causes it to be still more frightened; but it is necessary to practise this expansion and gradually overcome fear. It should not be a forcing process, because any concentration upon opening the mind tends to close it! Try a simple approach, applying yourself to the task with constant clear awareness. Then the mind will not be broken up, but will open itself.

Buddhism teaches that energy and contemplation must be balanced by awareness, and this will bring inner stability and steadiness. Without this, energy is dissipated and we become tired or bored. Fatigue and boredom are experienced by the superficial mind which does not understand itself, so that it cannot enjoy itself either. Do not think of this mind in terms of concepts. It is not something to be *thought about*, but we can see its movements going on endlessly. If you are aware of what is going on in your head you may say the mind is "working," doing something; but if you continue to observe it carefully you will see moments when its flow momentarily stops. At such moments you feel great relief, but before this you may experience psychological pain. You may perceive happiness on the surface, yet a deep suffering underneath. To see this, you must remain attentive, but usually we cannot remain passive; clarity fails to come and the mind continues to hunt ideas.

You may feel that to become passive will deprive you of things you need – you feel you must have things. This is the acquisitive mind, not the meditative one, and it will bring difficulties to its possessor. The listener must become the listening, otherwise there is a gap between the "entity" which is listening and the listening itself. This does not bring about understanding. But when the listener is absorbed into the listening, it becomes wise listening, which can understand what is being said. The gap is not there, and this is the Buddhist way of being objective – being free from the idea of doing anything. This kind of mind is very simple, but as we know, simplicity is profound. It is not so easy to be simple, but it is easy to slip into complications.

To be really simple requires freedom from thoughts and ideas. It is difficult not to conform to the knowledge you have already accumulated, but immediately you begin to practise this, the profounder aspects of your mind can be seen. How can we become simple? First of all we have to watch and understand our complications and our conformity to habits and tendencies. The only technique is to observe the way you think and feel, and the way you create problems. Deeply rooted habits have to be seen in an immediate way, not with any expectation of freedom from them, because this is a form of desire which leads in the opposite direction, away from liberation. Instead, the meditative mind should be used to look at the confusion and to clarify everything through awareness, without expecting any result. In awareness, desire is not carried within the mind, although in words we may express an intention to see. Our language has been built upon subject-object concepts and logical reasoning, but in talking about the application of awareness without desire we have to go beyond these concepts. If we remain aware of what is going on within us, and of how we are behaving, we shall be honest with ourselves. The meditative mind is an honest mind, because it deceives neither itself nor others. Therefore it can perceive dishonesty in everyday actions without rejection or approval.

Usually we deceive ourselves by trying to hide what is actually occurring. We seek to avoid it because we fear it, but instead of admitting this we enter the world of illusion and regard that as the reality. Perhaps our first step should be to learn to be honest with ourselves. Lying to others is only possible when we have already accepted the lie ourselves. If we can see our own self-deception, we are not so likely to encourage illusion in others, and instead will help each other to advance along the path to reality.

You may say there are certain pretences, such as politeness, which are necessary to avoid conflict or even cruelty. Awareness will not give rise to rudeness or harshness, but will automatically give rise to humility, gentleness, and genuine consideration for others, without conforming to conventions. Otherwise there is always a gap between the idea of what "should" be done, and the practice of it. The meditative mind does not say this will happen, or this should be done, because these are thoughts and plans concerning the future, whereas the meditative mind only operates in the present. It carries with it neither the past nor the future. You may think that such a mind would be lazy or irresponsible, without a care for past or future; but care can mean a kind of uneasy concern which interferes with true care or love. To really care means to give and forgive, without expecting anything in return. This also includes caring for yourself, without guilt or rejection – just accepting what is there and continuing to look at it. Then things will flow naturally, according to their nature. There is no point in life without this kind of love, which does not conform to imposed concepts.

In the meditative mind there is no conformity. Instead, there is a continuous breaking down of the walls surrounding ourselves and other people. If we observe ourselves, we shall immediately see that there are walls within us which prevent us from knowing ourselves. We live in a small room with four walls, so that when we look at something, it is usually seen in a narrow perspective. The truth lies beyond these walls and will be seen if the walls are broken down, but we are afraid to do this because we believe that walls mean security. We want to be convinced first that we shall be safe without them, but it is not possible to find this out unless we practise being without them. This is why we so often continue to live in a confined world, refusing to leave our "womb" and therefore unable to grow or move onwards.

We can also observe this in our opinions, which reflect what we are holding in our mind. If a view is held when looking at something, what is perceived will be limited by what is already in the mind and the thing will not be seen as it is, but only according to the viewpoint already held. This, of course, also happens to Buddhists who look at things "from the Buddhist point of view." This may be a convenient way of explaining things, but just as the Buddha had to find out everything for himself, so we need to approach things with a fresh mind, aware of all possibilities. People may say, "If we don't have a Buddhist viewpoint, what is the point of practising Buddhism?" The Buddha was a very tolerant and broad-minded man, who used to say that his teaching, or Dharma, should not be held on to. Instead, it is like a boat carrying us across the ocean of life, which we must be able to leave, otherwise we shall never be able to step out on to dry land. The whole purpose of Buddhism is to develop a mind free from the necessity to grasp or retain. When looking at what is there, forget Buddhist ideas completely, otherwise they will stand in your way. Do not trust even learned men, but trust yourself. Put aside all the Buddhist knowledge you have and look at things with a wide open mind unclouded by knowledge. The reality you see will then be in accordance with what the Buddha taught, because his teaching did not lead towards unreality. It is the interpretations and concepts arising from his teaching which tend to hinder the mind. True Buddhism springs from within not from books or speakers, and in order to contact this we need to meditate.

How can we meditate? It is hard – yet, as I have said, it is simple. Right effort – or perseverance – is very important, because the wrong kind of effort produces difficulties. Let yourself flow, aware of whatever arises without wanting to get anything out of it. The awareness will take care of itself, and of you. Remain as simple as possible, preferably giving yourself a quiet period every day to watch what is going on as steadily as you can.

People often feel the need to change their personality and their behaviour. This is a natural reaction, but we have to remember that such motives can hinder progress. If we keep practising the meditative mind, change is bound to occur by itself, without striving, and sometimes without one realising it. But usually one feels lighter within, as if one is in a clearer house. Such a change takes place through understanding, not through conditioning.

The understanding of change is a fundamental aspect of Buddhism. Life is always in the process of changing. Suppose you are looking at something beautiful which then disappears. You will feel sad because you want to see the beauty again. Instead of regretting the passing away of what you desire, look at what is desiring it, and immediately you will begin to understand.

It is the same with the meditative mind, which also comes and goes. Meditation cannot remain with us continuously – you can see that for yourself – and if you want it to stay with you, it will happen less. Let it come and go without trying to hold on, and as you become more tranquil it will remain with you longer. Why does the power of awareness leave us? Watch what happens and you will see. The meditative mind sees the whole, without being caught up in the parts or the whole. The trouble is that we tend to get caught up in things very easily and quickly. Perhaps we aim to remain completely still and quiet for half an hour without any inner talking or associations. Such an idea is itself a great obstacle to the flowing observation of everything arising, without which stillness cannot come. You will see that when you have an aim, the mind wishes to enter the goal as soon as possible, and tends to become more active.

Instead of opening itself, it gets caught in the desire for achievement and cannot remain aware of its own activities. When one does not want anything, the mind is without tension.

Tension can be built up unconsciously in the mind. Suppose you are climbing a mountain in order to reach the top. If your mind continually anticipates the peak, you will get tired and will not be fully aware of the steps you are taking. There is tension in both body and mind. But if you attend to the steps, they will automatically lead you to the top perfectly satisfactorily. Energy is wasted if it is used to anticipate an achievement, and this applies to the goal, nirvana. If you attend to all the movements of mind and body in life, this is like giving attention to your steps and your path instead of to the mountain peak. Then nirvana is not so far away.

Nirvana cannot be reached by thought, because thought is the product of a limited mind, a reaction of the conditioned mind. How can the limited give rise to the unlimited? It is not possible.

It is when the mind becomes aware of its limitations that it takes the first step in freeing itself from them. It becomes another mind, a meditative mind, which has begun the work of looking at itself. The mind changes all the time because of its different reactions and associations, and we tend to blame it for our unpleasant experiences, our negative tendencies and emotions. But it is our previous actions and attitudes which have conditioned the mind to produce what it does, and the more we resent and reject its negative aspects, the stronger they become. Do not keep thinking about what is there, but look at it for what it is. Close your mouth and open your eyes to what is within you, giving up the habit of seeking mere pleasure or laying blame.

The meditative mind will see what is within and outside you, not only during intensive meditation with the eyes closed, but also during daily living with the eyes open. There may be much noise both inner and outer, but the watching mind is silent. In this silence there is not nothing, but *clarity of being*, without words. When the silence is complete, you will hear things with your heart – the deep heart which is very sensitive to the true sound of life. At this stage of hearing, there is harmony, without the separation of itself; absolute objectivity.

The mind is never free, being continually caught up and confused to some extent. So there is no *newness*. The mind remains the old mind all the time, caught up in the memories of yesterday, last week, last year, and so on. Past experiences occupy it, making it *think* in an effort to escape or to seek satisfaction. But when the mind cannot get what it wants, it becomes frustrated and depressed. Such a mind cannot be fresh, or free. It lives in prison or, in religious terms, in hell. Hell is not somewhere down below; it arises in your mind, in your life.

A mind with fresh consciousness is clearly of enormous importance in life, yet people find its attainment very difficult. Some may question whether there can be such a thing as a fresh mind, but it can be found at any moment. If we seek it externally through studies or religious beliefs, it becomes clouded. It will only be found when there is quietness, alone and within. Otherwise the mind will repeat itself throughout its lifetime, occupied by what is superficial, tied to what it accumulates, exhausted by what it desires and experiences, and driven by its unconscious contents. Such a mind is overburdened, which is why so many people find it hard either to act freely or to relax. Because there is insufficient awareness and freedom, there is no tranquillity.

It is then essential to look at the mind and its burden, seeing it very clearly so as to penetrate what lies and works underneath. Gradually the mind will become lighter and fresher, and you will perceive the beauty of things without becoming attached to beauty. Yet there must be no effort at non-attachment, because in a sense this would be like running away instead of meeting what is presenting itself, whether pleasant or unpleasant.

The possibility of clarity of mind gives us the potential for freedom in all situations, and it can be achieved by meditation without any resistance to what may arise. Also, there should be no expectation about what will happen, or anticipation of a wonderful experience. With such ideas, any other result engenders disappointment, dismay, and impatience, and attention is distracted from what is *actually happening*. There is a tendency to exclude or fear what arises unexpectedly, and it is then resisted instead of observed. The mind is wrongly engaged in a battle, fighting and trying to push away what arises instead of just looking at it.

If you do not look for results, you are free to see what is there, which is what meditation really is. What matters is to be aware of the present, to be constantly watchful of what is going on within you. When your attention is used for this, and not distracted by thoughts about results, the mind cannot build up resistance. The mind is clever and it knows how to create protective barriers in order to maintain its own "progress." You have to understand its tricks, but nobody can show these to you – you have to know your own mind. You must not become ashamed or horrified through looking at what goes on. As one becomes sensitive to the undesirable aspects of the mind and of one's life, suffering will arise. But *one must not hold the idea of being free from suffering.* Such an idea hinders the work of facing and living through what is there. If there is no resistance to what arises, whether painful or pleasurable, gradually the *cause* of suffering will be extinguished.

Watching Thoughts and Emotions

Godwin Samararatne

Guided Meditation

You can sit in a comfortable position, because the posture is not really important. What is important is to have your spine erect, but relaxed. And you may have your eyes open or closed.

Now just allow the mind to do whatever it likes.[62]

If thoughts are arising, let thoughts arise – thoughts about the past, thoughts about the future . . . .

There's no need to repress thoughts, no need to control thoughts.

See how far you can be aware of each thought that arises. You need to have moment-to-moment awareness.

Just know how you relate to each thought that arises. Are you judging them? Are you getting involved with them? Or can you allow them to just arise and pass away?

You have enough space in your mind for any thought to arise. See how far you relate to each thought that arises.

Learning to make friends with your thoughts.

Make your own discoveries. Are the thoughts mostly about the past? Are they mostly about the future? Are the thoughts racing one after the other? Are they slowing down? Is there space between two thoughts? Do you get involved in some thoughts? Do you judge your thoughts? Make your own discoveries about the different aspects, about the different dimensions, about the structure of your thoughts.

Have moment-to-moment awareness of the way you are relating to each thought that arises.

Now, can you do the same in relation to emotions? Can you allow emotions to arise? Especially the emotions that we don't like, that we resist, deny, repress, and control? Emotions like sadness, fear, anxiety, guilt. Can you just allow such emotions to arise if they need to arise? Can you make friends with them? Can you make enough space for them? Can you just allow them to come? Letting them be, without repressing them, without controlling them, without resisting them.

Thoughts and emotions. Learning to see them as they are, not as they should be or ought to be. Learning just to allow them to be. Just letting them be.

Can you make friends with the emotions that you don't like, that you resist, that you control? Can you create space for them?

Can you do the same in relation to sensations in your body? Tensions, pressures, unpleasant sensations. Can you allow any sensation to arise in your body, and just let it be? Just allowing it to be.

Thoughts, emotions, sensations, sounds. Learning to see them as they are. Learning to have a mirror-like mind, just reflecting things as they are. Not resisting anything, not grasping anything. Not liking anything, not disliking anything. Not accepting anything, not rejecting anything. Just being, just allowing. Surrendering to *what is.*

Be alert and awake from moment to moment.

Thank you. You may open your eyes now.

Discussion

Godwin: We will begin our discussion with thoughts. Let me hear your experiences in relation to thoughts.

Meditator: I'm used to the practice of focusing on the breath, in order to stop thoughts rather than letting thoughts arise freely.

Godwin: This brings up a very important point. We need to learn to focus on an object, such as the breathing; but we also need to learn to allow the mind to do what it likes. That is, we need both focusing and scanning. Otherwise, if you are used to only focusing, then you can't do anything else. So ideally we should learn to do both, focusing and scanning.

Meditator: I find that when I allow thoughts to arise, no thoughts arise.

Godwin: This is fascinating! So I'd like to discuss the implications of it. When we are focusing on the breathing, and we don't want thoughts to arise, what happens? They arise. And when we are allowing thoughts to arise, they don't arise. Now why should this be? Why is the mind always acting in opposition to us? How is it that when we allow things to happen in the mind, or when we invite things to happen, they're not forthcoming; but when we don't want things to happen, they seem to arise? This happens not only with thoughts but also with emotions, especially emotions that we don't like. When you invite emotions to arise, they don't seem to arise. They seem to be rather shy. But when we fight them, when we fear them, when we don't want them to arise, they seem to arise. Now what is the reason for this?

This brings up an important point which I often repeat and emphasize. Meditation consists in making an effort to understand how our mind works by making friends with it, by being gentle with it, by telling the mind to do this or that as we would tell a child. If you tell a child not to do something, what does the child do? It's the same principle. And then, what do the parents say? "My child is stubborn." We use the same word in relation to our mind. "I can never meditate successfully. My mind is stubborn."

So it is extremely important in the first place to have this right relationship with our mind and body, to make friends with our mind and body, to create space for them; and then to make an effort to understand how our mind works. It is extremely unfortunate if we are so involved with techniques and achieving particular states of mind that we miss this wonderful opportunity to *understand* our mind. So this is why I say meditation is understanding, exploring, discovering. Then there's an element of fun in it. Then you find meditation interesting. All the time we can make discoveries about what is happening in our mind. But if we are concerned only about a particular state of mind, we miss this important point.

Meditator: There seems to be a natural tendency to repel our negative thoughts, but you are encouraging us to be friendly with our negative thoughts. That goes against our conditioning.

Godwin: It's a very strong conditioning that we have, to judge our thoughts: negative thoughts, positive thoughts; good thoughts, bad thoughts; beautiful thoughts, ugly thoughts; important thoughts, unimportant thoughts. After all, they are only thoughts. But with our past, with our past conditioning, we tend to judge them. And then, what happens when we start judging them? We repress them. "Negative thoughts should not arise," so we push them away. "Ugly thoughts should not arise," so we start repressing. This is how we start to repress, to control, to deny. So it is extremely important in this technique to learn to relate to thoughts just as thoughts, without these value judgements. Then you will not be repressing them, controlling them, denying them. And when you start relating to thoughts without judging them, then whenever thoughts come you don't judge them, you just let them go. It is by judging them that we get involved in them. Our thoughts really grip us, and that's how suffering is created. There is a beautiful metaphor that is used in Tibetan Buddhism, in the Mahāmudrā practice. Relate to your mind as a clear spacious sky, and to thoughts as clouds. The clouds do not affect the sky, and the sky does not affect the clouds. Or take the metaphor of a mirror, which is used in many meditation traditions. It is there in the Zen tradition, in the Tibetan tradition, in the Theravāda tradition, in Taoism. Whatever object comes before the mirror does not affect the mirror, and the mirror does not affect the object. So relate to thoughts that way; and you can do that only if you can learn not to judge them. So please avoid the confused idea that meditation is about trying to stop thoughts. If you can relate to thoughts in the way I am describing, then whether thoughts are there or not, the mind remains like a clear mirror or like the clear, spacious sky. And that is a mind that is free.

Another point is that when you learn to do this, you don't have to confine it to the sitting posture. As we all know, thoughts are arising and passing away all the time. From the time we wake up to the time we go off to sleep, it is continuous, relentless – thoughts, the inner chatter. So if you can learn to work with thoughts in this way, then meditation becomes a way of life.

Meditator: How does this practice of watching thoughts differ from daydreaming?

Godwin: Interesting question! We know how thoughts generate stories and daydreams and fantasies. I would like to illustrate with an example. There was a meditator at the Centre, in Sri Lanka, a Western woman, and a mosquito bit her. So she thought, "I'll get malaria." And then she thought, "If I get malaria, I'll have to go to hospital. And if I go to hospital, I won't be able to leave Sri Lanka on the day I'm planning to leave. In which case I'll have to inform Mother. And when Mother learns that I won't be arriving on the day she's expecting me, she's bound to get depressed . . . . " Now I see that you are amused. But isn't that what we all do – creating stories from what has happened in the past, and from what we anticipate in the future? But we don't realize that *we* create these stories; we become victims of the stories that *we* create *ourselves*. And this is how suffering is created.

Sometimes I use the metaphor of films. We create our own films. We produce them, direct them, act in them. We do all that. And these films that we create ourselves again generate suffering and the emotions that arise in relation to it.

Some meditators' daydreams are terrible. One young meditator told me that in all her daydreams she becomes the victim. Fascinating! But then there was another meditator who said that in his daydreams he was always victorious, successful. So it seems there are differences. Now this is meditation: to understand the contents of all this, exploring whatever happens in our minds.

It's very significant that the term used is "day-*dream*." What is the difference between a day-dream and a night-dream?

Meditator: Not much. They're both involuntary.

Godwin: Very good. In other words, we hardly have any control. In both situations they become so real! In both situations we hardly have any control; they become real. And this we call living! During the day, perhaps most of the time, we are lost in stories, daydreaming, fantasizing. And that situation – that is how suffering is created, that is how emotions arise.

Hence the importance of our meditation. Hence the importance of being alert and awake.

It is very significant that in techniques like focusing on the breathing, there is no room for stories to arise. When thoughts do arise, ideally we learn to let go of them and come back to the present. Because, as I said, our stories are about what has happened in the past and what is going to happen in the future. So in focusing on the breathing we learn to be in the here-and-now, so that there is no room for daydreaming or fantasies to arise.

Anything else about thoughts? It's a very interesting area, a very important area. I'd like to raise a question for you to reflect on: Can there be suffering without a thought? It's an important question to reflect on. Can there be suffering without a thought? Find out for yourself.

Now I'd like to hear your experiences in relation to emotions. When we practise letting emotions arise, especially emotions that we don't like, what happens? It's extremely important this working with emotions, especially unpleasant emotions. In meditation one needs to realize, in one's experience, that trying to repress emotions, trying to get rid of emotions, actually gives them more power, more energy. This is a very important realization. One has to see this in one's experience.

But when we allow emotions to arise, when we invite them, then either they don't arise, or when they do arise they are not so powerful, they don't overwhelm us. There's a word one meditator used to describe unpleasant emotions, and I have been continuing to use it though I'm not very happy with it. The word is "monsters." So you invite all the monsters you dislike to your party, and guess what happens: they don't come! They don't come. But if we are afraid of them, if they come when we are trying to get rid of them, then the small monsters become bigger. We don't realize how we make our monsters bigger. This is again a very important experience in meditation, to realize how we create our own suffering by making our monsters bigger.

So I have my own definition of meditation. Meditation is an attempt to create space in our minds so our monsters can become our friends. And when they have become our friends, it makes no difference whether they are there or not. And that is a very important breakthrough: the pleasant/unpleasant dichotomy disappears. Now what happens in meditation if we identify only with pleasant experiences and dislike unpleasant experiences? We like only angels but not monsters. So there's a split in us, a dichotomy, a duality. So what has happened is that in the name of meditation we have become divided; our meditation has become a battle, of resisting the monsters and going for the angels. One has to transcend this dichotomy, one has to go beyond this pleasant/unpleasant division. And this technique of watching emotions enables one to do that. It is an important breakthrough. You learn to have a mirror-like mind that reflects things as they are. And that is a mind that is free.

Meditator: When I invite unpleasant emotions to arise, they don't arise.

Godwin: So is there a problem? In fact some people tell me they want monsters to arise, and when they don't arise that's a problem! We are so used to them that when they don't arise, it's a problem. See what a lot of energy we have given to them. What is presented in the Dhamma is very simple: when they are there, just to know that they are there; when they are not there, just to know that they are not there. In both situations just have a mirror-like mind. That is freedom.

Meditator: When I invite them in meditation they don't come, but in certain situations in everyday life they come up and are a problem.

Godwin: A very important practical question, because in everyday life there are situations where these emotions may arise – anger, fear, depression, guilt, tension, jealousy, and so on. I think we are all familiar with these. And we also know from practical experience how they just come up in unexpected situations. Now how does a meditator work with such situations? We have a very strong conditioning, maybe from childhood, to dislike them, to repress them, to control them, especially the unpleasant experiences. Take anger. When we were small our parents didn't like us when we got angry. A girl once told me that when she was small her mother would say, "Don't get angry. Your beautiful face becomes ugly." And you will have heard similar things. So what happens? As children we learn to repress anger. We learn to pretend, to repress, to control. This is a very strong conditioning we have.

And then what happens when you take to the spiritual life, when you take up meditation? We are told the same thing: "Meditators don't get angry. They have only positive experiences." It is extremely important to change this perspective. And how does one change it? By realizing that we should first *learn* about these emotions. We have already taken up a position about them – that they are bad, undesirable – without even learning about them, without even experiencing them. This is why it is said so clearly in the Dhamma: When they are there, just be aware that they are there. We don't really experience these emotions fully and completely because of the positions we have taken. So if we have these emotions in everyday life – fear, anger, whatever – we can learn to be completely aware of them, completely *with* those emotions. This is the first point.

The second point is to learn to experiment with them, to explore them. Experimenting with them means not taking up a position. Consider anger; suppose that in everyday life you get angry. How does the meditator work with that anger? Why do we get angry? Because we have an expectation of how the other person should behave, we have a model or an ideal of how the other person should behave, or of how we should behave, or of how life should be. When we realize this, that the problem is with ourselves in having such an idea, having such a concept, then we learn to look at *ourselves*. And we learn to take responsibility for that anger. Otherwise we take up the position that the other person has provoked us, so we don't have to do anything about it, we can continue to get angry and not realize the reason for it by experimenting and exploring. Such a person will never get an opportunity to work with such states of mind. So one should look at *oneself*. This is the second point.

So rather than focus your attention on the object that is provoking you, you look at yourself and try to explore, to understand the nature of anger. And then at that moment you will realize: It's my problem, for having this idea, this model or image.

Then there is another aspect to anger. Some very interesting physiological changes take place in anger. And here again one has to make an effort to experience it, to understand it. This is what I mean by experimenting. Now what happens in our body when we get angry? What happens to our face, our heartbeat, our stomach? One has to be aware of these changes that are taking place in the body. Different people may have different signals physically, but there is one that happens to everyone when they get angry: the breath speeds up. What happens to the breath when we meditate and the mind becomes calm? It slows down. So this shows that the breath is a very important indicator, a very useful monitor of what is happening in our mind. Maybe that's why focusing on the breathing is a meditation technique. Doing this with anger, you will be relating to it in an entirely different way.

This can be done in relation to every emotion in everyday life. One can change one's attitude toward them rather than repressing them, controlling them, denying them. Rather than pretend that we're not angry and so on, we make friends with them, by creating space for them, and learning about them.

And there's yet another aspect to it. When we have these emotions, we tend to own them, We tend to think of it as *my* anger, *my* depression, *my* anxiety. Now, is it possible to relate to them without this sense of ownership? Can we see just anger, just guilt, just fear. With this change of attitude toward emotions, they become learning experiences, valuable experiences for us. We can be learning about these emotions all the time, waiting for opportunities to arise to learn about them. Then your spiritual practice takes on an entirely different dimension. So rather than being afraid of them, rather than chastising yourself for having them, you relate to them in an entirely different way. And then, you realize when they are not there. When they are there you learn to work with them, to explore them, understand them; and when they are not there you realize that they are not there. So what is the difference? What is the result?

Meditator: You are living just in the present.

Godwin: Well, living in the present is an ideal. But here again, this phrase "living in the present" has various aspects. Of course you are right, if one can be completely in the present, in the here-and-now, one can be free to a great extent of what is happening. But there's another way of understanding what one means by being in the present. It means that in actual fact, although we assume that there is a past and a future, in a sense there is only the present. There is only the here-and-now. Even when we recall things, and when we anticipate things, we do it *now.* So when we realize that the only reality is the present, then we'll be relating to the past and the future in an entirely different way. So again, to put it in practical terms, when you realize that a story you are constructing is dependent on something that has happened and something you are anticipating, then the story loses its power.

Meditator: But expressing our emotions can bring problems.

Godwin: Generally there are two ways we relate to emotions. Either we repress and control them or we express and indulge them. As we have found out, repressing and controlling them has its problems; and expressing and indulging them has its problems too, as we all know. But what is attempted in meditation is, ideally, neither to repress nor to express, but just to be aware of it, just to create space for it, to make friends with it, to experiment.

Meditator: Does this practice eventually bring about a transformation in the mind – enlightenment?

Godwin: This again brings up an interesting point, that we should not be so concerned about results. In meditation, the spiritual life, we can become so involved in goals. Is there a difference between being ambitious materially, and having ambitions spiritually? Is there really a difference? The ambition is the same. The more you try to get rid of an emotion, the more power you give it. So we should find the work we do with emotions more interesting than the state of being rid of the emotions. In some cultures there is such an emphasis on achieving, on results. You want results, immediate results; but then you miss the fun. What is important is not the end result, but the doing of it. What is important is not what will happen when you reach the top of the hill, but rather the process of climbing it, the adventures involved in it. So in some traditions they say that the ordinary mind *is* the enlightened mind. The practice *is* enlightenment.

Often we are doing something in order to overcome things, to see a result from it. But if we can change our perspective and learn to see what we are doing as something interesting in itself, something enjoyable, then that is enough. That is enlightenment, that is freedom. So I'd like to emphasize this point: see importance in your practice itself, not in what will come out of the practice. I don't see any difference between material ambition and spiritual ambition. Both can generate suffering, both create tension and repression. But if you can relate to the practice itself in this different way, then your mind is free at the time you are practising, not when your practice is over.

Finally, I'd like to touch on some other aspects of this technique. It can have subtler levels. One is that you may have a glimpse, while you are doing this, that there is only thinking, that there is no thinker apart from thought. Normally when we have thoughts, we assume that *I* am thinking, that these are *my* thoughts. But working with this technique of observing the thoughts, you may have a glimpse of insight that there is only thinking, and that the thinker apart from the thoughts is something that we construct. You may have a similar experience in relation to sensations and emotions: that there is no feeler, apart from feeling. The idea of *my* thought, *my* pain, *my* anger, *my* fear, drops away, and that is a very important realization.

Another aspect of this technique is that when we learn to observe whatever happens without judging, when we learn not to repress things, not to control things, then in psychological terms, this will help make our unconscious conscious. In techniques like focusing on an object, what happens is that there is an element of suppression. When thoughts come, you learn to let go of them and come back to the object, so there is an element of control, of exclusion. But in this technique of watching there is no control, no exclusion, no denial. So in this process when you learn to allow things to happen, then whatever you have repressed can surface. And when your unconscious is made conscious in this way, your behaviour becomes integrated and harmonious.

Another way of looking at this technique is that we are learning to *surrender*, to surrender to whatever is happening.

Zen Mind

Shunryu Suzuki

Posture

"These forms are not the means of obtaining the right state of mind. To take this posture is itself to have the right state of mind. There is no need to obtain some special state of mind."

The most important thing in taking the zazen posture is to keep your spine straight. Your ears and your shoulders should be on one line. Relax your shoulders, and push up towards the ceiling with the back of your head. And you should pull your chin in. When your chin is tilted up, you have no strength in your posture; you are probably dreaming. Also to gain strength in your posture, press your diaphragm down towards your *hara*, or lower abdomen. This will help you maintain your physical and mental balance. When you try to keep this posture, at first you may find some difficulty breathing naturally, but when you get accustomed to it you will be able to breathe naturally and deeply.

Your hands should form the "cosmic *mudrā*". If you put your left hand on top of your right, middle joints of your middle fingers together, and touch your thumbs lightly together (as if you held a piece of paper between them), your hands will make a beautiful oval. You should keep this universal mudrā with great care, as if you were holding something very precious in your hand. Your hands should be held against your body, with your thumbs at about the height of your navel. Hold your arms freely and easily, and slightly away from your body, as if you held an egg under each arm without breaking it.

You should not be tilted sideways, backwards, or forwards. You should be sitting straight up as if you were supporting the sky with your head. This is not just form or breathing. It expresses the key point of Buddhism. It is a perfect expression of your Buddha nature.

If you want true understanding of Buddhism, you should practise this way. These forms are not a *means* of obtaining the right state of mind. To take this posture itself is the purpose of our practice. When you have this posture, you have the right state of mind, so there is no need to try to attain some special state. When you try to attain something, your mind starts to wander about somewhere else. When you do not try to attain anything, you have your own body and mind right here. A Zen master would say, "Kill the Buddha!" Kill the Buddha if the Buddha exists somewhere else. Kill the Buddha, because you should resume your own Buddha nature.

Doing something is expressing our own nature. We do not exist for the sake of something else. We exist for the sake of ourselves. This is the fundamental teaching expressed in the forms we observe. Just as for sitting, when we stand in the *zendō* we have some rules. But the purpose of these rules is not to make everyone the same, but to allow each to express his own self most freely. For instance, each one of us has his own way of standing, so our standing posture is based on the proportions of our own bodies. When you stand, your heels should be as far apart as the width of your own fist, your big toes in line with the centres of your breasts. As in zazen, put some strength in your abdomen. Here also your hands should express your self. Hold your left hand against your chest with fingers encircling your thumb, and put your right hand over it. Holding your thumb pointing downward, and your forearms parallel to the floor, you feel as if you have some round pillar in your grasp – a big round temple pillar – so you cannot be slumped or tilted to the side.

The most important point is to own your own physical body. If you slump, you will lose your self. Your mind will be wandering about somewhere else; you will not be in your body. This is not the way. We must exist right here, right now! This is the key point. You must have your own body and mind. Everything should exist in the right place, in the right way. Then there is no problem. If the microphone I use when I speak exists somewhere else, it will not serve its purpose. When we have our body and mind in order, everything else will exist in the right place, in the right way.

But usually, without being aware of it, we try to change something other than ourselves, we try to order things outside us. But it is impossible to organize things if you yourself are not in order. When you do things in the right way, at the right time, everything else will be organized. You are the "boss". When the boss is sleeping, everyone is sleeping. When the boss does something right, everyone will do everything right, and at the right time. That is the secret of Buddhism.

So try always to keep the right posture, not only when you practise zazen, but in all your activities. Take the right posture when you are driving your car, and when you are reading. If you read in a slumped position, you cannot stay awake long. Try. You will discover how important it is to keep the right posture. This is the true teaching. The teaching which is written on paper is not the true teaching. Written teaching is a kind of food for your brain. Of course it is necessary to take some food for your brain, but it is more important to be yourself by practising the right way of life.

That is why Buddha could not accept the religions existing at his time. He studied many religions, but he was not satisfied with their practices. He could not find the answer in asceticism or in philosophies. He was not interested in some metaphysical existence, but in his own body and mind, here and now. And when he found himself, he found that everything that exists has Buddha nature. That was his enlightenment. Enlightenment is not some good feeling or some particular state of mind. The state of mind that exists when you sit in the right posture is, itself, enlightenment. If you cannot be satisfied with the state of mind you have in zazen, it means your mind is still wandering about. Our body and mind should not be wobbling or wandering about. In this posture there is no need to talk about the right state of mind. You already have it. This is the conclusion of Buddhism.

Breathing

"What we call 'I' is just a swinging door which moves when we inhale and when we exhale."

When we practise zazen, our mind always follows our breathing. When we inhale, the air comes into the inner world. When we exhale, the air goes out to the outer world. The inner world is limitless, and the outer world is also limitless. We say "inner world" or "outer world," but actually there is just one whole world. In this limitless world, our throat is like a swinging door. The air comes in and goes out like someone passing through a swinging door. If you think, "I breathe," the "I" is extra. There is no you to say "I". What we call "I" is just a swinging door which moves when we inhale and when we exhale. It just moves; that is all. When your mind is pure and calm enough to follow this movement, there is nothing: no "I," no world, no mind nor body; just a swinging door.

So when we practise zazen, all that exists is the movement of the breathing, but we are aware of this movement. You should not be absent-minded. But to be aware of the movement does not mean to be aware of your small self, but rather of your universal nature, or Buddha nature. This kind of awareness is very important, because we are usually so one-sided. Our usual understanding of life is dualistic: you and I, this and that, good and bad. But actually these discriminations are themselves the awareness of the universal existence. "You" means to be aware of the universe in the form of you, and "I" means to be aware of it in the form of I. You and I are just swinging doors. This kind of understanding is necessary. This should not even be called understanding; it is actually the true experience of life through Zen practice.

So when you practise zazen, there is no idea of time or space. You may say, "We started sitting at a quarter to six in this room." Thus you have some idea of time (a quarter to six), and some idea of space (in this room). Actually what you are doing, however, is just sitting and being aware of the universal activity. That is all. This moment the swinging door is opening in one direction, and the next moment the swinging door will be opening in the opposite direction. Moment after moment each one of us repeats this activity. Here there is no idea of time or space. Time and space are one. You may say, "I must do something this afternoon," but actually there is no "this afternoon." We do things one after the other. That is all. There is no such time as "this afternoon" or "one o'clock" or "two o'clock." At one o'clock you will eat your lunch. To eat lunch is itself one o'clock. You will be somewhere, but that place cannot be separated from one o'clock. For someone who actually appreciates our life, they are the same. But when we become tired of our life we may say, "I shouldn't have come to this place. It may have been much better to have gone to some other place for lunch. This place is not so good." In your mind you create an idea of place separate from an actual time.

Or you may say, "This is bad, so I should not do this." Actually, when you say, "I should not do this," you are doing not-doing in that moment. So there is no choice for you. When you separate the idea of time and space, you feel as if you have some choice, but actually, you have to do something, or you have to do not-doing. Not-to-do something is doing something. Good and bad are only in your mind. So we should not say, "This is good," or "This is bad." Instead of saying "bad", you should say, "not-to-do"! If you think, "This is bad," it will create some confusion for you. So in the realm of pure religion there is no confusion of time and space, or good or bad. All that we should do is just do something as it comes. Do something! Whatever it is, we should do it, even if it is not-doing something. We should live in this moment. So when we sit we concentrate on our breathing, and we become a swinging door, and we do something we should do, something we must do. This is Zen practice. In this practice there is no confusion. If you establish this kind of life you have no confusion whatsoever.

Tozan, a famous Zen master, said, "The blue mountain is the father of the white cloud. The white cloud is the son of the blue mountain. All day long they depend on each other, without being dependent on each other. The white cloud is always the white cloud. The blue mountain is always the blue mountain." This is a pure, clear interpretation of life. There may be many things like the white cloud and blue mountain: man and woman, teacher and disciple. They depend on each other. But the white cloud should not be bothered by the blue mountain. The blue mountain should not be bothered by the white cloud. They are quite independent, but yet dependent. This is how we live, and how we practise zazen.

When we become truly ourselves, we just become a swinging door, and we are purely independent of, and at the same time dependent upon, everything. Without air, we cannot breathe. Each one of us is in the midst of myriads of worlds. We are in the centre of the world always, moment after moment. So we are completely dependent and independent. If you have this kind of experience, this kind of existence, you have absolute independence; you will not be bothered by anything. So when you practise zazen, your mind should be concentrated on your breathing. This kind of activity is the fundamental activity of the universal being. Without this experience, this practice, it is impossible to attain absolute freedom.

Control

"To give your sheep or cow a large, spacious meadow is the way to control him."

To live in the realm of Buddha nature means to die as a small being, moment after moment. When we lose our balance we die, but at the same time we also develop ourselves, we grow. Whatever we see is changing, losing its balance. The reason everything looks beautiful is because it is out of balance, but its background is always in perfect harmony. This is how everything exists in the realm of Buddha nature, losing its balance against a background of perfect balance. So if you see things without realizing the background of Buddha nature, everything appears to be in the form of suffering. But if you understand the background of existence, you realize that suffering itself is how we live, and how we extend our life. So in Zen sometimes we emphasize the imbalance or disorder of life.

Nowadays traditional Japanese painting has become pretty formal and lifeless. That is why modern art has developed. Ancient painters used to practise putting dots on paper in artistic disorder. This is rather difficult. Even though you try to do it, usually what you do is arranged in some order. You think you can control it, but you cannot; it is almost impossible to arrange your dots out of order. It is the same with taking care of your everyday life. Even though you try to put people under some control, it is impossible. You cannot do it. The best way to control people is to encourage them to be mischievous. Then they will be in control in its wider sense. To give your sheep or cow a large, spacious meadow is the way to control him. So it is with people: first let them do what they want, and watch them. This is the best policy. To ignore them is not good; that is the worst policy. The second worst is trying to control them. The best one is to watch them, just to watch them, without trying to control them. The same way works for you yourself as well. If you want to obtain perfect calmness in your zazen, you should not be bothered by the various images you find in your mind. Let them come, and let them go. Then they will be under control. But this policy is not so easy. It sounds easy, but it requires some special effort. How to make this kind of effort is the secret of practice. Suppose you are sitting under some extraordinary circumstances. If you try to calm your mind, you will be unable to sit, and if you try not to be disturbed, your effort will not be the right effort. The only effort that will help you is to count your breathing, or to concentrate on your inhaling and exhaling. We say concentration, but to concentrate your mind on something is not the true purpose of Zen. The true purpose is to see things as they are, to observe things as they are, and to let everything go as it goes. This is to put everything under control in its widest sense. Zen practice is to open up our small mind. So concentrating is just an aid to help you realize "big mind," or the mind that is everything. If you want to discover the true meaning of Zen in your everyday life, you have to understand the meaning of keeping your mind on your breathing and your body in the right posture in zazen. You should follow the rules of practice and your study should become more subtle and careful. Only in this way can you experience the vital freedom of Zen. Dōgen-zenji said, "Time goes from present to past." This is absurd, but in our practice sometimes it is true. Instead of time progressing from past to present, it goes backwards from present to past. Yoshitsune was a famous warrior who lived in medieval Japan. Because of the situation of the country at that time, he was sent to the northern provinces, where he was killed. Before he left he bade farewell to his wife, and soon after she wrote in a poem, "Just as you unreel the thread from a spool, I want the past to become present." When she said this, actually she made past time present. In her mind the past became alive and was the present. So as Dōgen said, "Time goes from present to past." This is not true in our logical mind, but it is in the actual experience of making past time present. There we have poetry, and there we have human life. When we experience this kind of truth it means we have found the true meaning of time. Time constantly goes from past to present and from present to future. This is true, but it is also true that time goes from future to present and from present to past. A Zen master once said, "To go eastward one mile is to go westward one mile." This is vital freedom. We should acquire this kind of perfect freedom.

But perfect freedom is not found without some rules. People, especially young people, think that freedom is to do just what they want, that in Zen there is no need for rules. But it is absolutely necessary for us to have some rules. But this does not mean always to be under control. As long as you have rules, you have a chance for freedom. To try to obtain freedom without being aware of the rules means nothing. It is to acquire this perfect freedom that we practise zazen.

Mind Waves

"Because we enjoy all aspects of life as an unfolding of big mind, we do not care for any excessive joy. So we have imperturbable composure."

When you are practising zazen, do not try to stop your thinking. Let it stop by itself. If something comes into your mind, let it come in, and let it go out. It will not stay long. When you try to stop your thinking, it means you are bothered by it. Do not be bothered by anything. It appears as if something comes from outside your mind, but actually it is only the waves of your mind, and if you are not bothered by the waves, gradually they will become calmer and calmer. In five or at most ten minutes, your mind will be completely serene and calm. At that time your breathing will become quite slow, while your pulse will become a little faster.

It will take quite a long time before you find your calm serene mind in your practice. Many sensations come, many thoughts or images arise, but they are just waves of your own mind. Nothing comes from outside your mind. Usually we think of our mind as receiving impressions and experiences from outside, but that is not a true understanding of our mind. The true understanding is that the mind includes everything; when you think something comes from outside it means only that something appears in your mind. Nothing outside yourself can cause any trouble. You yourself make the waves in your mind. If you leave your mind as it is, it will become calm. This mind is called big mind.

If your mind is related to something outside itself, that mind is a small mind, a limited mind. If your mind is not related to anything else, then there is no dualistic understanding in the activity of your mind. You understand activity as just waves of your mind. Big mind experiences everything within itself. Do you understand the difference between the two minds: the mind which includes everything, and the mind which is related to something? Actually they are the same thing, but the understanding is different, and your attitude towards your life will be different according to which understanding you have.

That everything is included within your mind is the essence of mind. To experience this is to have religious feeling. Even though waves arise, the essence of your mind is pure; it is just like clear water with a few waves. Actually water always has waves. Waves are the practice of the water. To speak of waves apart from water or water apart from waves is a delusion. Water and waves are one. Big mind and small mind are one. When you understand your mind in this way, you have some security in your feeling. As your mind does not expect anything from outside, it is always filled. A mind with waves in it is not a disturbed mind, but actually an amplified one. Whatever you experience is an expression of big mind.

The activity of big mind is to amplify itself through various experiences. In one sense our experiences coming one by one are always fresh and new, but in another sense they are nothing but a continuous or repeated unfolding of the one big mind. For instance, if you have something good for breakfast, you will say, "This is good."

"Good" is supplied as something experienced some time long ago, even though you may not remember when. With big mind we accept each of our experiences as if recognizing the face we see in a mirror as our own. For us there is no fear of losing this mind. There is nowhere to come or to go; there is no fear of death, no suffering from old age or sickness. Because we enjoy all aspects of life as an unfolding of big mind, we do not care for any excessive joy. So we have imperturbable composure, and it is with this imperturbable composure of big mind that we practise zazen.

Mind Weeds

"You should rather be grateful for the weeds you have in your mind, because eventually they will enrich your practice."

When the alarm rings early in the morning, and you get up, I think you do not feel so good. It is not easy to go and sit, and even after you arrive at the zendō and begin zazen you have to encourage yourself to sit well. These are just waves of your mind. In pure zazen there should not be any waves in your mind. While you are sitting these waves will become smaller and smaller, and your effort will change into some subtle feeling.

We say, "Pulling out the weeds we give nourishment to the plant." We pull the weeds and bury them near the plant to give it nourishment. So even though you have some difficulty in your practice, even though you have some waves while you are sitting, those waves themselves will help you. So you should not be bothered by your mind. You should rather be grateful for the weeds, because eventually they will enrich your practice. If you have some experience of how the weeds in your mind change into mental nourishment, your practice will make remarkable progress. You will feel the progress. You will feel how they change into self-nourishment. Of course it is not so difficult to give some philosophical or psychological interpretation of our practice, but that is not enough. We must have the actual experience of how our weeds change into nourishment.

Strictly speaking, any effort we make is not good for our practice because it creates waves in our mind. It is impossible, however, to attain absolute calmness of our mind without any effort. We must make some effort, but we must forget ourselves in the effort we make. In this realm there is no subjectivity or objectivity. Our mind is just calm, without even any awareness. In this unawareness, every effort and every idea and thought will vanish. So it is necessary for us to encourage ourselves and to make an effort up to the last moment, when all effort disappears. You should keep your mind on your breathing until you are not aware of your breathing.

We should try to continue our effort forever, but we should not expect to reach some stage when we will forget all about it. We should just try to keep our mind on our breathing. That is our actual practice. That effort will be refined more and more while you are sitting. At first the effort you make is quite rough and impure, but by the power of practice the effort will become purer and purer. When your effort becomes pure, your body and mind become pure. This is the way we practise Zen. Once you understand our innate power to purify ourselves and our surroundings, you can act properly, and you will learn from those around you, and you will become friendly with others. This is the merit of Zen practice. But the way of practice is just to be concentrated on your breathing with the right posture and with great, pure effort. This is how we practise Zen.

To Polish a Tile

"When you become you, Zen becomes Zen. When you are you, you see things as they are, and you become one with your surroundings."

Zen stories, or kōans, are very difficult to understand before you know what we are doing moment after moment. But if you know exactly what we are doing in each moment, you will not find kōans so difficult. There are so many kōans. I have often talked to you about a frog, and each time everybody laughs. But a frog is very interesting. He sits like us, too, you know. But he does not think that he is doing anything so special. When you go to a zendō and sit, you may think you are doing some special thing. While your husband or wife is sleeping, you are practising zazen! You are doing some special thing, and your spouse is lazy! That may be your understanding of zazen. But look at the frog. A frog also sits like us, but he has no idea of zazen. Watch him. If something annoys him, he will make a face. If something comes along to eat, he will snap it up and eat, and he eats sitting. Actually that is our zazen − not any special thing.

Here is a kind of frog kōan for you. Baso was a famous Zen master called the Horse-master. He was the disciple of Nangaku, one of the Sixth Patriarch's disciples. One day while he was studying under Nangaku, Baso was sitting, practising zazen. He was a man of large physical build; when he talked, his tongue reached to his nose; his voice was loud; and his zazen must have been very good. Nangaku saw him sitting like a great mountain or like a frog. Nangaku asked, "What are you doing?" "I am practising zazen," Baso replied. "Why are you practising zazen?" "I want to attain enlightenment; I want to be a Buddha," the disciple said. Do you know what the teacher did? He picked up a tile, and he started to polish it. In Japan, after taking a tile from the kiln, we polish it to give it a beautiful finish. So Nangaku picked up a tile and started to polish it. Baso, his disciple, asked, "What are you doing?" "I want to make this tile into a jewel," Nangaku said. "How is it possible to make a tile a jewel?" Baso asked. "How is it possible to become a Buddha by practising zazen?" Nangaku replied. "Do you want to attain Buddhahood? There is no Buddhahood besides your ordinary mind. When a cart does not go, which do you whip, the cart or the horse?" the master asked.

Nangaku's meaning here is that whatever you do, that is zazen. True zazen is beyond being in bed or sitting in the zendō. If your husband or wife is in bed, that is zazen. If you think, "I am sitting here, and my spouse is in bed," then even though you are sitting here in the cross-legged position, that is not true zazen. You should be like a frog always. That is true zazen.

Dōgen-zenji commented on this kōan. He said, "When the Horse-master becomes the Horse-master, Zen becomes Zen." When Baso becomes Baso, his zazen becomes true zazen, and Zen becomes Zen. What is true zazen? When you become you! When you are you, then no matter what you do, that is zazen. Even though you are in bed, you may not be you most of the time. Even though you are sitting in the zendō, I wonder whether you are you in the true sense.

Here is another famous kōan. Zuikan was a Zen master who always used to address himself. "Zuikan?" he would call. And then he would answer. "Yes!" "Zuikan?" "Yes!" Of course he was living all alone in his small zendō, and of course he knew who he was, but sometimes he lost himself. And whenever he lost himself, he would address himself, "Zuikan?" "Yes!"

If we are like a frog, we are always ourselves. But even a frog sometimes loses himself, and he makes a sour face. And if something comes along, he will snap at it and eat it. So I think a frog is always addressing himself. I think you should do that also. Even in zazen you will lose yourself. When you become sleepy, or when your mind starts to wander about, you lose yourself. When your legs become painful – "Why are my legs so painful?" – you lose yourself. Because you lose yourself, your problem will be a problem for you. If you do not lose yourself, then even though you have difficulty, there is actually no problem whatsoever. You just sit in the midst of the problem; when you are a part of the problem, or when the problem is a part of you, there is no problem, because you are the problem itself. The problem is you yourself. If this is so, there is no problem.

When your life is always a part of your surroundings – in other words, when you are called back to yourself, in the present moment – then there is no problem. When you start to wander about in some delusion which is something apart from you yourself, then your surroundings are not real any more, and your mind is not real any more. If you yourself are deluded, then your surroundings are also a misty, foggy delusion. Once you are in the midst of delusion, there is no end to delusion. You will be involved in deluded ideas one after another. Most people live in delusion, involved in their problem, trying to solve their problem. But just to live is actually to live in problems. And to solve the problem is to be a part of it, to be one with it.

So which do you hit, the cart or the horse? Which do you hit, yourself or your problems? If you start questioning which you should hit, that means you have already started to wander about. But when you actually hit the horse, the cart will go. In truth, the cart and the horse are not different. When you are you, there is no problem of whether you should hit the cart or the horse. When you are you, zazen becomes true zazen. So when you practise zazen, your problem will practise zazen, and everything else will practise zazen too. Even though your spouse is in bed, he or she is also practising zazen – when you practise zazen! But when you do not practise true zazen, then there is your spouse, and there is yourself, each quite different, quite separate from the other. So if you yourself have true practice, then everything else is practising our way at the same time.

That is why we should always address ourselves, checking up on ourselves like a doctor tapping himself. This is very important. This kind of practice should be continued moment after moment, incessantly. We say, "When the night is here, the dawn comes." It means there is no gap between the dawn and the night. Before the summer is over, autumn comes. In this way we should understand our life. We should practise with this understanding, and solve our problems in this way. Actually, just to work on the problem, if you do it with single-minded effort, is enough. You should just polish the tile; that is our practice. The purpose of practice is not to make a tile a jewel. Just continue sitting; that is practice in its true sense. It is not a matter of whether or not it is possible to attain Buddhahood, whether or not it is possible to make a tile a jewel. Just to work and live in this world with this understanding is the most important point. That is our practice. That is true zazen. So we say, "When you eat, eat!" You should eat what is there, you know. Sometimes you do not eat it. Even though you are eating, your mind is somewhere else. You do not taste what you have in your mouth. As long as you can eat when you are eating, you are all right. Do not worry a bit. It means you are you yourself.

When you are you, you see things as they are, and you become one with your surroundings. There is your true self. There you have true practice; you have the practice of a frog. He is a good example of our practice – when a frog becomes a frog, Zen becomes Zen. When you understand a frog through and through, you attain enlightenment; you are Buddha. And you are good for others, too: husband or wife or son or daughter. This is zazen!

Some Tibetan Practices

Kathleen McDonald

The meditations presented here are solutions to a wide variety of problems and will help you develop a more realistic view of your inner and outer worlds.

A meditation on emptiness is given first, as this is the most powerful remedy to any difficulty. However, it might take time to develop sufficient grasp of this method for it to prove effective in dealing with strong, prevalent delusions. But persevere; it is well worth while.

The other meditations get us to look at our assumptions about life, suffering, death, and human relationships and to see that it is these assumptions and their attendant expectations that cause our unhappiness and frustrations.

The section on dealing with negative energy gives advice on how to handle problems as they occur in day-to-day life.

Begin the meditations with a few minutes – or as long as you like – of breathing meditation, slowing down the mind and observing its present state.

Then, start the analysis. Do not let your mind wander from the subject you are analyzing; the more concentrated you are, the better. Dissolve your mind in the subject, penetrating it with intellectual thought, questions, images, and illustrations from your own experience. Your meditation might take the form of an internal lecture, as though you were explaining a point to yourself; a debate, with yourself taking both sides; or a freestyle thought-adventure.

Doubts will inevitably arise, but do not gloss over them. Doubts are questions and questions need answers, so be clear about what you think, and why. Either come to a conclusion about the point in question or leave it aside for the moment and tackle it again later.

If during the analysis you should develop an intuitive experience of the subject, stop analyzing and hold the feeling with single-pointed concentration for as long as possible. When the feeling fades, resume the investigation or conclude the session. This union of analytical and stabilizing meditations is essential if we are to achieve true mind-transformation. In analytical meditation we think about and understand intellectually a particular point, and through stabilization meditation we gradually make it a part of our very experience of life.

Meditation on Emptiness

All Buddhist teachings are for the purpose of leading one gradually to the realization of emptiness. Here, emptiness means the emptiness of inherent, concrete existence; and the total eradication from our mind of this false way of seeing things marks our achievement of enlightenment, buddhahood.

What *is* "emptiness of inherent existence"? In practical terms, what does it mean? So-called inherent existence – of which all things are said to be empty – is a quality that we instinctively project on to every person and everything we experience. We see things as fully, solidly existing in and of themselves, from their own side, having their own nature, quite independent of any other cause and condition or of our own mind experiencing them.

Take a table, for example. We see a solid, independent table standing there, so obviously a table that it seems ridiculous to even question it. But where is the table? Where is its tableness located? Is it one of its legs? Or its top? Is it one of its parts? Or even one of its atoms? When did it start to be a table? How many parts do you take away before it ceases to be a table?

If you investigate thoroughly, you will discover that you simply cannot *find* the table you think is there. There is, however, an interdependent, changing from moment to moment, non-inherent table but this is not what we see. This is the crux of the problem. We experience not the bare reality of each thing, and each person but an exaggerated, filled-out image of it projected by our own mind. This mistake marks every one of our mental experiences, is quite instinctive, and is the very root of all our problems.

This pervasive mental disorder starts with the misapprehension of our own self. We are a composite of body – a mass of flesh, bones, and skin – and mind – a stream of thoughts, feelings and perceptions. The composite is conventionally known as "Mary," "Harold," "woman," "man." It is a temporary alliance that ends with the death of the body and the flowing on of the mind to other experiences.

These stark, unembellished facts can be rather disquieting. A part of us, the ego, craving security and immortality, invents an inherent, independent, permanent self. This is not a deliberate, conscious process but one that takes place deep in our sub-conscious mind.

This fantasized self appears especially strongly at times of stress, excitement, or fear. For example, when we narrowly escape an accident there is a powerful sense of an I that nearly suffered death or pain and must be protected. *That* I does not exist; it is an hallucination.

Our adherence to this false I – known as self-grasping ignorance – taints all our dealings with the world. We are attracted to people, places, and situations that gratify and uphold our self-image, and react with fear or animosity to whatever threatens it. We view all people and things as definitely this way or that. Thus this root, self-grasping, branches out into attachment, jealousy, anger, arrogance, depression, and the myriad other turbulent and unhappy states of mind.

The final solution is to eliminate this root ignorance with the wisdom that realizes the emptiness, in everything we experience, of the false qualities we project on to them. This is the ultimate transformation of mind.

Emptiness sounds pretty abstract but in fact is very practical and relevant to our lives. The first step towards understanding it is to try and get an idea of what it is we *think* exists; to locate, for example, the I that we believe in so strongly, and then, by using clear reasoning in analytical meditation, to see that it is a mere fabrication, that it is something that has never existed and could never exist in the first place.

But don't throw out too much! You definitely exist! There is a conventional, interdependent self that experiences happiness and suffering, that works, studies, eats, sleeps, meditates, and becomes enlightened. The first, most difficult task is to distinguish between this valid I and the fabricated one; usually we cannot tell them apart. In the concentration of meditation it is possible to see the difference, to recognize the illusory I and eradicate our long-habituated belief in it. The meditation here is a practical first step in that direction.

The Practice: Begin with a breathing meditation to relax and calm your mind. Motivate strongly to do this meditation in order to finally become enlightened for the sake of all beings.

Now, with the alertness of a spy, slowly and carefully become aware of the I. Who or what is thinking, feeling, and meditating? How does it seem to come into existence? How does it appear to you? Is your I a creation of your mind? Or is it something existing concretely and independently, in its own right?

If you think you can identify it, try to locate it. Where is this I? Is it in your head . . . in your eyes . . . in your heart . . . in your hands . . . in your stomach . . . in your feet? Carefully consider each part of your body, including the organs, blood vessels and nerves. Can you find your I? It might be very small and subtle, so consider the cells, the atoms, the parts of the atoms.

After considering the entire body, again ask yourself how your I manifests its apparent existence. Does it still appear to be vivid and concrete? Is your body the I or not? Perhaps you think your mind is the I. The mind is a constantly changing stream of thoughts, feelings, and other experiences, coming and going in rapid alternation. Which of these is the I? Is it a loving thought . . . an angry thought . . . a happy feeling . . . a depressed feeling? Is your I the meditating mind . . . the dreaming mind? Can you find the I in your mind?

Is there any other place to look for your I? Could it exist somewhere else or in some other way? Examine every possibility you can think of.

Again, look at the way your I actually appears, feels to you. After this search for the I, do you notice any change? Do you still believe that it is as solid and real as you felt before? Does it still appear to exist independently, in and of itself?

Next, mentally disintegrate your body. Imagine all the atoms separating and floating apart. Millions and billions of minute particles scatter throughout space. Imagine that you can actually see this.

Now, disintegrate your mind. Let every thought, feeling, sensation, and perception float away.

Stay in this experience of space without being distracted by thoughts. When the feeling of an independent inherent I recurs, analyze it again. Does it exist in the body? In the mind? How does it exist?

Do not make the mistake of thinking, "My body is the I and my mind is not the I, therefore I don't exist." You exist, but not in the way you instinctively feel, that is as independent and inherent. Conventionally your self exists *in dependence upon* mind and body, and this combination is the basis to which conceptual thinking ascribes a name "I" or "self" or "Mary" or "Harold." This is the you that is sitting and meditating and wondering, "Maybe I don't exist!"

Whatever exists is necessarily dependent upon causes and conditions, or parts and names, for its existence. This is how things exist conventionally, and understanding interdependence is the principal cause for understanding a thing's ultimate nature, its emptiness. The conventional nature of something is its dependence upon causes and conditions and its ultimate nature is its emptiness of inherent, independent existence.

Think now about how your body exists conventionally: *in dependence upon* skin, blood, bones, legs, arms, organs, and so forth. In turn, each of these exists *in dependence upon* their own parts: cells, atoms, and sub-atomic particles.

Think about your mind, how it exists *in dependence upon* thoughts, feelings, perceptions, sensations. And how, in turn, each of these exists *in dependence upon* the previous conscious experiences that gave rise to them.

Now, go back to your feeling of self or I. Think about how *you* exist conventionally, *in dependence upon* mind and body and name – the self's parts.

When the body feels hungry or cold, for example, you think "I am hungry," "I am cold." When the mind has an idea about something, you say "I think." When you feel love for someone you say "I love you." When introducing yourself to someone you say "I am so-and-so."

Apart from this sense of I that depends upon the ever-flowing, ever-changing streams of body and mind, is there an I that is solid, unchanging and independent?

The mere absence of such an inherently-existing I is the emptiness of the self.

Finish the session with a conclusion as to how you, your self, exists. Conclude by dedicating sincerely any positive energy and insight you have gained to the enlightenment of all beings. Think that this meditation is just one step along the path to finally achieving direct insight into emptiness and thus cutting the root of suffering and dissatisfaction.

About Visualization

In your attempts to calm and concentrate your mind, you have probably noticed visual images among the many things that distract your attention from the object of meditation: faces of loved ones, your home, other familiar places, appetizing food, or memories of films you have seen. Such images arise spontaneously throughout the day but we are often too engrossed in external sensations to notice them. And each night our mind creates vivid scenes in which we interact with dream-people and dream-events. Visualization, or imagination, is thus a mental technique we are all familiar with, but unless our work lies in, say, art, design, or film, we do little or nothing to develop and utilize it.

This natural capacity to think in pictures can be used to deepen our meditative experiences. Visualization is used in several ways in the Tibetan tradition of spiritual development. It adds another dimension to analytical meditations – for example, visualizing ourselves dying in order to sharpen the awareness of our mortality. A mental image of the Buddha is recommended as the focus of attention in the development of single-pointed concentration, and visualizing enlightened beings while praying helps to enhance our faith and conviction.

But the art of visualization is used to its optimum in Vajrayana, or tantra, the most profound and rapid means of reaching enlightenment. The practices of this path involve identifying oneself completely, body and mind, with an enlightened being and seeing one's environment as a pure realm. The ordinary, mistaken perceptions of oneself and all other phenomena are thus gradually abandoned as one's potential for enlightenment is allowed to express itself.

The meditational deities visualized in Vajrayana practice, such as Tara and Avalokiteshvara, are symbols of the enlightened state. Each is a manifestation of a specific quality – Avalokiteshvara, for example, is the buddha of compassion – but each also represents the total experience of enlightenment. The details of the visualization, such as colours, implements, hand gestures, posture, and so forth, symbolize different aspects of the path to spiritual fulfilment.

Meditation on these deities (or images from other traditions that you are more comfortable with, for example, Christ or Mary) helps us to open our hearts to the pure energies of love, compassion, wisdom, and strength that are ever-present, all around us, wherever we may be. And, as the potential for these enlightened qualities lies within us, we should consider the images we contemplate to be reflections of our own true nature. Although ultimate reality is inexpressible, words lead us to discover it; so too can images remind us of the experience of enlightenment until it becomes a living reality.

The two kinds of meditation – analytical and stabilizing – are used together in visualization techniques. We need analytical thought to construct the image at the beginning of the meditation and to recall it whenever it is lost during the session. Analysis is also used to deal with other problems that might occur, such as distraction or negative thoughts.

But developing a clear visualization depends primarily on stabilizing meditation. Once the image has been established and we feel comfortable with it, we should hold it with single-pointed attention, not letting the mind be distracted to other objects. Initially, our concentration will last only a few seconds, but with continual practice we will be able to maintain it for increasingly longer periods of time. Each time our attention wanders or we lose the object, we should again bring it to mind. This way of meditating both increases our familiarity with positive images and strengthens our ability to control and concentrate the mind.

It is common to find visualization difficult. If you are having problems, it could be that you are trying too hard or expecting too much. The mind needs to be in the right state – relaxed, clear and open. Too much effort creates tension, and the only vision that can appear is darkness. Too little concentration means the mind is crowded with distractions, leaving no space for a visualized image. We should learn to adjust our concentration as we would tune a musical instrument – with sensitivity and patience – until we have found the proper mental state in which the object can appear clearly.

Remember too that visualization utilizes only the *mental* faculty, not the eyes. If you find that you are straining to see something, you misunderstand the technique. Relax and let the image appear from within your mind.

Furthermore, we should be satisfied with whatever does appear, even if it is just a blur of colour or a minor detail. It is more important to have a sense or feeling of the presence of an enlightened being than be too concerned about seeing a mental image. Thus it is very important to be relaxed and free of expectations. It is self-defeating to expect a complete, perfect visualization after one or two attempts; it may take years of practice before you can really see the image. Again, it is a matter of tuning the mind to the right balance; learning to work with the energies and elements of the mind to produce a positive, joyful meditative experience.

You might find it useful to practise visualization with familiar objects. Sit quietly with your eyes closed and bring to mind the image of a friend, for example. Try to see the details: the colour and shape of the eyes, nose, and mouth, the style of the hair, the shape of the body, and so forth. Experiment with other objects: your house, the view from your window, even your own face.

Visualizing deities is made easier by gazing at a picture or statue, then closing your eyes and trying to recall the image in detail. However, this helps you with the details only; don't think your visualized figure should be flat like a drawing or cold and lifeless like a statue. It should be warm, full of life and feeling, three-dimensional, and made of pure, radiant light. Feel that you are actually in the presence of a blissful, compassionate, enlightened being.

Finally, it might be useful to practise the following simple visualization before attempting more complicated techniques.

Body of Light Meditation

Sit comfortably, with your back straight, and breathe naturally. When your mind is calm and clear, visualize in the space above your head a sphere of white light, somewhat smaller than the size of your head, and pure, transparent, and formless. Spend several minutes concentrating on the presence of the light. Don't worry if it does not appear sharply; it is enough just to feel it is there.

Contemplate that the sphere of light represents all universal goodness, love, and wisdom: the fulfilment of your own highest potential. Then visualize that it decreases in size until it is about one inch in diameter and descends through the top of your head to your heart-centre. From there it begins to expand once more, slowly spreading to fill your entire body. As it does, all the solid parts of your body dissolve and become light – your organs, bones, blood vessels, tissue, and skin all become pure, formless white light.

Concentrate on the experience of your body as a body of light. Think that all problems, negativities, and hindrances have completely vanished, and that you have reached a state of wholeness and perfection. Feel serene and joyful. If any thought or distracting object should appear in your mind, let it also dissolve into white light. Meditate in this way for as long as you can.

Purification Meditation

There are both positive and negative aspects to our personality. On the one hand we have love, wisdom, joy, and generosity, but on the other we have anger, selfishness, laziness, and a long list of other problems. All these traits are just mental experiences, waves on the ocean of our consciousness; all have the same basic, clear nature.

They are not static and permanent but constantly in flux, coming and going.

There are, however, two important distinctions to be made: positive states of mind are productive, beneficial for ourselves and others, whereas negative states are harmful and bring only confusion and pain. Peace of mind is achieved by cultivating what is positive and abandoning what is negative.

The second point is that anger and the other mental disorders arise from our misconceptions about the way things exist, while positive states of mind are realistic and arise from right understanding. When we recognize this and develop a correct view of reality, our negativities gradually lessen and eventually disappear altogether. As our wisdom develops, our spontaneous good feelings grow and our personality gradually transforms. At the end of this path is enlightenment, the perfection of all beneficial qualities – a state of great clarity and loving compassion.

Often we identify ourselves more with our negative side than our positive, and feel guilty about mistakes we have made. We believe, "I am hopeless; I can't control my anger; I don't do anything right; I'm completely cold and unable to love anyone." Although we may have faults and problems, it is wrong to think that they are permanent. We *can* free ourselves from negative energy and the burden of guilt, as long as we are willing to work. One way of doing this is through the process of purification.

Purification is a recurring theme in Buddhist meditation. It is chiefly a question of changing our way of thinking. When we think we are impure and negative, we become just that. A low, depressed self-image gradually permeates our behaviour and outlook on life. We feel limited and inadequate and don't even give ourselves a chance to change. But, by recognizing our potential for perfection and sincerely putting energy into developing it, we cultivate a more positive self-image. Believing that we are basically pure is the first step in becoming pure. What needs to be purified, therefore, is our lack of self-confidence and tendency to identify with our negative energy, as well as the negative energy itself.

This simplified meditation contains the essence of purification: letting go of problems and mistakes, seeing them as temporary obscurations, not as an intrinsic part of our nature. It helps us to get in touch with and develop our natural good energy.

The Practice: Be comfortable and relaxed. Take a few minutes to settle your mind in the here and now.

Then turn your attention to your breath. Breathe normally and observe the full duration of each inhalation and exhalation.

When you exhale, imagine that all your negative energy, past mistakes, distorted conceptions, and emotions leave your body with the breath. Visualize this energy as black smoke and send it out into space, where it disappears completely. Feel confident that you have freed yourself from every trace of faults and negativity.

When you inhale, imagine that all the positive energy in the universe enters your body with the breath in the form of pure, radiant white light. Visualize this light flowing to every part of your body, filling every cell and atom, and making you relaxed, light, and blissful.

Concentrate on this experience – breathing out the black smoke of your problems and breathing in the white light of good energy – for the duration of the session. When you are distracted by feelings, simply observe them without reacting or getting involved, transform them into the black smoke, and breathe them out into oblivion.

Conclude the meditation by dedicating your positive energy to all beings finding everlasting happiness and peace of mind.

Meditation on Compassion

Whereas love is the desire for others to be happy, compassion is the desire actually to bring about their happiness by freeing them from their suffering.

Compassion is not the sad, anxious feeling we often experience when we see or hear about people's pain. Neither is it a sentimental involvement in their problems, nor, on the other hand, a self-conscious holding-back. All these responses are inappropriate and show that we do not understand the causes of the problems, or the solution.

With true compassion we are more wise: we understand how and why suffering occurs and can deal realistically with the situation. It gives us the energy to do what we can to help and the wisdom to accept our limitations and not worry about what we cannot do.

An *attitude* of compassion is what really counts; we cannot expect to actually eliminate someone else's unhappiness while our own mind is still troubled by misconceptions and confused emotions. We should, therefore, work simultaneously on developing the wisdom to see clearly how things are, and on the compassionate wish to alleviate others' suffering – then our actions will be truly skilful.

Compassion benefits not only others but ourselves as well. As the

Dalai Lama has said, "If you want others to be happy, practise loving-compassion; if you want yourself to be happy, practise loving-compassion."

We all possess the potential to be limitlessly compassionate. A powerful way of awakening and developing this potential is by visualizing Avalokiteshvara (Tibetan: Chenrezig), the embodiment of compassion, and contemplating his mantra.

A mantra is a series of syllables that corresponds to certain subtle vibrations within us. A mantra has built up its energy for good by being used by millions of people for thousands of years. Its effectiveness does not lie in our understanding its literal meaning but in concentrating on its sound as we recite it aloud or silently.

Avalokiteshvara's mantra, *om mani padme hum*, expresses the pure energy of compassion that exists in every being. Reciting it, either in meditation or while going about our daily activities, not only awakens our own compassion but, by joining with the millions of other people saying it too, adds to the growth of peaceful, loving energy in the world. At the very least, concentrating on the compassion-mantra helps our mind stay alert and positive rather than scattered and negative.

This practice combines an analytical meditation for generating compassion with a stabilizing meditation on the image and mantra of Avalokiteshvara.

The Practice: Relax your body and mind and bring your awareness to the present by mindfully watching your breath. Check your thoughts and feelings and generate a positive motivation for doing the meditation.

Imagine that all of space is filled with beings, sitting around you and extending beyond the horizon. Contemplate their suffering. First, think of the suffering of your parents and the other people you are close to. Open your heart to the physical and psychological problems they are experiencing and think that, just like you, they want to be free of all suffering. Feel how wonderful it would be if they *were* free and could enjoy the peace and bliss of enlightenment.

Then think of the people you do not like or who have hurt you. Imagine their suffering: physical pain and discomfort, feelings of loneliness, insecurity, fear, dissatisfaction. Just like you, they don't want problems but they have no choice; as long as the mind is confused and ignorant of reality, it cannot find peace. Open your heart to these people for whom normally you feel irritation or anger.

Expand your awareness to take in the troubles and pain of other human beings and of animals; whoever has an uncontrolled mind necessarily has suffering.

But don't be overwhelmed by all of this! Remember that suffering, unhappiness, and pain are mental experiences, impermanent and changeable. They arise because of misunderstanding and confused emotions, and once their causes have been eliminated they disappear. It is a matter of each one of us working on our own mind, dealing with our misconceptions and negative energy and gradually developing a correct understanding of the way things actually exist.

Feel strongly the aspiration to do this yourself, so that you can help others to be free of their suffering.

Now, visualize just above your head, and facing the same way as you, Avalokiteshvara, the manifestation of pure unobstructed compassion, love and wisdom. His body is of white light, transparent and radiant. Try to feel his living presence.

His face is peaceful and smiling and he radiates his love to you and all the beings surrounding you. He has four arms. His first two hands are together at his heart and hold a jewel that fulfils all wishes; his second two are raised to the level of his shoulders, the right holding a crystal rosary and the left a white lotus. He is sitting on a white moon disc upon an open lotus, his legs crossed in the full-lotus posture. He wears exquisite silk and precious jewels.

Hold your awareness on this visualization until it is stable. Stay relaxed and comfortable and open to Avalokiteshvara's serene and loving energy.

Now, make a prayer from your heart, to overcome your misconceptions and negative energy and to develop pure love and compassion for all beings. Feel that you are connecting with your own true nature, your highest potential.

In response to your request, Avalokiteshvara lovingly sends streams of white light, filling every cell and atom of your body. It purifies all your negativities and problems, all your past harmful actions, and your potential to give harm in the future, and completely fills you with his limitless love and compassion. Your body feels light and blissful, your mind peaceful and clear.

The light from Avalokiteshvara radiates out to every living being, purifying their negative energy and filling them with bliss.

Now, while concentrating on this visualization, recite the mantra, *om mani padme hum,* aloud for a while and then silently, as many times as you like.

When you have finished the recitation, visualize Avalokiteshvara dissolving into white light, which flows down through the crown of your head and reaches your heart centre. Your mind merges indistinguishably with Avalokiteshvara's mind and you experience complete tranquillity and bliss.

Hold this feeling as long as possible. Whenever your usual sense of I starts to arise – an I that is bored, restless, hungry, whatever – think that this is not your real self. Simply bring your attention back again and again to the experience of being one with the qualities of Avalokiteshvara's mind: infinite love and compassion.

Finally, dedicate the positive energy you have created by doing this meditation to the happiness of all living beings.

Inner Heat Meditation

This meditation is an especially powerful Vajrayāna method for tapping and skilfully utilizing our innate blissful mental energy.

There is an intimate relationship between our mind and our subtle nervous system. Mental energy flows through the body within a psychic nervous system composed of thousands of thin, transparent, subtle channels. The principal ones – known as the central, right, and left channels – run parallel to and just in front of the spinal column. Pure mental energy can function only within the central channel, whereas deluded energy flows through all the others.

At present, our central channel is blocked by knots of negative energy – anger, jealousy, desire, pride, and so forth at points (*chakras*) corresponding to the base of the spine, navel, heart, throat, and crown. To the extent that this deluded energy is active, the pure energy of mind is blocked and unable to function. Recall, for example, the enormous physical and mental tension created by strong desire or anger; there is no space at all for calmness and clarity.

The inner heat meditation is an excellent method for transforming this powerful energy and developing spontaneous control over all our actions of body, speech, and mind. Mere suppression of attachment, anger, and other emotions does not eliminate them; it compounds them. The solution is literally to transform this energy – which by its nature is neither good nor bad – into blissful, free-flowing energy.

Skilful practice of the meditation will show us that we are capable of happiness and satisfaction without needing to rely upon external objects – an idea that is inconceivable for most of us.

This practice also helps us in our development of singlepointed concentration. Normally, our dissatisfied mind wanders uncontrollably, blown here and there by the force of deluded energy in the psychic channels; yet if we could have an experience of bliss pleasurable enough to concentrate on, we simply would not want to wander elsewhere.

The Practice: Sit comfortably in your meditation place and generate a strong positive motivation for doing this inner heat practice. Determine to keep your mind relaxed, concentrated, and free of expectations for the entire session.

Start by visualizing the central channel as a transparent, hollow tube, a finger's breadth in diameter. It runs straight down through the centre of the body, just in front of the spinal column from the crown of your head to the base of your spine.

Next, visualize the right and left lateral channels, slightly thinner than the central one. They start from the right and left nostrils respectively, travel upwards to the top of the head and then curve over to run downwards on either side of the central channel. They curve inwards and join the central channel at a point approximately four fingers' breadth below the level of the navel.

Take as long as you like to construct this visualization. Once it is stable, imagine a red-hot ember the size of a tiny seed inside the central channel at the level of the navel. To strengthen this visualization, imagine reaching into a fire, taking out a tiny glowing ember and placing it in your central channel. Once it is there, really feel its intense heat.

Now, in order to increase the heat, gently contract the muscles of the pelvic floor, concentrating on the internal rather than the external muscles, and in this way bring air energy up from the lowest chakra to the ember.

Next, gently take a full breath through both nostrils. The air travels from the nostrils down through the right and left channels to where they enter the central channel just below the level of the navel. The air joins with the heat there and with the energy brought up from below.

As you stop inhaling, immediately swallow and push down gently with your diaphragm in order to firmly compress the energy brought down from above: now the air energy is completely locked in, compressed from above and below.

Now, hold your breath as long as it is comfortable to do so. Concentrate completely on the ember in the navel area, whose heat is increasing and spreading as a result of the compressed air energy.

When you are ready, relax your lightly tensed muscles and exhale gently and completely. Although the air leaves through the nostrils, visualize that it rises up through the central channel and dissolves there. The heat emanating from the burning ember at the navel continually increases and spreads and starts to burn away the blockages at each chakra and starts also to warm the concentration of silvery blissful energy found at the crown chakra.

However, the focal point of your concentration is always the heat of the burning ember in the navel area.

Once your first exhalation is complete, again tighten the lower muscles, inhale a second time, swallow, and push down with the diaphragm, thus again compressing the air and intensifying the heat. Hold your breath and concentrate on the heat, then exhale, releasing the air up the central channel once again.

Repeat the entire cycle rhythmically seven times altogether, the intensity of the heat growing with each breath.

At the seventh exhalation, imagine that the now burning hot ember explodes into flames. They shoot up the central channel, completely consuming and purifying the deluded energy at each chakra. At the crown, the flames finally melt and release the silvery blissful energy, which pours down the purified central channel giving increasing pleasure at each chakra it passes. Finally, when it meets the blazing ember at the navel chakra, there is an explosion of bliss. This blissful heat flows out to every atom and cell of your body, completely filling you, making your mind very happy.

Concentrate on this pleasure without tension or expectation; without clinging to it or analyzing it. Just relax and enjoy it.

You will notice that, no matter how strong the pleasure is, your mind and body are calm and controlled, unlike our usual experiences of physical pleasure when the mind is excited and uncontrolled.

If your mind should wander from its concentration to other objects – the past or future, objects of attachment or aversion – focus your attention on the *subject* of the thought, the mind that perceives the distracting object, the thinker. Watch the subject until the distracting thought disappears, then concentrate again on the blissful feeling.

Analysis of Feeling: Having reached a state of clarity, it is good to use it to discover the nature of your mind. After concentrating on your feeling, being absorbed in it for some time, analyze it by contemplating each of the following questions. Take as long as you like.

Is the feeling permanent or impermanent? How? Why?

Is the feeling blissful or suffering? How? Why?

Is the feeling related or unrelated to the nervous system and the mind? How? Why?

Does the feeling exist inherently, from its own side, without depending on anything else, or not? How? Why?

Examine each point from every angle. Finish the session by summing up your conclusion, then dedicate any positive energy and insight gained during the meditation to your speedy enlightenment for the sake of all living beings.

Meditation in Tantra

Lama Yeshe

Clear Spaciousness of Mind

Renunciation, *bodhicitta*,[63] and the correct view of emptiness are three of the prerequisites for the practice of tantra. This does not mean, however, that our realization of these three has to be complete and perfect before we can start following the tantric path. An approximate understanding is sufficient for us to begin.

Take the realization of emptiness, for example. To gain a perfect understanding of the ultimate nature of all phenomena is a profound accomplishment. If we were to wait until then before we could practise tantra, when would we ever begin? Perhaps never! Fortunately, this is not a problem. In order to train in the various transformations of tantra, it is enough for us to be able to relax our ordinary sense of ego-identification somewhat. We do not need a perfect realization of our lack of self-existence, but we do need to be able to give ourselves some space from our ordinary, compulsive role-playing.

Tibetan lamas often say: "Not seeing is the perfect seeing." Strange words, perhaps, but they have a profound meaning. They describe the advanced meditator's experience of spacious, universal reality, the experience beyond dualism.

In our ordinary experience we are overwhelmed by countless dualistic perceptions and conceptions. Every day we are attracted to pleasurable objects and repulsed by unpleasant ones. Burdened with a narrow idea of who we are, we spend our time running towards this and away from that. As we have already seen, this deeply ingrained habit of viewing things dualistically and believing in our dualistic discriminations leads to nothing but confusion and repeated dissatisfaction. But it is possible to cultivate a completely different view of reality. Fed up with the endless rat-race of our compulsive cyclic existence, we can train in penetrative awareness and cultivate a direct perception of the actual way things exist.

This training proceeds in different stages, some of them highly analytical and conceptual and others more direct and experiential. Eventually, as we become more and more deeply absorbed in the experience of spaciousness, the ordinary, concrete appearances normally crowding our vision begin to dissolve. Like summer clouds disappearing back into the clear blue expanse of the sky, our dualistic visions cease and we are left with nothing but the clear, empty space of non-duality. In this space empty of all concrete discriminations of this and that, our mind feels calm and boundless, free of limitation. No longer occupied with "seeing" and believing in the ultimate reality of ordinary appearances, we enter into the "perfect seeing" of the non-duality experience.

Far from being in a state of sleep-like blank-mindedness, our mind at such a time is awake and alert – rejecting nothing, asserting nothing, yet accepting everything. Instead of feeling trapped and limited, forced to play the same pointless ego games over and over again, we begin to taste the true liberation of unencumbered consciousness. This liberation is possible because the superficial, conventional, fantasy, dualistic mind is *not* the fundamental nature of human beings. Our fundamental nature is as clean clear as crystal, and there is no place for the self-pitying imagination. It automatically dissolves. And with it dissolve all our imprisoning limitations.

If we can enter and then remain within the naturally clear state of our own mind, we will have the time and space to see things without confusion. We will even be able to handle the business of everyday life more skilfully. Many people wonder about this. "If I allow my mind to return to its natural, uncomplicated state, how will I be able to function in this complicated world? How can I get from one place to another? How can I hold down a job? How can I cook a meal? How can I do anything?" But there is no reason to carry on this type of argument with yourself. The fact is that when you are in a clean clear state of mind you will be free to pay full attention to what you are doing and you will therefore naturally do it well. Problems come when you are *not* living in a natural state of mind. Then, no matter what you are doing your mind will be on something else. You are supposed to be cleaning your house but your mind is thinking about going to the beach and eating ice cream. That is when you run into difficulties.

Clarity and Non-duality

By contemplating our stream of consciousness in meditation we can be led naturally to this spacious experience of non-duality. As we observe our thoughts carefully we will notice that they arise, abide and disappear themselves. There is no need to expel thoughts from our mind forcefully; just as each thought arises from the clear nature of our mind, so too does it naturally dissolve back into this clear nature. When thoughts eventually dissolve in this way, we should keep our mind concentrated on the resulting clarity as undistractedly as we can.

We should train ourselves not to become engrossed in any of the thoughts continuously arising in our mind. Our consciousness is like a vast ocean with plenty of space for thoughts and emotions to swim about in, and we should not allow our attention to be distracted by any of them. It does not matter if a certain "fish" is particularly beautiful or repulsive: without being distracted one way or the other we should remain focused on our mind's basic clarity. Even if a magnificent vision arises – the kind we have been waiting years to see – we should not engage it in conversation. We should, of course, remain aware of what is going on; the point is not to become so dull-minded that we do not notice anything. However, while remaining aware of thoughts as they arise, we should not become entranced by any of them. Instead, we should remain mindful of the underlying clarity out of which these thoughts arose.

Why is it so important to contemplate the clarity of our consciousness in this way? Because the source of all our happiness and suffering, the root of both the pains of samsara and the bliss of nirvana, is the mind. And within the mind it is our habitual wrong view – our ignorant, insecure ego-grasping – that holds on to the hallucination of concrete self-existence as if it were reality. The way to break the spell of this hallucination is to see the illusory nature of things and recognize that all phenomena are nothing but fleeting appearances arising in the clear space of our mind. Thus the more we contemplate the clarity of our own consciousness, the less we hold on to any appearance as being concrete and real – and the less we suffer.

By watching our thoughts come and go in this way, we move ever closer to the correct view of emptiness. Seemingly concrete appearances will arise, remain for a while and then disappear back into the clear nature of our mind. As each thought disappears in this way, we should train ourselves to feel that this disappearance is even more real than the thought's original concrete appearance. The more we train in this type of "not seeing," the more familiar we become with the clear spaciousness of our mind. Then, even when extremely destructive thoughts and emotions such as anger and jealousy arise, we will remain in contact with the underlying purity of our consciousness. This purity is always with us and whatever delusions we may experience are only superficial obscurations that will eventually pass, leaving us with the essentially clear nature of our mind.

When you contemplate your own consciousness with intense awareness, leaving aside all thoughts of good and bad, you are automatically led to the experience of non-duality. How is this possible? Think of it like this: the clean clear blue sky is like consciousness, while the smoke and pollution pumped into the sky are like the unnatural, artificial concepts manufactured by ego-grasping ignorance. Now, even though we say the pollutants are contaminating the atmosphere, the sky itself never really becomes contaminated by the pollution. The sky and the pollution each retains its own characteristic nature. In other words, on a fundamental level the sky remains unaffected no matter how much toxic energy enters it. The proof of this is that when conditions change, the sky can become clear once again. In the same way, no matter how many problems may be created by artificial ego concepts, they never affect the clean clear nature of our consciousness itself. From the relative point of view, our consciousness remains pure because its clear nature never becomes mixed with the nature of confusion.

From an ultimate point of view as well, our consciousness always remains clear and pure. The non-dual characteristic of the mind is never damaged by the dualistic concepts that arise in it. In this respect consciousness is pure, always was pure, and will always remain pure.

Is the nature of deluded minds such as jealousy and anger also clear? you may ask. Yes, *all* minds equally possess this clear, immaterial nature. Whether they are positive or negative, unmistaken or deluded, all minds clearly reflect their own appropriate objects. Just as a mirror has to be clear and uncovered for it to reflect the image of the face before it, whether the face is handsome or ugly, so too must the mind be clear. If any state of mind were *not* clear, it would not reflect anything, good or bad.

We can compare positive states of mind to water at rest and deluded states of mind to turbulent, boiling water. If we investigate the nature of the boiling water we will discover that, despite the turbulence, each individual droplet is still clear. The same is true of the mind: whether it is calm or boiled into turbulence by the overwhelming complexity of dualistic views, its basic nature remains clear and conscious.

The conclusion, then, is that we all have the capacity to move from the confused, polluted state of ego-conflict to the natural clean clear state of pure consciousness itself. We should never think that our mind has somehow become irreversibly contaminated. This is impossible. If we can train ourselves to identify and enter into the natural, unaffected state of our consciousness, we will eventually experience the freedom of non-dual awareness.

Manifestations of Consciousness

From the Buddhist point of view, all the circumstances of our life are manifestations of our own consciousness. This is the central understanding of Buddhism. Painful and confusing situations derive from a painful and confused mind, and whatever happiness we experience – from ordinary pleasure to the highest realization of enlightenment – is also rooted in our own mind.

If we look at our life we can easily see how it is completely controlled by our mind, especially by our mind of desirous attachment. We are continually thinking of going here and there, having this and that, and then acting on these desires, in our pursuit of satisfaction.

Not only does our restless mind continuously give birth to new thoughts and ideas, but we tend to follow them wherever they lead us. As a result we are lured from one situation to another by the promise of happiness, yet in the end we experience nothing but fatigue and disappointment. The solution is not to suppress our thoughts and desires, for this would be impossible; it would be like trying to keep a pot of water from boiling by pressing down tightly on the lid. The only sensible approach is to train ourselves to observe our thoughts without following them. This deprives them of their compulsive energy and is therefore like removing the pot of boiling water from the fire. Eventually calmness and clarity will prevail.

We humans are very proud of our ability to think, yet much of our thinking often makes things incredibly complicated. Look at the way even the wrapping of a simple piece of chocolate is crammed full of information and advertizing. We may feel that this ability to generate a great number of thoughts and ideas about a single object is a sign of our intelligence, but much of what we do with this intelligence is unnatural and totally unnecessary.

Of course our rational mind – the gross mind that is caught up in society's values – believes in the importance of everything we do. But we should not be fooled into believing that all this complicated thinking is the truth. There may be a lot of things we have to go along with in order to live our daily lives, but we don't have to believe in them. And when we are being complicated we shouldn't even believe in ourselves!

Does this mean that everything we do and think is false? No, there is some truth in what is going on. For example, even though the sky is fundamentally clear and pure, there is some truth to the pollution floating around in it. What I am saying is that we shouldn't believe that our thoughts about this and that are *absolutely* true. Air pollution may have some truth to it but it is not concrete, self-existent, or ultimately real. Similarly, our thoughts may have a certain amount of truth to them, but it would be a mistake to believe in them ultimately.

What we need to learn, then, is how to maintain clear awareness while cutting off our habitual reaction to things. Ordinarily, our immediate response when something happens – when, for instance, someone gives a piece of chocolate to our friend – is to react dualistically. "Why did she give it to *him*? Why didn't she give it to *me*? He is so lucky; I'm so unlucky." Our mind constantly churns out all kinds of dualistic garbage like this and our life reflects the confusion. One result is that our relationships with people and things are fickle and unstable. First we are interested in a new friend; the next day we discard him. One day we desire to own some beautiful new thing; the next day we cannot even stand to look at it. This constant changing of our likes and dislikes is another sign that our ordinary concrete concepts of reality are mistaken and nothing but the projections of a confused and superstitious mind.

There are times both in and out of meditation, however, when this dualistic confusion subsides and we experience the calm clarity of pure awareness. The peace of mind we experience at such times is indescribable and far superior to the fleeting pleasures our senses normally hunger after. But it is not enough to have an experience of this inner peace merely once or twice; this will not lead to any lasting realizations. Instead, we need continuous training so that we can repeatedly cut through our confused dualistic concepts and abide undistractedly in the underlying clarity of our essential mind. If we rely on a valid, well-tested method, such as the practice of tantra, eventually our awareness of the mind's fundamental clarity will become indestructible and we will no longer be under the control of our dualistic superstitions.

Clarity, Love, and Peace

The deep, peaceful clarity of our essential mind is in the nature of love, and in this calm atmosphere the disturbances of hatred and anger have no place. While absorbed in this deep state of awareness, there is no chance for a harmful thought to agitate us. It is not a question of consciously deciding to refrain from anger and behave virtuously; this loving, benevolent feeling arises spontaneously and effortlessly, from the depths of our being.

As this feeling of spaciousness grows and as we become closer to the correct view of non-concrete, non-self-existence, a sense of unity between ourselves and everything else will arise. Instead of feeling suffocated and oppressed by our surroundings – it's me against them – we will feel as if there is room enough for everything in the world. There is space for everything. Within the clear space of non-duality, everything flows freely in a constant process of coming and going, growing and dying, arising and disappearing. Within this expanse of non-self-existent reality, all things function perfectly without obstructing one another. There is no conflict, no confusion, and no separation. Instead of feeling alienated from our environment, from others, or even from ourselves, we share in the experience of universal harmony.

Realizing that our fundamental human quality is clear and pure allows us to cut through all partial, limiting, and self-imprisoning concepts. In the clear space of the fully relaxed mind there is no distinction between *your* fundamental reality and *my* fundamental reality. One is not better than the other; one is not worse than the other. Ultimately, there is no good and bad, no pure and impure. The whole point of meditation or prayer or whatever we are trying to do is to discover the fundamental principle of human nature, to go into this deep nature, to touch our mind, the fundamental principle of totality, non-duality. The moment we reach this experience there is no room for heavy concepts, heavy emotions, or sentimentality. Just be! At the moment of this experience, there are no concepts labelled by the dualistic mind. At such a time there is no Buddha, no God, no heaven or hell. Just being. The great peace. The great satisfaction.

Clarity, Colour, and Bliss

Tantra contains powerful methods for awakening the very subtlest level of mind and for directing this blissful, subtle, clear-light consciousness towards the spacious and penetrating vision of non-duality. Yet even before we become highly skilled practitioners of tantra we can make contact with our mind's natural state of clarity, and taste the freedom of the non-duality experience. An easy technique to use in times of confusion is simply to look up into the blue sky. Without focusing on any object, merely gaze out into space with intensive awareness and let go of all ideas about yourself. You are there, the blue infinity of space is there, and nothing else appears. As we fill our consciousness with this experience of the clarity of space, we will naturally come to contemplate the clarity of our mind.

As human beings, as soon as we visualize expansive blue light in this way, our concrete conceptualizations begin to break down somehow. That is one reason why in tantric art blue is often used to symbolize non-duality, the state wherein the ordinary dualistic concepts of this and that no longer appear and are no longer held on to as real. Many people feel this freedom from conceptuality when gazing out at the vast expanse of the blue sky or the blue ocean. I am not talking about some complex philosophical notion or about something you have to accept on faith because a lama has told you it is true; I am merely relating an actual experience that many people have had and that you may have had as well.

From the tantric point of view, whenever we open our mind and senses to the objective world, our perception is always related to a particular colour. And each colour that we perceive – blue, red, green, or whatever – is directly related to what is happening in our internal world. That is why in the practice of tantra, with its visualization of deities and so forth, colour and light play such an important part.

To give an idea of what I mean, let us consider the colour blue again. As I said, the particular inner quality of radiant blue light is freedom from fantasy projections. If these projections are very strong – when, for example, we are so caught up in ourselves that we cannot break out of depression – then even on a perfectly clear day we are unable to see the blueness of the sky. All we see is greyness. This definitely happens and, along with the experience of seeing red when angry or being green with jealousy, shows the close relationship between colour and states of mind.

To return to what we were discussing, we can achieve temporary freedom from conceptuality by gazing at the rays of the early morning sun or at a calm lake. We merely watch without any discrimination of this and that and at a certain point our mind will experience nothing but its own clarity. Taking such opportunities to experience clarity outwardly and then integrate it inwardly with our consciousness is a powerful and direct way of cutting through the confusion crowding our mind and of experiencing peace.

In addition to peace, whenever we contemplate the clarity of our consciousness we automatically experience a feeling of bliss as well. Normally, our dualistic mind with its confusing chatter and constant judgements about this and that tires us out. Thus it is a welcome relief when these conflicting thoughts and emotions subside and eventually disappear. The resulting clarity is experienced as peaceful, joyful, and extremely pleasurable. Unlike ordinary sensory pleasures, however, the bliss that comes from such an experience brings real satisfaction. Instead of agitating our mind the way sensory pleasures ordinarily do, this bliss actually increases the strength and sharpness of our concentration.

Blissful Absorption into Reality

Anyone who has ever tried to meditate knows that one of the biggest hindrances to concentration is the wandering thoughts that keep diverting our attention. We try to focus on a particular object only to discover that our mind has drifted somewhere else. Our attention span is almost as short as a young child's and we have great difficulty penetrating deeply into any one thing. As a result we find it impossible to gain true realizations. What is the cause of all this mental wandering? It is our overwhelming sense of dissatisfaction. We are continuously searching for something that will satisfy an undefined, inner longing, but this search is never successful. Even when we do find something pleasurable, the satisfaction it gives us is short-lived and soon we are on the look-out for something new. This restlessness is a characteristic of our dualistic mind and becomes all the more obvious when we sit down and try to concentrate in meditation.

The bliss that arises while contemplating the clarity of our consciousness is a powerful antidote to this restlessness. It has the ability to provide a calm and deep satisfaction unmatched by ordinary pleasures. Because you feel fulfilled experiencing this bliss, your mind is not even tempted to wander elsewhere, and your concentration increases effortlessly.

We have all had the experience of being so absorbed in something that we remain oblivious to things that would ordinarily distract or disturb us. Similarly, if we contemplate deeply and continuously enough upon the formless clarity of our own mind, it is possible to stop perceiving the forms, sounds, smells, and so forth that come to us through the doors of our senses. As these sensory experiences and our gross conceptual thoughts subside, the gateway to superstition closes and we become aware of an upsurge of ecstatic, blissful energy from within. This tremendous surge of bliss happens spontaneously; we do not have to fabricate it in any way. And the more we experience this deep internal state of bliss, the more profound our absorption into it will become. This opens the way for us to experience expansive, liberated, and all-encompassing states of consciousness that are presently unknown to us.

Ripening Our Enlightened Potential

The clear, pure, and blissful state of mind that we have been describing exists within each one of us right now. Yet the fact that we have this fundamentally pure nature does not mean that we are already enlightened. Until we rid ourselves of hatred, greed, jealousy, and all the other symptoms of the false ego shrouding our mind, we are certainly not enlightened. There is no such thing as a buddha with delusions. But beneath the gross levels at which these delusions function there is something more subtle, more basic to our nature. And it is this essential aspect of our human consciousness that has the potential of becoming fully awakened and everlastingly blissful.

The question, then, is: "How can we get in touch with and fulfil the enlightened potential of our essential nature?" The practices of tantra are specifically designed to accomplish this extraordinary transformation as quickly as possible but we cannot jump into these practices unprepared. In other words, we need to ripen ourselves by means of the various preliminaries. The three principal aspects of the path that we have discussed – renunciation, bodhicitta, and emptiness – are the common preliminaries to tantra. In addition, it is important to train in what are sometimes called the uncommon preliminaries. These include such things as receiving the appropriate tantric initiation, or empowerment, and keeping the various commitments of the empowerment, purifying oneself of obstacles to successful practice, accumulating a store of positive energy, and gaining inspiration through the profound practice of *guru-yoga*.

The Spiritual Guide and Model

For the teachings of enlightened beings to reach us, and for their insights to make an impression on our mind, there should be an unbroken lineage of successive gurus and disciples carrying these living insights down to the present day. As a member of this lineage, the spiritual guide who makes the four noble truths come alive for you does so through his or her inspiration or blessings. Familiar with your character and aptitudes, such a guide can make these noble truths so clean clear for you that your mind itself *becomes* the path of realization. This is what is meant by inspiration or blessing, just this. And the practice of guru-yoga, or guru devotion, is nothing more than opening ourselves to this inspiration.

Furthermore, we need an experienced guide to show us exactly how to put the teachings we receive into practice. We will not get anywhere if we try to learn from a book, hoping to figure things out by ourselves. The information may all be there, but nearly all tantric texts are cryptic, revealing their meaning only when studied together with the explanations of a skilled practitioner, and it is not easy to know just how to go about implementing this information. We need someone to show us, to give us a practical demonstration. This person is the guru.

The need for such an experienced guide is crucial when it comes to following tantra because tantra is a very technical, *internally* technical, system of development. We have to be shown how everything fits together until we actually feel it for ourselves. Without the proper guidance we would be as confused as someone who instead of getting a Rolls Royce gets only a pile of unassembled parts and an instruction book. Unless the person were already a highly skilled mechanic, he or she would be completely lost.

The main reason that religion in both the East and the West has degenerated so much nowadays is the rarity of meeting good spiritual examples. If people never meet highly realized beings they have no way of knowing the limitless possibilities of their own human consciousness. It is not enough that there are texts recording the deeds and accomplishments of past masters. By themselves, such stories cannot inspire us very much. In fact, they may only increase our feeling of remoteness: "Buddha and Jesus lived such a long time ago," we may think, "and their purity belongs to another age. It is impossible for someone like myself living in this degenerate twentieth century to attain anything resembling their level of purity." Or we may reject these accounts of past masters completely, dismissing them as fairy tales fit only for gullible children. The only way we can lay to rest these feelings of doubt, incapability, and cynicism is by coming face to face with someone who has activated his or her highest potential. Only then do we have an example of purity and spiritual evolution whom we can actually see and relate to ourselves.

Thus the outer guru is of utmost importance. We need the example of someone who, while human like ourselves, has developed beyond the bounds of what we presently think possible. When we see someone who has reached beyond selfishness, who has transcended the petty concerns of this world while still living in the world, who speaks and acts from intuitive wisdom, and who is truly dedicated to the welfare of others, then we can have faith and conviction that these attainments are possible for ourselves as well. Otherwise, if our only models are those of greed and aggression, our vision of what we are and what we can become will be sadly limited.

A good model is important not only for those interested in following a spiritual path. The most urgent need in the world today is for peace and harmony, and we all feel this need, whether we call ourselves religious or not. But peace cannot be brought about through mere words, and it certainly will not come about through force. Instead, we need the example of those who have made peace and harmony the centre of their lives. It is only the example of such people, living lives of strength and purity, that will convince a disillusioned world that peace – internal and external – is truly possible here and now.

Transmission through Empowerment

For us to progress along the tantric path to complete self-fulfilment there must be a meeting of the inner and outer gurus. Our own enlightened potential must be energized and inspired by contact with someone who has already developed this potential to the full. Each tantric *sādhana*, or method of accomplishment, focuses on a meditational deity who embodies a particular aspect of the fully evolved, enlightened mind. And just as the ordinary, egocentric mind creates its own limited environment, the fully realized mind of the deity creates its own transformed environment within which it functions to benefit others. This combination of deity and transformed surroundings is known as a maṇḍala, and if we wish to actualize a particular deity within ourselves we must first be introduced into his or her maṇḍala by a qualified tantric master.

Only then will our subsequent practices of self-transformation have the possibility of succeeding.

Each tantric deity has its own unbroken lineage of practitioners. To be authentic and reliable this lineage must have had its source in the fully enlightened experience of a true master. Furthermore, this experience must have been passed down to us through an unbroken succession of adepts, each of whom attained realizations by accomplishing the practices of this deity. The strength of tantra – which has the literal meaning of "continuous" or "continuity" – lies in its preservation and transmission of the enlightened experience through a continuous, unbroken lineage of practitioners. Therefore, it is necessary that we establish contact with this vital lineage of transmission if we wish to transform ourselves; and the way this contact is made is through *initiation,* or *empowerment.* Receiving an empowerment serves to awaken a special type of energy within us. By establishing an intimate communication with the guru, it arouses our potential to travel the tantric path to completion. Initiation is a shared act of meditation; it does not mean that some exotically dressed monk from Tibet is magically going to confer incredible powers on you so that you can control snakes and scorpions! We should not think of initiation in this way. Nor should we be preoccupied with the external aspects of the ceremony – the prayers, chanting, bell-ringing, and so forth. What we must understand is that initiation has great *inner* significance.

Many people, both Eastern and Western, have mistaken ideas about what happens at a tantric empowerment. They think that all they have to do is attend the initiation and the lama will do the rest. "He is giving something special and as long as I am there I will receive it." But this is much too passive. True empowerment only occurs when there is active participation by both the disciple and the teacher. It is an act of two consciousnesses sharing the same experience. Only when this happens can it truly be said that empowerment has taken place.

Formal Practice of Guru-yoga

Once we have received an initiation into the practice of a particular meditational deity we may begin our daily practice of that deity's sādhana, and one of the first meditations of the sādhana is the practice of guru-yoga, done in a way similar to the following. Either in front of us or above the crown of our head we visualize the main meditational deity of the tantra we are practising, surrounded by the various gurus of its lineage. These lineage gurus are the successive masters who have passed on the teachings and realizations of that particular practice, and include everyone from the first master of the lineage through to our own spiritual guide, the guru from whom we received the empowerment.

We then request the members of this assembly to bestow their inspiration and blessings upon us and, in response to this request, they merge with one another, enter us through the crown of our head in the form of light, descend our central channel, and dissolve into our heart centre. As this happens, all ordinary dualistic appearances and conceptions dissolve into the clear space of emptiness. We then meditate upon the feeling that our guru, who in essence is identical with the deity, and our own subtle consciousness have become indistinguishably one.

The essence of the guru is wisdom, the perfectly clear and radiant state of mind in which bliss and the realization of emptiness are inseparably unified. Therefore, when we visualize the guru absorbing into our heart we should feel that an indestructible impression of that wisdom is being made upon our fundamental mind. From this time onwards we should try to recall this inner experience of great bliss and non-dual wisdom repeatedly, no matter what circumstances we may encounter. If we let our mindfulness of this inner experience deteriorate, we will easily fall under the influence of grosser sensory experiences, and the inner bliss of non-dual wisdom will eventually vanish completely.

When we visualize our spiritual guide as the meditational deity, we should think especially about his or her great kindness and concern for us. Simply speaking, although the guru-deity is not my father, not my mother, not my wife, not my husband, still he is as concerned about me and my situation as if he were. It is as if he exists solely for my sake, so that I might develop a supremely healthy body and mind. This is how we should relate to the visualized guru-deity.

By visualizing in this way and thinking of the personal kindness shown to you by your guru, a powerful connection is established. Instead of being some vague, impersonal image, the deity is seen as being inseparable in essence from your own immeasurably kind spiritual guide. In this way a feeling of incredible closeness develops. Because of this feeling of intimacy, and because the deity is visualized as a radiantly beautiful being of light, inspiration can come to you very quickly. Your visualization magnetically attracts such inspiration, such blessing, and this enables you to develop clear realizations. This, after all, is the entire point of the guru-yoga practice. The purpose for seeing the guru in an exalted aspect has nothing to do with benefiting the guru – a true guru has no use of such homage – but is solely to speed your own spiritual evolution.

Continuous Recognition of Unity

Seeing the underlying unity of our guru, the deity, and ourselves is not something we do only during formal meditational practice. We need to practise guru-yoga – identifying ourselves with the guru's essential buddha nature – during every moment of our life. Instead of always thinking about our miserable, dissatisfied mind, we should cultivate the recognition of our fundamental unity with the absolute guru residing within. Even if our most egotistical mind is arising, instead of adding fuel to it by identifying strongly with this deluded state, we should try to recognize *that very mind* as the enlightened totality of the guru-buddha nature: the so-called *dharmakāya* experience. Then suddenly even this deluded mental energy can be utilized and transformed in such a way that it is digested into great wisdom. This is the outstanding teaching of tantra.

To be able to accomplish such a profound transformation, however, we must practise guru-yoga continuously. We must become intimately familiar with the essential oneness of the guru, the deity and our own innermost nature. In *Offering to the Spiritual Master* it is said, "You are the guru, you are the deity, you are the *ḍāka/ḍākinī*, you are the dharma protector." To interpret this we can borrow an image from Christianity, a spiritual tradition based on the existence of one God, one absolute reality. Although God manifests in the three aspects of Father, Son, and Holy Spirit, God is essentially one: the principle of totality. Similarly, although tantra speaks about many different deities, *ḍākas*, *ḍākinīs*, protectors and so forth, at a certain point all these apparently different entities are to be seen as a unity, one all-embracing totality. That is the fundamental concern of tantra. When you develop yourself fully so that your entire inner potential is realized, then you yourself *become* a deity, you yourself *become* a buddha. This is the ultimate aim of guru-yoga.

The Vajra Body and Resident Mind

According to highest yoga tantra, our body and mind exist not only on the gross level we are normally familiar with but also on subtle levels about which most of us are completely unaware. Our ordinary physical form, composed of various material elements, is subject to the inevitable sufferings of sickness, decay, and death: merely possessing it binds us to the recurring miseries of our ordinary existence. But within the boundaries, or atmosphere, of this body is another, far more subtle, body: the so-called *vajra body*, "vajra" having the connotation of "indestructible". Just as our gross and perishable physical body is pervaded by the ordinary nervous system, this subtle vajra body is pervaded by thousands of channels (*nāḍi*) through which flow the energy winds (*prāṇa*) and drops (*bindu*) that are the source of the bliss so vital to highest tantric practice.

As is true of our essentially pure and blissful mind, this subtle conscious body exists within us right at the present moment, and the job of the tantric practitioner is to discover and make use of it. Once we have made contact with this clear, conscious body of light through meditation, our gross physical body will no longer be a problem for us, for we will have transcended it. Physical limitations are just another symptom of ego-grasping, and once we merge with our essentially pure nature all such restrictions will be overcome. At that point, the attainment of the radiant light body of the deity ceases to be merely a visualized goal and becomes a reality.

This is not the place to discuss the vajra body and its channels, winds, and drops in detail, but it will be helpful to mention the central channel (*avadhuti* or *shushumna*) at least briefly because it is of particular importance. This channel runs in a straight line from the crown of our head down to an area in front of the base of our spine, and along it are several focal points known as *cakras*, or energy wheels. Each one serves a different function in the practice of tantra. Depending upon which tantra we are following and which stage or function we are focusing upon in our meditation, we turn our concentrated attention towards and penetrate a particular centre. It is not a matter of guessing which centre to choose; these things are described in precise detail in the tantric texts and their commentaries and are explained to the qualified practitioner by the spiritual guide.

The most important cakra, however, is the one located at the level of the heart, for the heart cakra is the home of our very subtle mind: the priceless treasure of all tantric practitioners. This very subtle mind has been with us from conception; in fact, together with its supporting energy winds the continuum of this mind has been with us for lifetimes without beginning. As the fundamental conscious-ness abiding at our heart centre throughout this life, the very subtle mind is sometimes referred to as our residential mind. However, although it has flowed continuously from life to life, it has rarely had the opportunity to function. What prevents it from becoming activated – and from performing its most valued function: penetrating the universal nature of reality – is the continual arising of our numerous gross states of mind. These are like tourists, temporary visitors who come and go in constant movement, and they completely overwhelm the stationary resident mind.

The activity of all types of mind, both gross and subtle, depends upon their supporting energy winds and upon where these winds are travelling. As long as they flow through any of the thousands of channels other than the central one, these winds activate the gross tourist minds that repeatedly give rise to superstition and confusion – our ordinary life experiences. But when these winds enter, abide, and dissolve into the central channel – as happens naturally at the time of death, for example – these gross minds subside and the very subtle mind of clear light arises instead.

With the dissolution of the energy winds into the central channel, the environment in which our gross minds normally function automatically disappears; the tourist department is closed and our superstitious thoughts can no longer come and go. In the resulting quietness our original, fundamental consciousness – the resident mind – awakens.

This entire process happens automatically during the death process but very few people are trained to take advantage of the very subtle clear light consciousness that arises at that critical time. In fact, few people even recognize it. But the tantric yogi and yogini train themselves not merely to recognize this blissful consciousness at the time of death but to awaken this penetrating clear light mind during their life in meditation, thereby gaining complete control over it. By cultivating a profound concentration on the vajra body in general and upon the central channel in particular, they are able to cut through the gross levels of mental functioning and make contact with their original mind. They can use this powerfully concentrated mind to meditate on the emptiness of self-existence and penetrate the ultimate nature of reality, thereby freeing themselves of all delusions. At the same time that this total absorption into the clear space of non-duality takes place, they experience an explosion of indescribably blissful energy. The unity of great bliss and the simultaneous comprehension of emptiness (the tantric experience known as *mahāmudrā*, the great seal) is the quickest path to full enlightenment.

Section IV

Personal Accounts

INTRODUCTION

This section presents five examples of a genre that is all too rare in the meditation literature: personal accounts, by practising meditators, of their own meditative experiences.

A major reason why such accounts are rare is that meditators are often instructed not to discuss their experiences with anyone but their own teachers. This restriction is rationalized in various ways: talking about one's meditative attainments might generate conceit, which would hinder one's further progress; other meditators, if told what lies ahead, would tend to anticipate, to the detriment of their practice; partial knowledge about meditative practice could be dangerous if imparted by anyone but an experienced teacher; and so on. For the present purpose such considerations, if indeed they have any validity, are judged to be far outweighed by the obvious benefits of making the relevant information available as material for research and discussion.

The five accounts presented here are all in the Theravādan tradition, for reasons mentioned earlier. They necessarily cover only a fairly limited range of meditative techniques; nevertheless, the information they contain is extensive in scope. Furthermore, the meditators themselves represent a wide range of types – from committed Asian Buddhist to rigorous Western psychologist. The order of presentation adopted here corresponds roughly to the meditative sequence implied in traditional summaries of the path of practice.

The first account, Chris Kang's *Experiences in Meditation* (Reading 24), is a previously unpublished report on two major types of practice: meditation on loving-kindness and mindfulness of breathing. The writer first gives a detailed phenomenological description of his experiences with these practices over a two-year period, and then offers an insightful assessment of how they appear to correlate with the textual accounts.

From a Meditator's Diary (Reading 25) is an extract from Jane Hamilton-Merritt's book, *A Meditator's Diary: A Western Woman's Encounter with Buddhism in Thailand Monasteries.* The technique she practised was Burmese satipaṭṭhāna, originally taught by Mahasi Sayadaw (Reading 18). Although this extract covers only a small part of her time in Thai meditation centres, it includes many valuable observations, some quoted directly from the meditation notebook she wrote up at the end of each day's practice.

The item entitled *A Student's Response to Meditation* (Reading 26) is another day-by-day report by a meditator, this time an unnamed university student participating in a four-week meditation workshop. The principal technique being taught was mindfulness of breathing. However, the meditator also describes other, less well known techniques, which he discovered on his own account and then incorporated into his practice. His report subsequently appeared in the book *Secrets of the Lotus* by Donald K. Swearer, who organized the workshop.

Roger Walsh's *Initial Meditative Experiences* (Reading 27) deserves recognition as a model example of this type of writing. It is a detailed and careful report of the author's experiences with vipassanā practice, presented in precise psychological language. As originally published, it incorporated numerous interpretive comments and comparisons drawing on the mainstream psychological literature. Most of these have been deleted here, leaving the bare description and the writer's keen personal insights.

Finally, in *Experiments in Insight Meditation* (Reading 28), Rod Bucknell describes how, having tried Burmese satipaṭṭhāna, he went on to develop, on his own account, a technique of insight meditation in three integrated stages. He describes these stages in full and discusses the significance of the insights they yield. He acknowledges that this three-stage technique is nowhere explicitly mentioned in the Buddhist texts, but leaves aside the question whether it is an "authentic" Buddhist practice.

The five items in this section represent a valuable body of data on the experiential side of meditative practice. It is to be hoped that their appearance in this volume will help persuade other meditators to disregard the old taboos and publish accounts of their own meditative experiences.

Experiences in Meditation

Chris Kang

It was some eight years ago, amid the material comforts of city living and the demanding pressures of academic pursuits, that I first encountered the gentle and profound teachings of the Buddha. At that time a natural curiosity about the nature of the mind, and encounters with the concepts of biology and theoretical physics, had awakened in me a healthy appetite for intellectual nourishment. It is therefore not surprising that I was immediately attracted to the philosophical and psychological genius of the Buddha. What I at that time accepted intellectually of Buddhism led me, in due course, to the practice of Buddhist meditation, which is the central axis of Buddhist spiritual life.

I began my meditation practice with mindfulness of breathing (*ānāpāna-sati*) and cultivation of loving-kindness (*mettā-bhāvanā*), two techniques widely practised by Theravādan Buddhists in Sri Lanka, Thailand, and Burma. As I had no teacher at that time, and consequently had to rely on a small paperback manual on Buddhist meditation, my practice did not really take off. It remained intermittent and rather unenthusiastic until some five years ago, when I met my Buddhist teacher, the Venerable Shravasti Dhammika.[64] He became instrumental in launching me into serious and committed meditation practice, practice that has continued to the present day.

The above preamble sets the background for this account of my subjective experiences during some two years of practising mindfulness of breathing and loving-kindness meditation. In the first half-year, this comprised a daily average of fifteen minutes of mindfulness of breathing followed by ten minutes of loving-kindness meditation. By the second year, the daily average for the two types of meditation had increased to about forty minutes and twenty minutes respectively. That second year also included two semi-intensive retreats. The first retreat lasted four days, during which the daily practice time totalled four and a half hours; the second was of three days duration, with the daily practice time increased to six hours. This, however, was not the whole of my meditative regime during the period in question. I was also practising general mindfulness (*satipaṭṭhāna*) as far as possible when not engaged in formal mindfulness of breathing and loving-kindness meditation. However, that mindfulness practice is not described here.

The Meditative Techniques

Mindfulness of breathing, or ānāpāna-sati, is a traditional Buddhist meditation technique aimed at purifying and unifying the mind through sustained concentration on the breath during inhalation and exhalation. Attention is fixed at the nostrils, at the point against which the moving air strikes, because it is there that the entry and exit of the breath can be observed. No attempt is made to hold or stop the breath, or to deliberately deepen or force it into a definite time rhythm. As Nyanaponika states, "The only task here is to follow the natural flow of the breath mindfully and continuously, without a break or without unnoticed break."[65] Any thoughts that arise in the course of the meditation are merely noted, and attention is gently returned to the point of observation. A major goal of this practice is the attainment of states of deep mental unification called *jhānas*, characterised by total immersion of the mind in its object and a progressive elimination of thoughts and emotions.

Meditation on loving-kindness, or mettā-bhāvanā, is another traditional Buddhist meditation technique. It has the twofold aim of (a) strengthening the quality of unbounded and universal loving-kindness within the mind, and (b) attaining the first three jhānas. The practice begins with sitting quietly with fully or half closed eyes and back erect, and arousing within oneself the emotions of joy and kindness. One then silently wishes "May I be well and happy," while suffusing oneself with kind and loving emotions. This is followed by evoking the image of someone that one respects or likes, and extending these emotions to him or her, while wishing "May you be well and happy." The same procedure is then used in turn for a neutral person, a disliked person, and finally for all sentient beings. It thus involves a gradual progression in the extension of loving-kindness, from the individual to all living beings without exception, and in all directions: in front, to the right, behind, to the left, below and above. The commentarial advice given for beginners in this practice is not to extend loving-kindness to someone of the opposite sex, as this might evoke emotions of lust or attachment. A dead person who was dear to one is also an unsuitable object, as this might arouse emotions of grief and sadness. It is stressed that the first person to be suffused with loving-kindness should be oneself, since self-acceptance forms the basis of any genuine acceptance of other beings.

The First Four Months

I began meditating with fifteen minutes of mindfulness of breathing each day. During the first few weeks of practice, I was overwhelmed by a barrage of thoughts, images, emotions, and even sounds or voices, that were constantly "swimming" in the mind. This was not evident to me until I had to make repeated attempts to focus attention on a single object (the breathing). I started becoming aware of how unaware I had always been of these ubiquitous mental states and contents. The constant flow of images and inner sounds would so often occupy the entire field of consciousness that it was extremely difficult to pay concentrated attention to the breath. This led to a gradual build-up of frustration and doubt, which on certain days grew almost unbearable. On such days I would abandon my fruitless attempts to attend to the breath and instead engage in chanting traditional Buddhist praises to the Buddha, Dhamma, and Sangha. This would often result in a certain degree of upliftment and purity of mind that imparted a quiet tranquillity to my otherwise difficult practice.

Devotional practices, such as chanting and symbolic offerings of light, flowers, and incense, while not essential to Buddhist practice, have often been found useful in calming and unifying the mind – a valuable preliminary to formal meditation practice. With persistent effort, and a firm, affirming confidence in the Dhamma, I was gradually able to maintain concentration on the breath for increasingly longer periods without unnoticed break. By the end of the fourth month of practice, I was able to maintain intermittent concentration for twenty minutes at a time, with comparative ease.

Each day, following my mindfulness of breathing, I would proceed to the practice of loving-kindness meditation. This involved extending loving thoughts and feelings to myself and others without undue thinking and emotional involvement. My initial attempts brought a feeling that the whole procedure was rather contrived and artificial. I had felt, at that time, that the practice was not very different from the psychological technique of auto-suggestion and therefore was suspect. Nevertheless, I decided to temporarily suspend my skepticism and critical appraisal of the practice so as to give it a fair trial.

Another difficulty I encountered in the course of this practice was constant emotional involvement in the images I had evoked, whether of a loved one or of a disliked one, often resulting in a whole train of discursive thinking connected with the images. At such times I would forget the aim of the practice and become completely immersed in my personal mental melodramas. It usually took me some time to notice that I had wandered. This recognition had the effect of automatically re-establishing the practice. By the end of the first two months, I was feeling increasingly doubtful about the value of this practice. The sense of its artificiality came to me with greater intensity than before. I persisted nevertheless. By the fourth month of practice, I found myself more able to stay with the practice without being sidetracked. I also began to feel more natural and at ease with the procedure.

The First Year

By this time in my breath-watching practice, the flow of thoughts was no longer the main problem. Instead, the increased ability to sustain attention elicited an intensifying boredom in the observation process. The breath was by nature not at all interesting to watch, and I was very quickly overcome by a dullness and drowsiness of mind. There came a point when brief periods of awareness would be interrupted by longer periods of a semi-conscious, sleep-like state, during which the mind was totally inattentive to the breath. The meditation sessions often resulted in a heavy, uncomfortable pressure in the head that would subside whenever the mind was aroused by some object or activity of great interest. This made me more aware of the intimate link between the body and the mind, and of how profoundly psychological states influence one's physical condition.

By the beginning of the seventh month of practice, I was sitting in meditation for a total of forty-five minutes per day: half an hour of mindfulness of breathing, followed by fifteen minutes of loving-kindness meditation. Drowsiness continued to be a problem in observing the breath, but never seemed to interfere with the practice of extending kind and loving thoughts. This seemed to be because radiating loving-kindness to mentally-evoked images aroused more interest than watching the breath at the nostrils. It was not until the end of the seventh month of breathing practice that I began to experience a relative freedom from drowsy episodes, except on days when I was physically tired.

There were days when the benefits of meditation practice became apparent to me, as the mind began to grow in calmness and alertness. Such times were often characterized by a pliancy and lightness of mind coupled with a seemingly effortless attention to the breathing process. During these periods, I noted a sense of enthusiastic interest in the practice. Whenever this mental quality was present, boredom and drowsiness would be absent. With this noticing of the mutual exclusivity of incompatible mental states, I felt I had realized a simple but significant and fundamental aspect of the nature of the mind. On certain occasions, this enthusiastic interest in Dhamma practice would manifest as an emotion of uplifting joy which would pervade the whole upper body. Any thoughts that were still present seemed to have lost much of their force and energy, such that they no longer had the power to distract the focused attention.

Upon terminating the meditation session, I would experience a deep sense of peace and relaxation, which would linger on throughout the day, as long as activities were not too rushed or emotionally intense. Also, such occasions would often result in a spontaneous and expansive flow of warm and kind feelings, which naturally led to a deep and genuine experience of loving-kindness for all beings. On such days, and for a long time after that, my earlier doubts about, and resistance to, loving-kindness practice dissolved. I was finally able to touch a deep and loving part of my heart to a degree I had never thought possible. The gradual extension of loving-kindness from myself to all beings resulted in a state of consciousness which, though brief, was blissful, expansive, and non-limiting.

The Second Year

In the second year of practice, I increased the mindfulness of breathing to forty minutes daily and the loving-kindness meditation to twenty minutes. It was also during this period that I did the two semi-intensive retreats mentioned earlier. My ability to attend to the breath without unnoticed break steadily improved, though it was still not without the regressions into excessive discursive thinking, worries, fantasies, and occasional bouts of drowsiness. I noticed that whenever the mind was immersed in trains of thoughts, there was almost invariably some underlying emotional state that seemed to be generating these thoughts: worry, fear, anticipation, excitement, or (more subtly) a state of apathy or lack of interest (resulting in thoughts as a means of distraction or entertainment). Generally, however, there was improved concentration and a heightened capacity to be relaxed yet alert and relatively tranquil in the course of my daily life.

In loving-kindness practice there was becoming evident an increased ability to feel genuine and sincere acceptance of, even warmth for, a disliked person. As I practised looking deeply at the image of the disliked person in question, with a non-judgemental mind, and without entering into unprofitable conceptual proliferation about her faults and weaknesses, I found myself more able to appreciate her as another being who shares in the universal ailments of greed, aversion, delusion, and hence suffering. With this change in perspective came a corresponding decrease in dislike and an increase in warm, positive feelings for the person. These manifested in an improved and more harmonious relationship between us. It was also becoming increasingly easy for me to extend deep feelings of love and acceptance to myself, to those dear to me, and in fact to all beings. While it was technically impossible to conceptualize each and every living being in the universe, it remained possible for me to visualize as many beings as I could recall (both human and non-human) and to radiate similar feelings of warmth and love to them without judging or discriminating.

One profound experience I had in the course of this practice left a deep and lasting impression on me. On the occasion in question, I sat and commenced with mindfulness of breathing as usual, which left my mind with a sense of lightness and happiness. As I proceeded to wish myself well and happy, a sudden gush of rapturous joy welled up within me in the region of the middle chest, then spread and permeated my neck, face, head, shoulders, hands, and even down to my lower abdomen. With this pervasive and uplifting feeling came a momentary mental one-pointedness and an expansion of the spatial boundaries of consciousness. In retrospect, I realised that in that moment of oneness and expansion the mind was totally still with not a single thought. However, slight trickles of thought soon re-emerged as the experience of mental concentration and expansion gradually faded. These thoughts seemed to move much more slowly than usual and lacked the power to disturb my tranquillity. In such a state, I continued with the extension of loving-kindness to a dear one, a neutral person, a disliked person, and finally to all beings, with a depth, authenticity, and naturalness that previous sessions had lacked. I was left with an openness of heart and a sensitivity of spirit that carried over into the next two days or so.

There were also three related experiences worth mentioning here. The first was an ability to notice increasingly minute details of the breathing process. I noticed that every inhalation ended with a short pause, during which no movement of the breath occurred; then followed the movement of exhalation, which ended in another short pause. This cycle repeated itself with the commencement of the next inhalation. I also observed that even the fleeting phenomenon of a single breath (one inhalation or exhalation) had extension in time, a distinct beginning, middle, and end of movement. The attention, however, was not equally keen and clear in all three phases, the middle and end of each breath often being more distinct than the beginning. It seemed to me that the reason for this was that breathing had been so much an unconscious and involuntary process that I was normally unaware of its existence, let alone of the distinct phases of the whole process. It was thus to be expected that any attempt to observe the process keenly would result in an intermittent awareness, which often arose somewhat more slowly than the inhalation itself. The task was, therefore, to cultivate an evenly-applied mindfulness that would sustain itself through all three phases of the inhalation – and indeed through the whole breathing cycle, incorporating the pauses and the three phases of each inhalation and exhalation. The recognition that an evenly-applied mindfulness was my next task proved to be another important insight into how the mind is to be focused – an insight that has greatly facilitated my concentration practice since then.

I therefore put an increased amount of energy into watching clearly the distinct phases of both inhalation and exhalation together with the pauses, with the aim of sustaining an even, continuous attention throughout. With repeated effort, I finally succeeded in achieving this for an extended period. Following this a new type of sensory experience became apparent. I felt vivid tactile sensations, in the form of subtle rapid vibrations, at the tip of each nostril and around the upper lip. These tactile sensations became more distinct and concrete whenever mindfulness increased in intensity and duration. At this stage, when strong continuous mindfulness was present, the three phases of the breathing were no longer apparent, as they seemed to have dissolved into a rapid succession of minute vibrations. The flow of rapid vibrations occupied the whole field of consciousness, and there was a deep one-pointedness and an immense vacuity of mind. For an instant, my whole physical world would seem to have collapsed into oblivion, with a total loss of bodily perceptions except for the concentrated awareness of rapid vibrations.

From this second experience, and apparently as a direct consequence of it, there immediately followed the third experience. Sustained application of attention to the vibratory sensations would gradually lead to a point where the vibrations would suddenly disappear, leaving a spacious ground of greatly expanded awareness that seemed to have no distinct boundaries. It was as if the threshold of consciousness had been reached. This altered state of consciousness was, however, very short-lived, lasting only for a finger-snap. Its termination was followed by a return to the preceding experience of tactile vibrations. This profound experience occurred very rarely, and mostly during the periods of retreat when the pressures and distractions of mundane existence were largely absent. It would invariably result in a state of strong mindfulness and mental clarity, heightened perceptual sensitivity, increased energy, and emotional stability and calmness, which would then persist for hours or even days on end.

Critical Appraisal

The above is a phenomenological account of my experience with mindfulness of breathing and loving-kindness meditation. It is of interest to compare this account with the Buddha's descriptions of meditative experience as recorded in the Pali suttas.

The first jhāna, the first stage in the process of mental unification, is repeatedly described in the suttas as follows:

> Being thus detached from sense desires, detached from unwholesome states, he enters and remains in the first jhāna, which is with thinking and pondering, born of detachment, filled with delight and joy.[66]

As mentioned earlier, there was a time during my breath-watching practice when, in the absence of certain "unwholesome" states (namely frustration, doubt, drowsiness, excessive thinking) and the presence of enthusiasm and joy, the mind was effortlessly attentive to the breathing process, pliant, and light. "Thinking" and "pondering" were present but the thoughts lacked the energy and power to distract the mind from its object of concentration. This experience seems to correspond very closely to the Buddha's description of the first jhāna.

In the Tevijjā Sutta, the Buddha describes how the noble disciple goes forth into the holy life, practises the moralities, attains the first jhāna (account similar to the one above), and then proceeds to loving-kindness meditation:

> Then, with his heart filled with loving-kindness, he dwells suffusing one quarter, the second, the third, the fourth. Thus he dwells suffusing the whole world, upwards, downwards, across, everywhere, always with a heart filled with loving-kindness, abundant, unbounded without hate or ill-will.[67]

As mentioned before, when my loving-kindness meditation was preceded by a pliancy and lightness of mind with relative freedom from thoughts, spontaneous feelings of joy and warmth would arise from within and lead to an almost effortless pervasion of the whole world with loving-kindness. In that state, the mind was filled with a sense of delight and openness. This experience seems to correspond with the Buddha's description just quoted. More importantly, it lends credence to the idea of sequential progression in meditative training: prior attainment of the first jhāna greatly facilitates successful practice of extending loving-kindness.

The sutta description of the second jhāna is as follows:

> Again, a monk, with the subsiding of thinking and pondering, by gaining inner tranquillity and oneness of mind, enters and remains in the second *jhāna*, which is without thinking and pondering, born of concentration, filled with delight and joy.[68]

In describing one profound experience I had in the course of loving-kindness practice, I mentioned three specific mental factors present, namely an uplifting joy permeating my body, mental one-pointedness, and a momentary but total absence of thoughts. This experience was, therefore, significantly similar to the Buddha's description of the second jhāna.

The suttas describe a further set of advanced meditative attainments, namely the *arūpa* or formless jhānas, four distinct and progressively more subtle stages. The first arūpa jhāna is described as follows:

> By completely transcending all perception of matter, by the vanishing of the perception of sense reactions, and by non-attention to the perception of variety, realising: "Space is infinite," one enters and abides in the Sphere of Infinite Space.[69]

I described above the experience of rapid subtle vibrations that occupied the whole field of consciousness, with loss of body sense and of perception of distinct breath phases. This bears a loose similarity to the sutta account just quoted. The disappearance of body sense and of distinct breath phases seems to correspond to the "vanishing of the perception of sense reactions" and "non-attention to the perception of variety." The sense of limitless expansion of the mind-space – filled completely by the perception of subtle vibrations – and the apparent disappearance of the breath and the physical world, further suggest that my experience was of the first arūpa jhāna.

The second arūpa jhāna is described thus:

> By transcending the Sphere of Infinite Space, thinking: "Consciousness is infinite," one enters and abides in the Sphere of Infinite Consciousness.[70]

This invites comparison with the third set of experiences described earlier. The sudden disappearance of the vibrations, accompanied by dissolution of the boundaries of consciousness and thus attainment of a wider-encompassing awareness, can be seen as corresponding to the characteristics of the second arūpa jhāna as just quoted.

Some Final Thoughts

Diligent and sustained practice of mindfulness of breathing and loving-kindness meditation is a fruitful and spiritually fulfilling endeavour that results in an enhanced state of awareness and a transformation of unwholesome mental patterns in one's daily life. The above comparison indicates, furthermore, that the altered states of consciousness to which these practices lead correspond closely to certain of the jhānas as described in the Pali texts.

An important point to note is that the jhānas are not permanent states which, once arisen, will remain unfluctuating. Persistent, diligent, and insightful practice is essential to the consolidation of such positive mental states in one's meditation and life.

Personally, I find that these practices have brought a deeper understanding of the following words of the well-known meditation master, Sumedho Thera:

> [The Buddhist texts] are not meant to be "sacred scriptures" that tell us what to believe. One should read them, listen to them, think about them, contemplate them, and investigate the present

reality, the present experience with them. Then, and only then, can one insightfully know the truth beyond words.[71]

From a Meditator's Diary

Jane Hamilton-Merritt

I awoke the next few mornings thinking of the abbot and the special consideration which he was giving me, the beginner, at the Dhamma classes. These pleasant thoughts seemed to prompt me to slip from my bed each morning to try again to practise mindfulness of breathing.

Each day it became easier to get into a comfortable half-lotus sitting position and it seemed easier to concentrate on my breathing. The counting had advanced to four, sometimes even five, without interruptions, but most of the time I managed only a count of three.

This morning I practised for twenty-five minutes; it was considerably more relaxed than previous sessions, which was encouraging, but I was still apprehensive. Why was I unable to hold my mind still for anything more than a mere dot in time? I had always thought that I had control over my mind. So why couldn't I do this seemingly simple exercise? Why not? Then I recalled the familiar warning that was repeated so often at Wat Bovornives: "Don't force meditation; be patient."

Placated by the thought that there still might be hope for me, I decided that today was the day to explore the stack of books on Buddhism which had been given to me by a Thai lady who was steeped in Buddhist philosophy. As I looked through the stack, I realized that I was familiar with only one book. I felt very ignorant and humble.

I had experienced this same feeling earlier when this lady had informed me that a popular Western book on Buddhism that I had with me was no good, misleading, and incorrect. This morning I pushed that book far beneath my bed and turned to the new books, written in English and published in either Sri Lanka or Thailand by Buddhists.

I read until noon. Then, inspired undoubtedly by the small

success in the morning's meditation, I tried mindfulness of breathing again for another thirty minutes. The results were not very different from the morning, but now it seemed more natural.

In the evening I decided not to use the counting system but to be mindful of the in-breath and the out-breath – by thinking breathing in and breathing out. This method seemed more suitable for me.

After this practice, I sat alone in my small room reflecting on the past days, the results of which I entered in my meditation notebook.

A routine has developed for me which changes little day to day. There are Dhamma and meditation classes at Wat Bovornives and Buddhist writings to read. There are discussions on Buddhism with friends and lay scholars at other wats,[72] particularly Wat Sraket.

While my physical world changes little with each passing day, I'm becoming aware that something quite new and different is beginning to take place within me. But I'm not certain I understand it.

A few days later I entered another synopsis of my progress.

I practise mindfulness of breathing three times a day – early morning, early afternoon, and evening. At first the sessions lasted approximately twenty-five to thirty minutes. Now the length of time is increasing, but not by any conscious effort on my part. It appears to be a natural occurrence as it becomes easier and easier for me to become mindful of my breathing.

I have abandoned the counting system as not the proper method for me. My mind still has its fits of skittering about uncontrollably, but, unlike the initial days, I don't try to force my mind. Each time it wanders, I gently acknowledge to what it has roamed and then bring it back to being aware of my breathing.

There are bouts with pain and mosquitoes. I don't always meditate where there are fans to keep the mosquitoes away nor does the mosquito repellent always fend them off successfully. If only I weren't allergic to their bites.

Then there is the problem of my leg going to sleep and the itches and scratches that are so disconcerting in meditation. The monks told me that when pain occurs to think "paining, paining, paining," and it will go away; or when a mosquito is biting to think the same; or if it is a matter of an itch, to concentrate on the itch and repeat mentally, "itching, itching, itching." Previously I have always thought that if one could ignore the source of irritation or pain it would go away. But here I am being told to become more aware of it, to try to see the nature of it, to concentrate on the irritation or pain itself. I have been doubting that this method will work, since mosquito bites usually give me hives, so tonight I will test the theory.

While meditating in the abbot's *guti*,[73] the left side of my nose began to twitch and itch mercilessly. My mind seemed uncontrollable; there seemed to be no way that I could keep my attention on the breathing when this itch seemed to be spreading over my entire face. So, hesitantly and very skeptically, I allowed my mind to switch completely to the itch.

My mind became aware of the itch with great energy. I wanted desperately to scratch, but I held back, repeating "itching, itching, itching." The itching continued to spread. Again I concentrated on "itching, itching, itching" for what seemed a long time. Then it stopped!

As soon as the nose itching ceased, there came a strong itch beneath my left breast; one that couldn't be ignored. I allowed my mind to flow there and settle on the discomfort while I slowly repeated, "itching, itching, itching." I repeated it again and then again. Finally that discomfort was eliminated.

Then an itch on my right side sprang up. This was ridiculous! But I followed the instructions. This time the words had to be repeated only once, but very slowly and with full concentration.

I'm not certain I understand any of this, but it seems possible to eliminate pain with powerful concentration.

Pains and itches continued to trouble me in meditation, but I refused to give in to them. I neither rubbed nor scratched. There were other problems that also interfered with meditation.

For several days I was aware only of my breath coming in. I could not feel it coming out, which was most disturbing. Sometimes it felt as if my body, puffed up with all the inhaled air, would explode.

One evening after Dhamma class, I reported the problem. A monk in attendance told me that I was not being mindful or aware. "Of course, the air is coming out. If you were more aware you would be able to distinguish the change in temperature of the air that entered your nose and that being released."

Again he reminded me not to force breathing because it was a form of desire or grasping and that I was too anxious for success in meditation. He was undoubtedly right. I probably was obsessed with the "I" or "self" – because *I* wanted to succeed; *I* wanted to be a good meditator. It was true that *I* was determined to absorb all I could about Buddhism and meditation. The monk was right. I wanted too much and it was destroying or, at least, hindering my practice.

I knew that to eliminate the "I want" frame of reference I would have to become more relaxed – to be a participant in the middle way, a way that recommends no over-indulgence nor extreme asceticism.

That evening, after the discussion, the class went to the abbot's meditation room. This room was becoming a more friendly room for me partly because I knew the routine of the Dhamma and meditation classes and partly because the fear of making a grand "faux pas" was subsiding. Yet I was still edgy about the three *wai*[74] before and after meditation. The exact procedures involved in making the wai and the reason for it remained a mystery. My resolution of the problem was to wai once, keeping my head to the floor until the others had finished this ceremony.

Sitting in the soothing atmosphere, I reflected on what had transpired thus far in my meditation, trying to prepare myself to begin all over again – to try to be more mindful – to develop *sati*.[75] Samādhi, or concentration meditation as this form of meditation was called, no longer remained unknowable. I was beginning to understand something of the theory of sati; it seemed to be an attempt to teach the meditator to develop or control his mind so that he could reach some state of tranquillity.

However, I was finding great pain or suffering in the bouncing and leaping about of my mind as I tried to be aware of my breathing. I could physically feel my mind jumping from side to side, to and fro, and then back again in ridiculous fleeting bounds that seemed to lead nowhere. My mind was a muscle, twisting, pulling, and leaping. Its actions resembled muscular cramps that twitch on and on uncontrollably. Never before had I been aware of the mind's apparent physical energies.

I could not comprehend the depths of samādhi meditation, but, knowing that man has learned to use only a very small portion of his mind and now learning that man could be taught to expand his mind's range and abilities through the techniques of samādhi meditation, I began thinking that meditation could be a most desirable activity.

After all these thoughts had paraded through my mind, I settled into a comfortable position and began breathing in and breathing out. It seemed much easier now that I had accepted that I must start from the beginning.

My most recent problem seemed to be gone; my breath was flowing both ways. As the breathing in and breathing out became soft and routine, I became aware of a mass of amorphous grey putty that was hanging under my nose, or maybe it was between my eyes, I was not certain. Eventually I became aware that this was my mind! There it hung, outside of my head, congealed together in a most unattractive manner. The breathing in and breathing out continued rhythmically while the conglomerate of unknown textures floated about. It seemed as if my mind were there and not there at the same time. I acknowledged a force of concentrated energy in it, yet it seemed ethereal in that it wasn't anything that had a recognizable form.

It seemed as if there were at least two minds; one concentrating on the breathing and the other one looking at the greyish mass. The bulbous form was there, but recessed, as if it were on another plane, while the breathing was taking place on the same plane that I was on.

The bulb shimmered and moved about in fleeting movements, becoming dark grey and then lighter grey. It remained while I continued to be aware of both the breathing and my mind hanging outside my head. The intrigue of this configuration, heavy with energy, finally pulled my complete attention to it, or so it seemed. When I concentrated on it directly to have a good scientific look, it disappeared. I returned to breathing in and breathing out, but it failed to reappear.

Then, seemingly without any suggestion from me, the meditation seemed to be ending. Concentration on my breathing began to wane, and a soft, fragile feeling followed. I wanted to keep my eyes closed, to keep the meditation going, yet I knew that it was over. I had to make a conscious effort to open my eyes and to move my hands. It was difficult to move, yet there was awareness that it must be done.

I looked at my watch, which I always placed on the floor beside me since I didn't like anything touching me during meditation; I had been sitting in meditation for forty-five minutes while it seemed that only five or ten had passed.

I remained sitting on the little saffron rug for some time. There was a feeling of quietness both in the room and in myself that was a new experience. It felt good and I rejoiced in this feeling – which was undoubtedly wrong for I was "clinging" to something again. It was the first time that I had been aware of this kind of delicate quietness.

Then I became aware that I was alone except for a temple boy who was peeping at me from an adjoining room. I supposed he was waiting for me to leave so that he could turn off the fans. It seemed that my meditation practice was progressing, although slowly. Yet I was constantly reminded by meditation instructors and from readings that a meditator who worries about his progress is caught by delusion and greed, and these defilements will prevent him from practising satisfactorily.

One evening in the abbot's guti, not long after the appearance of the grey amorphous mass hanging somewhere under my nose, a new experience unfolded. I did not understand why new directions always seemed to take place first in the abbot's meditation room. Was it because of the inspiration of the Dhamma class prior to meditation, the inspiration of the abbot himself sitting in meditation before me, or the atmosphere of this room which seemed so conducive to meditation? Or what?

This particular meditation session began in the usual way: getting comfortable, making certain that no clothes were binding my body; taking off my watch; getting my left leg as comfortable as possible since it inevitably went to sleep; straightening my back and body so that my body seemed to be firmly supported by my legs and buttocks. I was much more comfortable with the breathing awareness exercises now. It was becoming easier and easier to still the mind and for longer periods of time. In fact, meditation was something that I, in the past days, had come to welcome.

This night, the breathing in and breathing out brought with it a pin prick of blue, ever so tiny. This pin prick of blue was in infinity, far, far away. It flickered and grew larger until it filled my horizons. It spread and grew to unlimited proportions. The original colour changed into multitudes of various intensities and shades of blue, ranging from deep purples to the lightest of aquas. Like a gigantic kaleidoscope, the patterned colours twisted, turned, increased, and diminished in a swirl of exquisite shapes, designs, and shades.

The breathing remained close to me and dominant. The kaleidoscoping colours and patterns remained distant, beyond me – free, undulating, creating, moving at rapid speeds, tumbling throughout entire universes. The colours played and danced in an infinite distance just beyond my reach, yet I was aware of an exhilaration in this beauty. I seemed, however, to be afraid to release my mind from the breathing in and breathing out.

Later I wondered how it was possible to be aware of the breathing process and at the same time to be aware of infinite fields of colours? How many minds did I have? How does perception take place in the mind?

For some days to come, my meditation seemed invariably to include psychedelic displays which began with a minute speck in a huge vastness. Sometimes the speck was a tiny, very intense light, piercingly brilliant, from which evolved a massive amount of bluish colour that flowed out and captivated an entire universe, bringing me joy from the beauty of its art. Often at the beginning of meditation, the grey bulb – what seemed to be my mind – would appear somewhere beneath my nose, holding within its elusive shape a sense of energy.

Then, one day, before the colour parade began, the energy mass which was usually light grey took on a tinge of yellow, a glowing yellow, almost luminous. It wavered and jumped evasively. At times it seemed very near, or was it the fact that its amorphous nature seemed to be taking more detailed shapes and forms which, perhaps, made it seem closer?

Although it continued to quiver and wiggle, a design was forming, one that I could not absolutely recognize. Once it seemed to be the shape of a small Buddhist charm that many Thais wear around their necks for good fortune. Another time it seemed to be the silhouette of a Buddha sitting in a meditating position. And another time it took a shape resembling the unfolding of a lotus blossom.

It continued to appear in mystifying forms, and I often wondered what it was. Did it have any meaning? Probably not, I decided, but why was it so persistent? Why did this attractive, luminescent image try to lure the engagement of my concentration? I thought it might pass in time, but it did not.

Then, one night during an after-meditation discussion session, although I was still shy about my ignorance of meditation, I asked why my meditation was accompanied by blues. Why not other colours?

The presiding monk, a young man of about twenty-five, did not have an explanation, but turned the question around a bit. "What do you do with the blue colours?"

"Nothing," I answered. "I enjoy them and try to be mindful of my breathing."

"It's *dukkha* to enjoy them," he reminded me. "You are liking and wanting the colours. Do not become attached to them. Since blue is considered a calming colour, the next time, instead of enjoying the colours, try pulling them into your body through your breathing."

Almost as a footnote he added, "But you shouldn't do that with the nimitta. You should ignore it."

I didn't understand his warning because I didn't know the word *nimitta*. Thinking it was probably a stupid question, I gathered courage to ask what he meant by *nimitta*.

"Nimitta is a symbol or shape, a visual image, that often appears at some point in meditation. It's often called an acquired sign. This sign seems to be different for each person, but," the monk explained in a soft voice, "it indicates a calming or stilling of the mind. When a nimitta is developing, concentration is beginning to work.

"Remember that the nimitta is not *yours* nor *you*. The coming and disappearing of the nimitta, like all impermanent things, exemplifies impermanence, which is a cause of suffering or dukkha. The nimitta comes and goes as conditions arise or cease; it is the result of causes and effects. Don't be a slave to the nimitta. The beauty should not be in the nimitta but in the fact that the mind is relatively calm and tranquil.

"Concentration," he continued, "is the key to meditation, but meditation must always be on the immediate present. Be careful of the nimitta because it can be extremely powerful. Be alert to it. Remember, do not become enslaved to it!"

He concluded by suggesting that if I would come by his guti, he would give me a book in English that explained the nimitta in detail.

On my long walk home, I wondered about the monk's warning on the dangers of attachment to a nimitta. I did not understand what he meant, so l decided that it would be wise to follow his advice and read about this phenomenon.

The next day I borrowed the monk's book and found the following explanation of nimitta written by one of Thailand's leading, though highly controversial Buddhist intellectuals, a monk named Buddhadasa.

In a discussion on the steps involved in learning mindfulness of breathing, he wrote that the first step is to become aware of how long or how short the breath is, and where the centre of the breath seems to be. The second step involves fixing the mind on the gate, or nostrils. In this second step, the breathing, he concluded, should be soft and calm. Next he discussed the nimitta and I copied a passage from his book into my diary:

> When the acquired sign (the nimitta) is well maintained, it tends to be still, and the mind is calmed down. After this the acquired sign begins to change in shape. How big or small it appears, or how beautiful it is, or where it is placed, is different to different individuals. For example, to some this mental image appears as something white right in front of their face, or as a huge moon in the sky or on the top of a tree or in the nostril; this depends on individuals and their slightest idiosyncrasies, which are more or

less automatic. But finally, after having taken some particular shape and place, this mental image becomes invariable without the least change.[76]

I was fascinated by all this. Did this mean that I was making some progress? Was this repeating image a nimitta? Undoubtedly it was. But the most interesting part of it all was that I had not known about nimitta until after it had occurred in my own meditation.

But why should I be alert to its powers? I read on and recorded the following:

This is the stage (of the acquired sign) where mind, like a well tamed monkey, becomes peaceful and calm. One feels showered with bliss owing to pervasion by the feeling of happiness. One can notice applied and sustained thoughts, rapture, happiness, and one-pointedness being present in complete harmony with the mind . . . This is the stage in which we have the *patibhāga-nimitta*, the absorption sign. The moment we arrive at this stage, the mind is completely freed from the unwholesome mental objects which are technically called the five *nīvaraṇas* (mental hindrances, namely: lust, ill-will, torpor and sloth, restlessness and mental worry, and doubt).[77]

The word "absorption" startled me. I thought of absorption in connection with yogas and trance states which I understood to be periods of extraordinarily powerful concentration. I knew that I did not have to worry about reaching any state of absorption, not if it meant being free of restlessness, worry, doubt. I had enough of these qualities to last a life-time.

What was the danger of a nimitta? Was it allowing the nimitta to become an unchecked source of power for concentration so that all else was eliminated?

It was interesting to speculate on all this, but I felt that it was something with which I would never have to be concerned.

In meditation the next evening my breathing was soft and calm. It was so much easier to be mindful of my breathing now. The nimitta appeared with its quaking and shimmering luminous outlines along with the omnipresent blues. In a kind of modern abstract painting of chromatic colours, the dark blues at the bottom expanded into lighter and lighter blues, rounding off with the most delicate of light blues.

As recommended, instead of enjoying the colours or becoming attached to them, I attempted to pull them into my body with my breathing as I slowly, calmly, and somewhat languidly breathed in and breathed out. The colours easily came toward me, but I wasn't aware of them actually entering my body, though I could see them coming in, in a flowing stream to the call of my breathing. At the point where they touched my nose, I became unaware of them. At moments it seemed that I was aware of the nimitta, the breathing, and the flowing, restful blueness. I could not consume all the blueness; there was always a universe more to be drawn in.

Then slowly, so slowly, the blues receded and swirled away down a pin prick hole. I was mindful only of breathing and tranquillity and then a knowing that meditation was ceasing.

The cessation of meditation is intriguing. It all happens so naturally, yet there is a distinct longing for it to continue. There is a sense of joy in meditating, there's an anticipation for more of it with its resulting joy – all of which is undoubtedly bad, since meditation seeks to lead one to develop the mind to the levels where wanting of any kind is completely extinguished.

This sense of joy and calmness remained with me after meditation. As I headed home through the noisy and crowded market streets, I felt so light that I was certain that I would faint before reaching my room. I did not, though this buoyant feeling remained for several hours.

From the beginning days of meditation practice, I found it impossible to eat after meditating. Sometimes I would drink a glass of water, iced tea, or some fruit juice, but tonight I could not force myself to drink anything. Later, I discovered that this is a common experience among meditators.

Often, after coming from the wat, I would sit on my bed, sometimes sipping a cool drink, and ponder meditation. This night was no exception. As I thought about the relative ease with which I had entered tonight's meditation and the calmness that followed, I recalled the warnings of knowledgeable friends . . . "Don't be deluded by thinking that you are making progress in meditation and in the understanding of Dhamma. Meditation is a long and painful process. There are no short-cuts. Never!"

I knew these warnings were valid. Yet tonight, while I was meditating, it seemed that I was able to be mindful on my breathing, to be aware of the nimitta and the blues, and, at the same time, to be aware of the temple dogs barking and temple boys playing.

As it occurred, I recorded in my mind that I was hearing dogs and boys, but it was a neutral recording. I was conscious of them, but not distracted. Was this a kind of detachment?

I began to think about the troublesome Buddhist concept of detachment and the four qualities of *mettā* or loving-kindness, of *karuṇā* or compassion, of *muditā* or sympathetic joy, and of *upekkhā* or equanimity.[78] I understood that if we cultivated these qualities then we would know something of a higher level of being.

Worrying about the seeming conflict between detachment and these four qualities, I wrote in my notebook:

Is detachment being aware of all things but not relating or reacting to them – an acknowledgement but no involvement? But if I don't relate, how can I show loving-kindness or mettā? The monks always speak of developing mettā. It seems a basic and simple meditation goal, but how can I extend loving-kindness, without any delusions or pretensions, to *every* being – whether human, animal, or insect. This is no easy task. Experiencing mettā might be easier than knowing the other three so-called divine abidings or sublime states of consciousness of compassion, joy or gladness, and equanimity. These are words that I thought were familiar to me, for often I write about love, joy, and compassion. But the compassion, joy, and equanimity of Buddhism are strangers to me. According to Buddhist theories, these qualities, to be pure, have to exist without attachment. I cannot understand how compassion can be compassion if it has to exist without attachment.

A Student's Response to Meditation

Donald K. Swearer

In January 1969 an unusual workshop was held at Oberlin College, Oberlin, Ohio – an experimental project in Buddhist meditation. The workshop brought together a Thai Buddhist meditation teacher, the Venerable Chao Khun Sobhana Dhammasudhi, and a Zen priest, the Reverend Eshin Nishimura, to share in instructing a group of twenty-eight students in the theory and practice of *satipaṭṭhāna* and *zazen*, two forms of Buddhist meditation.

For the first two weeks of the project the Venerable Dhammasudhi instructed in Theravāda meditation practice. He began by teaching the students how to sit in the half-lotus or full lotus position, and instructed them in *ānāpāna-sati*, or breathing mindfulness. Sore backs and legs were gradually overcome, and they proved to be apt and serious pupils.

The project began the fifth of January and lasted for four weeks. The schedule included two periods of daily meditation practice between 10:30 and 12:00 each morning, and discussion groups twice weekly. In addition to these group meetings, the meditation teachers made themselves available to individual students throughout the day and evening.

One emphasis throughout the month was the importance of the application of mindfulness. The Venerable Dhammasudhi and the Reverend Nishimura were both very concerned that students not think of the practice of mindfulness solely in terms of sitting meditation. They stressed the fact that mindfulness should be relevant to all one's activities. This aspect of meditation seemed to surprise some of the participants, who had thought only in terms of a formally practised religious discipline. One girl observed:

This type of mindfulness gave me a new perspective in examining myself, calmly observing, and from this distance I gained some self-knowledge. For instance, I learned the kinds of things that occupy my mind; I observed that my head is filled with memories of odd little things, and with worries about often insignificant problems. I also realized that mindfulness of action is valuable, for when one is aware of the situation and the action, time is not wasted because it is lived in full.

Each member of the project was required to submit some kind of written response at the end of the experiment. These responses varied from a paragraph-length statement to a multi-paged diary. The following is one of the more detailed responses.

Preamble to Meditator's Journal

After serious thought I've decided to attach the daily journal in hopes that you may find it useful, even though I have some misgivings about it. There is the obvious difficulty of trying to translate expressively and yet honestly and objectively into verbal form experiences of an essentially non-verbal nature. Also I thought and agonized over too many of the entries, playing with words in trying to be descriptively honest until much of the spontaneity was probably bled out of them. Keeping the journal itself became a stumbling block to meditation during the Zen training because I began to think about, analyze, and compare everything that was occurring in terms of how I was going to record it later. In being committed to the pattern of scrutinizing my experiences on a daily basis, sometimes I had the feeling of not seeing the forest for the trees. Perhaps in retrospect some time hence, I will be able to see this experience as a whole and articulate just how it touched me – for I know it did not pass lightly over – and was part of my own religious quest and process of becoming a person. But from the perspective I have known, I can at best examine the parts to see how they have contributed to the ineffable whole.

During the period of Theravāda meditation, I felt a centre of calm spilling over into all aspects of living which I had experienced before but never with such continuity. The time to be introspective and to develop awareness of what was going on within and without me was invaluable. To a certain extent so was the detachment from emotion. But I was afraid of giving up the capacity to surge with powerful feelings. Though I never really experienced an enlightened realization of impermanence, suffering, and no-self in meditation, I became intellectually aware of their worth as concepts and was continually applying them to everything I experienced. I think I became a bit more self-understanding and self-accepting, both of which are basic to healthy relationships with other people.

The Zen experience of being thrown out to sea with nothing specific to look for as in the Theravāda pattern was extremely frustrating. It was much more difficult not to expect anything, perhaps because it took me almost until the final session to recognize the sort of intrinsic value in the discipline, which was readily apparent in the calming development of awareness of Theravāda training. I got caught in a dilemma of trying to choose between concentration and awareness, assuming that they were mutually incompatible. For a long time I didn't really feel that I was meditating at all but rather doing a great deal of fruitless thinking in an uncomfortable position. I wanted very much to feel into the Zen meditation because it seemed to be so much more accepting of individualization and human emotion. There have been moments when I have faced, not a dark night of the soul, but crisis moments when no rational answer was possible.

Meditator's Journal

– On this first day of meditation, I didn't have much problem with pain except between sessions when changing positions, but my mind was like a wild animal ranging from one disjointed thought to another. Attention to the breathing was completely lost in the chaos. This disturbed me even though the instructions had been not to deliberately shut out anything. Part of the frustration stemmed from the fact that I was quite sleepy and so not alert enough to try to maintain awareness of everything happening within and without me.

– Today I made the discovery that it is literally possible to sit back and watch the thoughts come and go just as it is possible to watch breath movements rise and fall. I was pleased with myself at being able to trace the links within the mental tangents back to their trigger points (e.g., sound of toilet flushing, twitching in the eyelid), some of which seemed ridiculous. In the first session, when we were to notice the up and down breath movements and the distinction between the movement and our awareness of it, my fascination with tracing the thought processes was so overpowering that I wasn't paying much attention to breathing. Later, when we were to try to be aware of the rising, duration, and cessation of both the up and down movements, a strong sensation of circular motion developed, and there were moments when the distinction between the physical aspect and the awareness was starkly clear. After the session I was ecstatic with the day but at the time retained a degree of passivity even in the midst of the "insight" experiences.

Several of us meditated in Chao Khun's room for forty-five minutes. The experience today was one of great calmness. There was a feeling of what I will have to call detachment, for lack of a more accurate way of expressing it, in sitting back and watching the breathing and flickering thoughts without working at maintaining concentration on the breathing or tracing back the thoughts. At one point toward the close of the fleeting session the euphoric feeling became one of height, of being above myself and looking down.

– The initial stiffness in the knees and ankles soon disappeared without my having to direct full attention to it, and I was able to maintain relatively uninterrupted awareness of the three-part breathing movements for a few minutes. The rising movement was usually more pronounced. I first noticed my attention beginning to wane when realizing that I was mentally counting – arising, duration, falling – for both up and down movements without truly being aware of an accompanying physical movement. While intellectually recognizing impermanence in all this, I found myself thinking about it and then daydreaming (usually sparked by external sounds when bothering to trace the tangents back to their sources) without truly experiencing anything. My mind was slothful. It did not fight the daydreaming but was slow in becoming aware of it. In the second session I lowered my level of aspiration to maintaining awareness of the distinct physical movements and then to the difference between awareness and the actual movement. There were moments when the distinction was clear. The time passed quickly without anxiousness for the end of the session.

– Chao Khun turned us loose on our own, feeling that we'd had sufficient previous instruction. Today the movement in the abdomen was most pronounced, rather than in the chest as it usually is, so I directed my attention there. Found myself quite passive, even withdrawing from the seemingly increased noise. My mind did not jump about as much in its usual scrambled way or desire to dwell on memories, but a couple of times I caught myself quite involved in pure fantasy. This would disappear as soon as my attention was turned fully to it but would resume when I became bored with following the breathing. In connection with the fantasy I was aware of a slight feeling of pleasure which was unusual. Ordinarily I feel emotionally neutral during meditation. During the second part there was more wandering of the mind rather than fantasy. Also I experienced a feeling of coldness which became strong enough to cause shivers, although it didn't seem so much within the body as enveloping it and wasn't uncomfortable.

– Most of the way through the first session, my mind seemed clear. It was also energetic and refused to be confined to awareness of breathing only. I could view the mental gymnastics detachedly, tracing the links back to their sources in some cases. Awareness was also clear regarding physical sensations (slight twitching of facial muscles, ringing in the left ear, etc.). I became acutely aware of a sharp pain in my left hip socket. When attention was focused on this area, it seemed to spread throughout the leg and lower side while increasing in intensity. This caused an uneasiness (because such a strong pain had never arisen before, and the method of coping with it didn't seem to work), which might have accelerated into panic if the end of the session hadn't come shortly. Evidently this "blew my mind" for the opening stretch of the second part; my thoughts were tangled and crowded. The will to sort them out just wasn't there. Gradually the mind became a bit calmer. As attention was directed to the three-part breath movements, the familiar feeling of circular motion grew, which seemed this time to be trying to jar or pull away from the physical body but which couldn't get completely free. At one point there was a sensation of swinging around to "view" myself as part of the group. None of the figures were really sharply defined as human but were only vague in outline. This may have been pure fantasy – I couldn't tell.

– Today in the initial moments my awareness seemed sharper than usual and focused easily on the breath movements. But then, perhaps out of pride that it seemed to be going so well or out of subconscious desire to have a good day since this was the last official meditation with Chao Khun, my mind began to be very capricious and the pain in my right leg became strong. After the 11:00 chimes sounded and I knew we were to break soon, the session was a total loss. Both legs were hot and in the pins and needles stage. I kept thinking, "Man, is this killing me! Why doesn't the session end?" In the other half, I maintained awareness of breathing for a little while and then seemed to settle into some kind of strange emptiness which wasn't sleep . . . maybe some kind of stupor. There was a sensation which can only be rather inadequately described as a slight weight on the brain. This sensation remained relatively unbroken until the end of the period, which did not startle me.

– For a solid forty-five minutes I felt very alert for the most part, and at the same time pleasantly tranquil. At first I was preoccupied with the breathing and other physical processes going on within. For a time, the slight undulating movement of the torso seemingly caused by a strong heartbeat was compelling enough to become the object of meditation. Then my thoughts took the centre of attention. The mental process was less like a hurricane and more like a train of thought, which could be watched disinterestedly even when people or memories of events ordinarily arousing strong feelings entered my consciousness. The fact that I remained passive did not bother me as it has sometimes before. Sensitivity to sounds was sharp, both external ones and those associated with my own body. There was also a new sensation of prickly warmth throughout the whole body. Toward the latter part there was an experience of seeing colours and shapes, which seemed to be moving rapidly, similar to the experience when one has been leaning heavily on the heels of the hands with closed eyes.

– In this first day of Zen meditation practice my excitement, curiosity at the newness of the experience, the more disciplined form, and the emotional reaction (some fear, shock, disturbance) to hearing others being smacked with the stick kept my attention and alertness keen throughout the entire period. Up to the time Nishimura began walking around to correct us, my mind remained concentrated on counting the breathing. I never lost count although when I tried to draw out the breaths they were shakier, my head began to feel very light and empty, and concentration was not quite so solid. There was no conscious attempt to deliberately shut everything else out, but nevertheless I was aware of my mind straying only briefly from counting. When the first person was struck, I became very disturbed. My own breathing speeded up, and I winced at the impact of the blows. Then as other meditators were "encouraged," my agitation grew less. I became calm again until he came down my row. There was a momentary conflict between wanting to find out what the blows would be like and fearing what they might be like, which dissolved with the realization that there was no real need to ask for the stick for encouragement then, because my attention had not been slack. After the session I had the feeling that I'd worked hard but not that I had meditated, at least in the sense of Theravāda meditation.

– My legs were very painful at first. Distractions seemed much greater today, especially sounds in the building. Counting the breathing became quite mechanical and would continue even while my mind was off on a tangent. Sometimes when the number ten was approached, my attention would suddenly come back to focus again with the realization that counting had gone on without mindfulness. The general feeling was one of attempted concentration, not meditation. The physical discipline seemed a barrier to awareness. The first time Nishimura used the stick it very much startled me, but subsequently the disturbance was not as great as yesterday. When he passed me, I asked for the "encouragement" without fear or hesitation. The blow was heavy – yes. But I almost wanted it to be; it was a good pain. It was very easy to sit perfectly erect after that. The tingling was a reminder. The walking phase didn't seem like meditation at all but rather a welcome break from sitting. During the last long segment my attention became caught up in the pattern of light and dark on the floor which shifted in configurations, something like watching clouds. Faces and head shapes were the most frequent patterns emerging.

– There was a certain feeling of calmness in the beginning. Still, there was not a very strong feeling of detachment, perhaps partly due to the fact that my eyes were open and I "saw" myself as part of a physical environment. Though the counting was lost only a few times, much of the time it was not being done mindfully. I got very hung-up today in *thinking*: about how things were going, how it compared to yesterday and to Theravāda, what I should remember to write in this journal, whether or not I should be trying to concentrate exclusively on the breathing, and in being concerned about the fact that I was thinking. I probably should have asked for the stick today, but Nishimura had whacked the two people in front of me, so at the time I didn't need it for alertness and hesitated, knowing he doesn't want to over-use it. The walking meditation was the best part. Breathing came naturally and was easy to keep track of. There was no anxiety, no pressure about keeping up. A feeling almost of disembodiment became strong at one point. I noticed it, was pleased with it, and lost it; then it arose again and lasted longer.

– My senses were seemingly a little sharper than usual, picking up smells and temperature changes as well as the usual inner and outer sounds. There also seemed to be more moments (at least up through walking meditation) when there was a feeling of detachment from sense perceptions, although not from mental processes. My mind wandered considerably today, though I did maintain the counting, with some total breakdowns and many lapses of attention, throughout the session. Some of the wandering was thinking – which didn't bother me as much as it had yesterday – some playing with memories, and mostly daydreaming. I asked for the stick and was surprised at how much it hurt. Though it helped as far as holding the physical pose, it didn't really aid the meditation because I became wrapped up in thinking about the pain (how much it hurt, why it stung more than last time, and whether or not my frame of mind had influenced my reaction, etc.), not simply noticing it. The first part of today's session followed the general pattern of mechanical counting, daydreaming, thinking, and being bothered by thinking, except that pain was the predominant sense impression. After the walking meditation when Nishimura gave someone the first blow, I was very much startled and completely lost track of the breathing. Then, partly still being confused by the question whether or not I should be concentrating or being "aware," I seriously began to wonder why I was sitting there enduring the ache in my hip joint and struggling to do exactly as I was told. I just sat there and forgot about the breathing while the room echoed with subsequent blows, and was disturbed because I had been detached neither from my body nor my mind, nor could even be certain that that was desirable any more – and waited for it to end.

– The concentration versus awareness dilemma continued unresolved but was not quite so traumatic. Maintaining real concentration on the breathing was a very elusive thing – conscious effort to do this only seemed to make it more difficult. The disembodied feeling arose again during walking meditation. I enjoyed it and tried to sustain it. The blows of the stick were as they had been the first time – sweet pain. But at the end of the period I did something I had not done before: I gave in to the ache in my legs in a sudden impulsive desire for relief, which the change of position did not bring. Then I had to wait out the last few seconds washed over not only by the continuing physical pain but also by guilt and disgust with myself.

– I wanted today to be a "good" day, especially since it was the last session ever with Nishimura. But at first I could not force myself by sheer willpower to overcome sleepiness. I would catch myself not just preoccupied with thought fragments and bits of memories, but really involved in thinking about them. It seemed that whenever I had resolved this time to give full attention to the breathing I became caught up in thinking about something else, This didn't greatly disturb me but was faintly disappointing. Walking meditation was a welcome relief in the struggle and to my cramped legs also. Nishimura's words of reminder that this was our final time together and his admonition to pour all possible energy into it caused me to decide, though I don't think consciously, to concentrate everything on the sitting posture itself. For the first time there was a real satisfaction in the discipline of sitting itself and an acceptance of the value of doing simply that. Of course there were still flickerings of thoughts and memories through my mind, but neither this nor the fact that I wasn't maintaining constant awareness in counting the breathing ruptured the calmness. The blows of the stick were not sharp and painful but a definite reinforcement of my efforts at sitting. I was conscious of a feeling of exhilaration in these final minutes.

Reading 27

Initial Meditative Experiences

Roger Walsh

This is an account of the subjective experiences of some two years of *vipassanā* or insight meditation. During the first year this comprised an average of approximately one hour per day and during the second was increased to about two hours, as well as some six weeks of intensive meditation retreats, usually of two weeks duration. These retreats comprised about 18 to 20 hours daily of continuous walking and sitting meditation performed in total silence and without eye contact, reading, or writing. While this amount of practice may be vastly less than that of more experienced practitioners, it has certainly proved sufficient to elicit a range of experiences beyond the ken of day-to-day non-meditative living.

Vipassanā, or insight, meditation aims at a simple, non-judgmental, non-interfering, precise awareness and examination of whatever mental or physical phenomena enter awareness (mindfulness). Usually one object is observed at a time, the object being selected by a process of "choiceless awareness," in which the attention is allowed to settle effortlessly on whatever percept is predominant. If judgments, distractions, aversions, thoughts, etc. arise in response to the percept, then these reactions are themselves allowed to become the primary object of awareness. This differs from the usual state in which there is no experiential recognition of the phenomenon of awareness per se, of the distinction between awareness and the object of awareness, and a greater number of reactions go unnoticed.

I began meditation with one-half hour each day, and during the first three to six months there were few times during which I could honestly say with complete certainty that I was definitely experiencing benefits from it. However, with continued perseverance, subtle effects just at the limit of my perceptual threshold did begin to become apparent. I had expected the eruption into awareness of powerful, concrete experiences, of sufficient intensity to make it very clear that I had "gotten it," whatever "it" was. What "it" actually turned out to be was not the appearance of formerly non-existent mental phenomena, but rather a gradual incremental increase in perceptual sensitivity to the formerly subliminal portions of my own inner stream of consciousness.

At first this was apparent as the occasional ephemeral appearance of a sense of peace, or some other subtle, hard to categorize affect, interspersed among innumerable pains, itches, doubts, questions, fears, and fantasies, which occupied the majority of meditation sitting time. Usually one or more or these "events" would be deemed important enough to divert my attention from meditation. With increased practice the disruptive nature of these breaks became more and more apparent, and the stringency of the criteria for disrupting meditation became progressively higher. The order in which the different kinds of distractions were given up seemed to provide an index of the strengths of my attachments. For example, I am an analytic, intellectually curious person who loves to understand things. This predilection runs counter to the vipassanā process, which emphasizes just watching and observing the arising and passing away of all mental phenomena, thoughts, feelings, sensations, without analyzing or changing them in any way. Therefore, when something unusual occurred in meditation, I may have thought, "Wow, I could really learn something from that." This thought was usually sufficient to jolt me out of a relaxed meditative watching and into an active analytic probing and changing of the experience.

Fantasy

The more sensitive I became, the more I was forced to recognize that what I had formerly believed to be my rational mind, preoccupied with cognition, planning, problem solving, etc., actually comprised a frantic torrent of forceful, demanding, loud, and often unrelated thoughts and fantasies, which filled an unbelievable proportion of consciousness even during purposive behaviour. The incredible proportion of consciousness which this fantasy world occupied, my powerlessness to remove it for more than a few seconds, and my former state of mindlessness or ignorance of its existence, staggered me. (I am here using "mindlessness" in an opposite sense to the vipassanā term "mindful," which means "aware of the nature of the object to which the mind is attending.") Foremost among the implicit beliefs of orthodox Western psychology is the assumption that man spends most of his time reasoning and problem solving, and that only neurotics and other abnormals spend much time, outside of leisure, in fantasy. However, it is my impression that prolonged self-observation will show that at most times we are living almost in a dream world, in which we skilfully and automatically yet unknowingly blend inputs from reality and fantasy in accordance with our needs and defences.

The presence of inner dialogue and fantasy seems to present a limiting factor for the sense of closeness and unity with another person. If I am with another person, and free of dialogue and fantasy, and feeling an emotion, especially a positive one such as love, which I know the other person to be also experiencing, then it feels as though there are no detectable ego boundaries; we are together in love. But if part of my mind is preoccupied with dialogue and fantasies, then my awareness is split; I know that my experience is different from the other individual's, and feel correspondingly distanced and separated.

The subtlety, complexity, infinite range and number, and entrapping power of the fantasies which the mind creates seems impossible to comprehend, to differentiate from reality while in them, and even more so to describe to one who has not experienced them. Layer upon layer of imagery and quasi-logic open up in any point to which attention is directed. Indeed, it gradually becomes apparent that it is impossible to question and reason one's way out of this all-encompassing fantasy, since the very process of questioning, thinking, and seeking only creates further fantasy.

Meditation Exercise

Since the power and extent of this entrapment is so difficult to convey to someone without personal experience of it, I'd strongly encourage any non-meditator to use the following concentration exercise before continuing.

Set an alarm for a minimum of ten minutes. Then take a comfortable seat, close your eyes, and turn your attention to the sensations of breathing in your abdomen. Feel the abdominal wall rising and falling, and focus your attention as carefully, precisely, and microscopically as possible on the instant-to-instant sensations that occur in your abdomen. Don't let your attention wander for a moment. If thoughts and feelings arise, just let them be there, and continue to focus your awareness on the sensations.

Now, as you remain aware of the sensations, start counting each breath until you reach ten, and then start again at one. However, if you lose count, or if your mind wanders from the sensations in the abdomen, even for an instant, go back to one. If you get lost in fantasy or distracted by outside stimuli, just recognize what has happened and gently bring your mind back to the breath. Continue this process until the alarm tells you to stop, and then attempt to estimate how much of the time you were actually mindfully focused. As your perception sharpens with more practice, you would probably recognize that you have greatly overestimated, but this should be sufficient to give a flavour of the extent of the problem.

The impossibility of working or thinking one's way out of this multilayered, multidimensional fantasy world into which one falls, rapidly becomes apparent. That leaves within the experiential meditative world only the primary sensations, e.g., pain and breathing, on which to focus as perceptual anchors. By focusing attention back on the breathing, it seems that the energy or arousal going into the fantasy by virtue of the attention being paid it is withdrawn, and it collapses under its own weight leaving only the primary sensations until the next fantasy arises.

The power and pervasiveness of these inner dialogues and fantasies left me amazed that we could be so unaware of them during our normal waking life, and reminded me of the Eastern concept of *māyā*, or all-consuming illusion. The question why we don't recognize them seems incredibly important, but to date I have seen no explanations other than the almost universal ones among the meditative-yogic traditions that normal man is an automaton, more asleep than awake. It is the contrast between the dialogues-fantasies and the background affective state which makes the detection of their pervasiveness easier. I have not infrequently found that, when I am what initially appears to be dialogue-free, closer examination of my consciousness reveals dialogue with which I had been completely and unconsciously identified, such as: "I'm really doing this well, I'm in a really clear place, I don't have any dialogue going, I'm really getting to be a good meditator." However, at such times a thought like "I'm not getting anything out of this," stands out strongly and is readily identified for what it is: yet another thought. Other factors possibly accounting for our inability or unwillingness to identify the extent of this dialogue-fantasy may be the extent to which we have habituated to its presence. It is only when we attempt to stop it that we become aware of its remarkable hold on us, a situation strongly reminiscent of addictions.

Traditionally fantasy has been seen as ranging from being a source of creativity and pleasure in well-adapted individuals to a central hallmark of psychopathology when excessive. When the individual believes his fantasies to be real, and they are discordant with those of the majority of society, the fantasies are called hallucinations and he is labelled psychotic. Also, when the fantasies are especially painful and egodystonic, the individual may experience himself as, and be diagnosed as, mentally ill, even though he knows them to be fantasies. Thus, in Western psychology fantasies are seen as normal or even beneficial, unless they prove especially painful or over-whelming.

However, a remarkably wide range of meditation and yogic disciplines from a variety of cultures hold a very different view. They assert that, whether we know it or not, untrained individuals are prisoners of their own minds, totally and unwittingly trapped by a continuous inner fantasy-dialogue which creates an all-consuming illusion or māyā. "Normal" man is thus seen as asleep or dreaming. When the dream is especially painful or disruptive, it becomes a nightmare and is recognized as psychopathology; but since the vast majority of the population dreams, the true state of affairs goes unrecognized. When the individual permanently disidentifies from or eradicates this dream, he is said to have awakened, and can now recognize the true nature of his former state and that of the population. This awakening or enlightenment is the aim of the meditative-yogic disciplines.

Perceiving and Labelling Fantasy

With continued practice the speed, power, loudness, and continuity of these thoughts and fantasies began to slowly diminish, leaving subtle sensations of greater peace and quiet. After a period of about four or five months there occurred episodes in which I would open my eyes at the end of meditation and look at the outside world without the presence of concomitant internal dialogue. This state would be rapidly terminated by a rising sense of anxiety and anomie accompanied by the thought, "I don't know what anything means." I could be looking at something completely familiar, such as a tree, a building, or the sky, and yet without an accompanying internal dialogue to label and categorize it, it felt totally strange and devoid of meaning. It seemed that what made something familiar and hence secure was not simply its recognition, but the actual cognitive process of matching, categorizing, and labelling it; and that once this was done, then more attention and reactivity was focused on the label and labelling process than on the stimulus itself. Thus the initial fantasy- and thought-free periods may feel both strange and distinctly unpleasant, so that we are at first punished by their unfamiliarity. We have created an unseen prison for ourselves, whose bars are comprised of thoughts and fantasies, of which we remain largely unaware unless we undertake intensive perceptual training. Moreover, if they are removed, we may be frightened by the unfamiliarity of the experience, and rapidly reinstate them.

Presumably this labelling process must modify our perception in many ways, including reducing our ability to experience each stimulus fully, richly, and newly, by reducing its multidimensional nature into a lesser-dimensional cognitive labelling framework. This must necessarily derive from the past, be less tolerant of ambiguity, less here-now, and perpetuative of a sense of sameness and continuity to the world.

The First Retreat

The first meditation retreat, begun about one year after commencing sitting, was a very painful and difficult two-week affair. I had never meditated for more than an hour at a time, so continuous walking and sitting brought me to a screaming halt. Within three hours I felt as though I had ingested a stimulant, and by six hours there were significant psychedelic effects. A marked hypersensitivity to all stimuli, both internal and external, rapidly developed, resulting in intense arousal, agitation, discomfort, and multiple chronic muscle contractions, especially around the shoulders. This agitation was associated with an increased sensitivity to pain, which seemed like part of a more general hypersensitivity. This was particularly apparent during the first three or four days, and any exercise such as running would result in extreme tenderness in the corresponding muscles.

One of the most amazing rediscoveries during this first retreat was the incredible proportion of time, well over ninety per cent, which I spent lost in fantasy. Most of these were of the ego-self-aggrandizing type, so that when eventually I realized I was in them, it proved quite a struggle to decide to give them up and return to the breath; but with practice this decision became slightly easier, faster, and more automatic. This by no means happened quickly, since over the first four or five days the proportion of time spent in fantasy actually increased as the meditation deepened, and on days three through five of the retreat reached psychotic proportions. During this period, each time I sat and closed my eyes I would be immediately swept away by vivid hallucinations, losing all contact with where I was or what I was doing, until after an unknown period of time a thought would creep in, such as "Am I really swimming, lying on the beach?" Then I would either get lost back into the fantasy, or another thought would come: "Wait a moment, I thought I was meditating." If the latter, then I would be left with the difficult problem of trying to ground myself, i.e. of differentiating between stimulus-produced percepts ("reality") and entirely endogenous ones ("hallucinations"). The only way this seemed possible was to try finding the breath, and so I would begin frantically searching around in this hypnagogic universe for the sensations of the breath. Such was the power of the hallucinations that sometimes I would be unable to find it and would fall back into the fantasy. If successful, I would recognize it and be reassured that I was in fact meditating. Then in the next moment I would be lost again in yet another fantasy. The clarity, power, persuasiveness, and continuity of these hallucinations is difficult to adequately express. However, the effect of living through three days during which time to close my eyes meant losing contact almost immediately with ordinary reality was extraordinarily draining. While this experience was uncomfortable and quite beyond my control, it was not particularly frightening; if anything, the opposite. For many years I had feared losing control if I let down defences and voyaged too far along the road of self investigation and discovery.

During this first retreat a lot of old, almost forgotten, highly charged memories would arise into consciousness, remain for a moment, then slowly sink back out of awareness. Not infrequently, as they did so I would be aware that the affective charge, e.g. anger, sadness, which was originally associated with them, would tend to diminish while they were held in awareness, and that they had attained a neutral status by the time they disappeared back into the unconscious. Some of these memories ranged all the way back to age three or four, and to the best of my recollection I had never recalled them previously since their original occurrence.

While a good ninety per cent or more of this first retreat was taken up with mindless fantasy and agitation, there did occur, during the second week, occasional short-lived periods of intense peace and tranquillity. These were so satisfying that I could begin to comprehend the possibility of the truth of the Buddhist saying that "peace is the highest form of happiness." Affective lability was also extreme. While more than eighty per cent of the time of the first retreat was sheer pain, there were not infrequently sudden, apparently unprecipitated wide mood swings to completely polar emotions. Shorn of all my props and distractions, there was just no way to pretend that I had more than the faintest inkling of self-control over either thoughts or feelings.

The type of material which forcibly erupted into awareness and disrupted concentration was most often material – ideas, fantasies, thoughts, etc. – to which I was attracted (addicted) and around which there was considerable affective charge. Indeed, it seemed that the stronger the attachment or charge, the more often the material would arise. There was a definite sense that attachments reduced the flexibility and power of the mind, since whenever I was preoccupied with a stimulus to which I was attached, then I had difficulty in withdrawing my attention from it to observe other stimuli which passed through awareness. The attachment or need to understand, itself proved a perceptual and information limiting factor. As long as I needed to understand something it was necessary to keep that something around in awareness until it was understood rather than allowing it to pass away of its own accord to be replaced by the next object; that is, "to understand" my experience I had to retain and analyze it and thereby stop the free flow of awareness.

Thoughts

During the last retreat I sometimes found myself experiencing mind as a vast space in which thoughts could be observed to materialize, move, and disappear. They would first be detectable as a physical sensation soon to be accompanied by a visual image. To the physical sensations would soon be added an affective tone, and then also a body of information. At my clearest I could watch thoughts materializing into consciousness in the form of a visual image of a bubble arising from the surface of some invisible material arching up into the mental space, and then, if not identified with, diminishing in size and brightness and disappearing, sometimes back into the material from which it arose. In some cases bubbles would begin to form but then would merge back into the invisible medium from which they appeared without breaking free and reaching clear awareness. The image of an individual thought appeared to be composed of two spherical parts of unequal size and intensity. The larger sphere appeared dull and amorphous, and seemed to be composed of affect and to be carrying a smaller sphere within it. The smaller one appeared to be brighter, to be situated within the upper portion of the larger, and composed of a highly compact body of information, i.e. the cognitive component of the thought.

It seemed that the positionality of the thought in the visual image was directly related to, and informative of, my degree of identification with it. Thus thoughts which I was clearly observing without identification appeared to be in front and to arise out of and return to unconsciousness below me (here I am using "me" in the sense of the observer). However, if a thought arose and, after it had appeared, I identified with it, then it seemed that in a very small fraction of a second my awareness moved towards and centred in the sphere, and perhaps especially the brighter information component. I would suddenly find myself in the middle of, and surrounded by, a complex three-dimensional fantasy. On the other hand, if I gradually became aware that I was already in, and identified with, a formerly unrecognized thought, then that thought would appear from behind and gradually separate from me.

The nature of the thoughts which would arise seemed clearly related to the affect which I was experiencing at that time. Furthermore, both would elicit further thoughts and feelings of a similar kind. Thus, if I was experiencing anxiety, then anxiety-provoking thoughts would appear and elicit more anxiety, in a self-perpetuating stimulus-response chain.

What, then, is a thought? Usually we tend to think of thoughts as being distinct from emotions, but these experiences suggest that the demarcation is not so clear. Rather, thoughts appear to be comprised of both informational and affective components. Subjectively it seemed that the affect acted as an energizer or carrier wave to power the information component or signal wave, into awareness. Certainly, at a grosser level it is clear that affective arousal tends to increase the number of thoughts, and this carrier-wave:signal-wave concept provides a rationale for the meditative approach of reducing desires and arousal as a means of reaching a thought-free state.

The obvious capacity of thoughts to act as components of stimulus-response chains raises questions concerning conditioning and identification. It seemed that if I was watching as a non-identified observer, then one thought did not necessarily stimulate another. However, if I did identify with it, then it seemed that there would very rapidly arise multiple cascades of further thoughts, so that I would rapidly be buried within thoughts and fantasies within thoughts and fantasies. That is, I would almost immediately be back again in my multi-layered fantasy universe. Thus, identification with a single thought may be all that is necessary to remove us from the here-and-now and to initiate stimulus-response chains.

Perceptual Sensitivity

One of the most fundamental changes has been an increase in perceptual sensitivity, which seems to include both absolute and discrimination thresholds. Examples of this include both a more subtle awareness of previously known percepts, and novel identification of previously unrecognized phenomena. It seems that I can discriminate visual forms and outlines more clearly. The experience feels like having a faint but discernible veil removed from my eyes, and that the veil is comprised of hundreds of subtle thoughts and feelings. Each one of these thoughts and feelings seems to act as a competing stimulus or "noise," which thus reduces sensitivity to any one object. After meditation any specific stimulus appears stronger and clearer, presumably because the signal:noise ratio is increased. These observations provide a phenomenological basis and possible perceptual mechanism to explain the findings that meditators in general tend to exhibit heightened perceptual sensitivity and empathy.

Visual images during meditation constitute another example. Visual images go through a process of appearing and then, after a variable period of time, disappearing, or rising and passing away. When an image arises there is the possibility that I will become completely lost in and identified with it, so that my experience is of living in the fantasy and experience created by the image. On the other hand, I may recognize the image for what it is, and be able to watch it without identification or getting lost in it and forgetting that I am meditating. This recognition may occur at various stages, which seem to come more rapidly with practice.

With increased sensitivity has seemed to come an increased awareness of the continuously changing nature of experience. More subtle awareness leads to finer and finer and more and more rapid discriminations of change within what formerly seemed to be a static experience. For example, during the periods between thoughts the general background of awareness may initially appear uniform and relatively constant, but with a finer awareness each of the smallest component areas seems to be in continuous flux.

One unexpected demonstration of greater sensitivity has been the occurrence of the synaesthetic perception of thoughts. Synaesthesia, or cross-modality perception, is the phenomenon in which stimulation of one sensory modality is perceived in several, as for example, when sound is seen and felt as well as heard. Following the enhanced perceptual sensitivity which occurred during my prior psychotherapy, I began to experience this phenomenon not infrequently, suggesting that it may well occur within all of us though usually below our thresholds. Now, during moments of greater meditative sensitivity I have begun to experience this cross-modality perception with purely mental stimuli, for example thoughts. Thus, as previously described, I may initially experience a thought as a feeling, and subsequently become aware of a visual image, before finally recognizing the more familiar cognitive information components.

Identity

Undoubtedly the most fundamental question raised by the practice of meditation is that of identity. Most commonly in the West this question is framed in the form "Who am I?" meaning "What kind of person am I?" During the last six months it has become apparent that intensive meditation raises the much more fundamental question "*What* am I?" Since the experiences that arise within meditation are so inconsistent with the concepts of identity which we usually hold, they call into question our usually unquestioned beliefs and assumptions about who and what we are. The following paragraphs, then, represent an attempt, first to describe some of my experiences, and then to examine some of their implications for different models of man.

The following experiences are described in the order in which they occurred over a period of some six months, most often while in meditation retreats. There is no clear progression, nor is their precise relationship to one another clear.

The first experience occurred during a moment or two of special clarity in which I was observing – in what I thought to be a non-identified manner – the arising of thoughts. However, I suddenly noticed that I was in fact identifying with, and hence unaware of, certain thoughts, mainly "I" thoughts, e.g. "I'm not identified with any of these thoughts." Having seen this process, I was able to observe without identification at least some of these "I" thoughts, although obviously I cannot say what percentage of them, since identification with them renders them impossible to observe. At this point there was a moment of heightened clarity, and I saw that "I" thoughts were somehow differentiated from others; they were somehow grabbed by and absorbed into consciousness. It seemed as though the "I" thoughts were recognized as belonging to a special category and were then somehow grasped and incorporated by the awareness which had been watching them. In the instant of recognizing this, the "I" thoughts ceased to be differentiated and grasped, and then existed as "just thoughts" without their former significance. Immediately there followed a powerful awareness, accompanied by intense emotion, that "I" did not exist, and all that existed were "I" thoughts following rapidly one after another. Almost simultaneously the thought, "My God, there's no one there!" arose, and my consciousness reverted to its accustomed state. It is difficult to convey the power of these seconds of experience, but it was sufficient to disrupt my meditation for the next two days.

A further sense of the non-existence of the observer or "I" has come from attempting to focus awareness on the observer. In this procedure, concentration on objects, such as the breath, is developed first, and then turned back on the observer. Due to the limits of my concentration, my attempts have seldom lasted more than a few seconds, but the experiences have all been somewhat similar. Often there is identification with that which is looking for the observer, the latter apparently having simply switched positions. However, on those occasions when I have been able to avoid this identification I have had the experience of looking into darkness and sensing that there is no one there.

Another, more frequent experience has arisen within the last few months as a result of a change in technique in which percepts and mental objects are named, e.g. "thought, thought; anger, anger." The process of naming objects seems to reduce the risk of identifying with them. Thus, there have been periods lasting several minutes in which I have had the experience of being a point in a vast space constituted by my awareness, in which thoughts, feelings, and percepts occurred, but which were separate from and did not necessarily influence me. During and after these states there is the feeling that what I usually identify with is the mental content, e.g. thoughts and feelings, and that this "I" represents a very narrowed, limited, and driven portion of awareness which has lost sight of that which is much larger. This progression from lesser to greater awareness seemed to begin with an initial identification with and failure to recognize thoughts; then came a recognition of some thoughts and a beginning awareness of the space between them, which usually had an affective quality attached to it; and finally a sense of vast space or context within which these phenomena occur.

One particularly powerful experience occurred during a meditation in which I was having great difficulty extricating myself from identification with numerous fantasies. I would realize that I was lost in a fantasy, bring my attention back to the breath, and then rapidly get lost in yet another fantasy with which I would stay identified for varying periods of time before recognizing what was happening and beginning the cycle again. Over the course of a sitting, this process of disidentification became more rapid. Eventually there came a point at which I seemed to be recognizing the fantasies for what they were almost as soon as they appeared, and I had a sense of sitting behind them, letting go of one after another at a faster and faster rate. This process seemed to speed up more and more until at one instant I found myself looking at what appeared to be another fantasy, and that fantasy was what I thought I was. That is, I felt that my sense of identity – e.g. the person, the striver, psychiatrist, writer, worrier, achiever, player – was just another fantasy, a creation of mine whose illusion of continuity and permanence was derived from the piecing together of salient patterns and behaviours; and that who I really was was the awareness which had created – and was now watching – this fantasy. In the next instant there arose a visual image of a huge sphere of consciousness, on one side of which was a small mask of a face called "Roger." "I," a sphere of consciousness, was looking at the world through the eyes of the mask, identifying with the mask, and forgetting everything else that I was. Immediately there appeared a sense of awe, followed by two thoughts: "Now I understand what they mean when they say, 'You are not who you think you are'," and: "I already am everything I am striving to be – I just don't recognize it."

A similar image arose during an experience of "big mind," as described earlier. The image comprised a large clear sphere representing a consciousness overlaid by an incredibly complex superstructure of desires, fears, and anxieties, together with plans, doings, and strivings aimed at fulfilling the desires. This superstructure was in ceaseless activity and of such incredible complexity that it was impossible to figure it out or work one's way out of it, especially since any effort to modify it only fed more energy into it and so was self-perpetuating and self-defeating. However, when this consciousness turned its attention towards itself – towards the big mind – and withdrew attention from the desires and merely allowed them to be, then the whole elaborate superstructure was drained of energy, collapsed, and disappeared.

Assuming that these experiences are at least partially valid sources of information, what do they indicate about identity? The one thing I am certain of is that I am not who and what I thought I was. The following represents an attempt to conceptualize my experiences and current understanding of this process. Clearly, these experiences and concepts lie close to the limits of my present perception and understanding, and hence must be regarded as highly tentative.

What seems clear is that who I thought I was represented a product of identification with mental content; that is, I thought I was my mental content. By identifying myself solely in this way, I lost sight of the broader context which held this content. It seems that what I identify with runs me, and provides the motivation and the context within which I interpret other content, determine my reality, and adopt a logic. Thus, identification with mental content transforms that content into the context which holds, interprets, attributes, and elicits other content, in a manner which is congruent with, and reinforces, this context. For example, if the thought arises "I'm scared," and I observe it as just another thought and do not identify with it, then it exerts little influence on me. However, if I identify with it, then the reality at that moment is that *I am scared,* and I am likely to identify with a whole series of fearful thoughts and to interpret any nondescript feelings as fear. Thus identification sets in train a self-fulfilling prophetic process. The thought "I'm scared," when identified with, constitutes a belief, or in behavioural terms, a self-attribution.

The two major (and to some extent mutually exclusive) factors determining the sense of who I am appear, then, to be mindfulness and identification with mental contents. Mindfulness of an experience affords the potential for disidentification and for reducing context to content, and in so doing minimizes its motivational influence. Awareness thus becomes the ultimate context for experience. If the "I" or observer, which is what I usually think myself to be, is also an illusion of identification with mental content, then this leaves only awareness and content, and both are effectively devoid of any "I"; that is, there remains just an impersonal flux of mental phenomena and the awareness of them. This concept seems analogous to the Buddhist doctrine of *anattā* or "not self," which states that both awareness and objects of awareness exist as automatic processes devoid of any "I." If this is true, and at this stage I am forced to agree that it probably is, then it provides a solution to a long unanswered mystery of neurophysiology. Researchers have been able to follow the perception-induced train of neural excitation up the sensory pathways into the brain, but have long been puzzled as to how the excitation of the brain's sensory areas is "observed." Various types of observing homunculi, "the ghost in the machine," have been hypothesized, but none have produced satisfying explanations. Now it seems that the subjective experience of the observer is an illusion, and the question becomes one of explaining the illusion rather than explaining an observer.

Re-entry

At the completion of a retreat the re-entry into the world may provide quite an experience in its own right. In my case, for a day or so I am aware of a heightened sensitivity, and this is particularly apparent with regard to negative experiences. Indeed, not infrequently I am dismayed at the amount of pain and suffering in the world. On more than one occasion I and other meditators with me have experienced marked discomfort during the first week. I can give one graphic illustration of this sensitivity by describing my reactions, and those of a friend, to a movie which we watched twenty-four hours after completing a retreat. We had decided to view the in-flight movie on our return flight home, and to watch it as mindfully as possible for half an hour as a type of meditation. However, we were unable to complete it, since this unremarkable police drama left us both so shaken that by the end of twenty minutes both of us were sweating, unwilling to continue, and felt the need to meditate to regain our equilibrium. Each picture of aggression, pain, and tension elicited strongly painful responses in us, which, in addition to being highly uncomfortable, made it extremely difficult to remain mindful. With this degree of sensitivity, it is perhaps not surprising that, on another occasion when I left a retreat for one evening, this produced sufficient agitation to require almost a full day of meditation to return to the calm which I had previously experienced there.

Conclusion

The reliability, validity and generality of the principles enumerated throughout this paper are as yet unknown, but most are open to testing. Hopefully, in the not too distant future, more precise descriptions employing groups of subjects, will expand far beyond the limits of this account. However, if this paper spurs the production of these more advanced reports, it will have served its function as the preliminary testing and reporting of a novel – but perhaps essential – experimental paradigm. In addition to being only a beginning from a scientific perspective, the same seems true for me personally; since the more I learn, the more I sense that what I and many of us have assumed ourselves to be, represents but the merest glimpse of our true nature.

Experiments in Insight Meditation

Rod Bucknell

This is a report on my experiences with insight meditation (*vipassanā-bhāvanā*) during a four-and-a-half year period spent in Thailand and India. It deals only in small part with my formal vipassanā training; that lasted barely two months and is only briefly summarized. For the most part it describes independent experiments with meditative techniques which I assumed, at the time, to be original and unorthodox. Subsequent reading has indicated that those techniques, though not widely practised, are in fact well known within certain schools of meditation. This has reinforced my belief in the value of the techniques, and has encouraged me to publish a report on my experiences.

Formal Vipassanā Training

The vipassanā centre in Bangkok where I began my meditative training claimed to teach the system of practice developed by Mahasi Sayadaw of Myanma, often called Burmese *satipaṭṭhāna*.[79] The practice was based on two related exercises: (1) concentration on a single object, namely the sensations accompanying the rising and falling movements of the abdomen in breathing, practised while sitting with eyes closed; and (2) constant attention to the various sensations experienced while engaged in simple activities (walking, eating, etc.), all of which had to be performed in slow motion. In both of these exercises any digressions from the assigned object of attention had to be mentally noted. Distracting sensations were identified as "itching," "pain," "hearing," etc., and distracting thoughts as "daydreaming," "planning," "theorizing," etc. The two exercises were alternated: half an hour of sitting, half an hour of walking, and so on throughout most of the eighteen-hour waking day.

Judged by my teacher's comments at our daily interviews, and by the published reports of other meditators which I subsequently read, my experiences under this rigorous regime were in most respects typical. Like most beginners in meditation, I initially had great difficulty in stemming the flow of thought and keeping attention on the prescribed object; I experienced astonishment and distress on realizing the triviality and worthlessness of most of my mental content; and I gained occasional useful insights into formerly hidden layers of my personality.

After two weeks of practice I was able to maintain concentration on the object for a minute or more at a time. This partial success in concentrating brought with it certain pleasant experiences. I increasingly found, on opening my eyes and rising from my seat, that my perception of the world and of myself had undergone subtle changes. Colours, textures, and shapes seemed to have become unusually clear and vivid; there was a refreshing newness, interest, and beauty in objects that had formerly been dull and humdrum; time seemed to have stood still, so that I lived in an eternal present moment – while the effect lasted; and I felt as if I had been somehow purified of negative emotions and was radiating benevolence toward all beings. These positive effects gave me much-needed encouragement, and I redoubled my meditative efforts.

At the end of three weeks I was able to maintain uninterrupted mental one-pointedness for prolonged periods. During such periods nothing was present in consciousness but the meditation object, the sensations in the abdomen. The rest of the body, and the world outside it, had ceased to exist. I identified completely with the sensations; I *was* the sensations. Increasingly I experienced synaesthetic effects. For example, I often "saw" the pattern of sensations in the abdomen in various forms – usually as an oscillating system of levers, or as a pulsating globe of light. On my teacher's advice I took this mental image as my new object of concentration. (The sitting practice had, by this stage, become the principal component of the meditative regime; mindful walking was now of secondary importance.) Then one day, as I was concentrating on my pulsating image, it suddenly disappeared, plunging me into a pitch-black emptiness. My teacher regarded this strange experience as an important meditative attainment, and told me to cultivate and prolong it. I followed his instruction for a time – until I learned that the objective was to prolong the state of emptiness to twenty-four hours. The achievement of that feat would constitute successful completion of the meditation course.

At that point I decided it was time to leave the vipassanā centre. I had begun to doubt the value of this state of mental emptiness, and of some of my other hard-won meditative skills as well. Thanking my teacher, I left Bangkok and moved to Chiangmai in the north of the country.

In Chiangmai I entered another vipassanā centre, to find out if their methods were significantly different. There were differences in detail, but they amounted simply to different ways of inducing the same concentrated state. After five days I left. I moved into a quiet *wat* (monastery) and, disregarding my former teacher's last words to me, gave up meditating. There followed a period of reflection and evaluation of the experience I had been through.

In retrospect my training in vipassanā meditation seemed to me the most important and valuable thing I had ever done. At the same time I found much to criticize. I came to the conclusion that "insight meditation" was hardly an appropriate term for the kind of practice I had been engaged in. While there had been some incipient insights, the nature of the practice had been such as to prevent my following them up. Repeatedly I had had to abandon promising lines of introspective observation in order to return to the concentration practice; concentration had always received the primary emphasis. I had once mentioned my frustration on this point to my teacher. He had told me that such curiosity about the mechanism of thought must be recognized as an alluring side-track, something that one had to forgo in order to progress; and he had gently reprimanded me for coming to the course with preconceptions about how it ought to proceed, and for having less than total faith in the method. At that time I had been prepared to suppress my introspective curiosity, to provisionally accept the method on faith, and to press on with concentrating on my abdomen. Now in retrospect it seemed that the emphasis had been wrongly placed. I had been taught how to *have* experiences rather than how to *observe* or *understand* them. For example, by mastering concentration I had experienced a remarkable clarity of perception and other effects, but I had not gained any insight into the nature or cause of those experiences. I had not been able to discover what change in the mind's mode of functioning was responsible for the supernormal clarity of perception, the *jamais vu* feeling, and so on. As for the normal, everyday processes of the mind, these remained almost as much a mystery as ever. I had hoped (here, admittedly, another preconception taken with me into the course) that I would be taught how to observe mental processes from the inside. But in that direction we had gone no further than labelling digressions as "daydreaming," "planning," etc.

I was unable to be more precise than this in identifying the reasons for my dissatisfaction with the practice. What I was sure of, however, was that I placed high value on insight into the mind, and that the course of practice had brought little of that. I discussed my problem with several monks at the wat, some of them meditators with years of experience. A few agreed that the emphasis on mental emptiness was a serious fault, and maintained that it represented a distortion of Mahasi Sayadaw's teaching. They said that the real objective was insight into the "three universal characteristics": transience, suffering, and non-selfhood. My teacher had in fact drawn my attention to these "characteristics"; for example, pains in the abdomen, formerly unnoticed but revealed during concentration, were evidence of the universality of suffering. I had been inclined to take such observations rather as evidence that an individual's interpretation of an altered state of consciousness reflects his or her religious conditioning. (The three characteristics are repeatedly mentioned in the Buddhist canon and in monks' teachings.)

One of the monks I consulted condemned the entire Burmese satipaṭṭhāna method as lacking textual authority. He advised me to practise instead mindfulness of breathing (ānāpāna-sati), textually the best authenticated of all meditative techniques.[80] Although this was again a form of concentration practice, and although I now had neither the guidance of a teacher nor the conducive environment of a meditation centre, I decided, without much enthusiasm, to try it.

In mindfulness of breathing as usually practised, the object of concentration is the fine tactile sensation experienced at the nostril as the breath moves in and out. I found this subtle object far more difficult to concentrate on than the abdomen had been. This difficulty, combined with the lack of guidance and my skepticism about the value of concentration, meant that, in spite of the experience gained in Bangkok, I made slow progress. But this unpromising situation brought unforeseen benefits; for in the course of attempting to control my unruly mind, I developed, almost by accident it seemed, a new meditative technique. This technique led to others, yielding in time my own version of a course in insight meditation.

Retracing

Like most meditators I had been struck by the fact that the topics to which my mind wandered were often totally unrelated to my actual situation, suggesting a lack of any coherence in the thinking process. I could be concentrating on my breathing one moment, and the next moment find myself speculating on the mechanical condition of my car, wondering if my washing was dry yet, or dwelling on a vivid fantasy of biting into a tasty cheese sandwich. In order to find out something about the unseen processes whereby such vast transitions came about, I introduced a variation into my practice. Instead of returning to the concentration object directly, as I had been taught to do, I carefully retraced my mental steps, making the mind return by the way it had come. The result was a reconstruction, in reverse, of the mental digression.

There is nothing original in this technique. Probably most people have at some time tried retracing their mental tracks. It is an interesting thing to do if, for example, one suddenly realizes, in the middle of some task, that one is thinking of something totally different, and is curious to find out how this came about. The following example (chosen at random from many such in a recent meditation session) illustrates how the procedure is applied in practice.

While attempting to keep my attention focused on the tactile sensation at the rim of my right nostril, I suddenly realize that I am, instead, pondering on a long-standing, though essentially trivial problem, namely the lack of sufficient shelves in my office at work. Instead of returning immediately to the nostril, I reconstruct, in reverse order, the sequence of thoughts. From my cluttered office, with its inadequate shelves, I go back to a set of white-painted shelves standing unused in the garage at home; then I go back to a similar white-painted set of shelves in a friend's house; then to the last occasion on which I visited that friend, when, seated near the set of shelves, he demonstrated his limited talents on the cello (the cello bow at one stage actually knocked against the shelves); then to a concert I once attended, featuring an impressive performance by a very stout male cellist with piano accompaniment; then to the pianist, regarding whom my principal impression was that he seemed to slouch instead of sitting upright as a pianist should; then, finally, to my own posture which in the prolonged meditation session has become very slouched, producing a slight pain in the back. With the identification of this pain in my back as the beginning point of the digression, the reconstruction is complete: aching back → slouching pianist → stout cellist → friend playing cello near shelves → shelves in garage → office with inadequate shelves.

Recognizing that this retracing procedure had potential as a means for revealing the formerly hidden processes of thought, I began practising it regularly in association with the mindfulness of breathing. My practice then comprised a repeated cycle of three stages:

1. concentration on the chosen object (the breathing);
2. a short thought sequence, as the mind wanders from the object;
3. retracing this thought sequence to its starting point.

Previously the practice had been limited to stages 1 and 2; now, with stage 3 added, it became possible to discover the nature of the digressions.

Practising in this way, I found that the same course of events was repeated again and again. Some initial stimulus (in the cited example, the pain in the back) would set in train a sequence of thoughts, which would rapidly lead far away from the starting point. By observing the general direction taken by thought sequences, I learned things about myself that I would otherwise perhaps never have suspected: unresolved conflicts, previously unrecognized interests, fears, etc. Reviewing this material had a perceptible therapeutic effect. Problems became less important, and I could smile at aspects of myself that I had previously taken too seriously. Retracing therefore became the principal component of my practice. Concentration was now of secondary importance. However, I found that concentration could not be abandoned altogether; indeed it proved to be an indispensable part of the meditative procedure, serving as an anchor to prevent the mind from drifting too far.

Since I was using mindfulness of breathing as the basis for my three-stage practice, I meditated initially in the accepted cross-legged posture and with eyes shut. Walking (as in the vipassanā course) had no place in my regime. However, I soon decided to introduce mindful walking, in order to overcome a problem I was having with physical fatigue. I would walk slowly along a quiet path – not, however, in the artificial, slow-motion fashion required by my vipassanā teacher – with eyes directed at the ground and attention focused on the changing visual pattern before me. Then, each time I realized the mind had wandered into a train of thought, I would retrace.

This modification of the procedure, prompted initially by

considerations of comfort and practical convenience, proved to have a profound effect on the nature of the meditation. Because the eyes were now open, the thoughts were seen contrasted with whatever was in the field of vision. Against that relatively substantial background each thought appeared as a semi-transparent picture, like a photographic slide projected on to a wall in a well lit room. I was now seeing my thoughts *as mental images*. Previously, when I had been meditating with the eyes closed, each image had occupied the whole of consciousness, because it had not been contrasted with direct visual sensation in this way. Like a slide projected on to a screen in a completely darkened room, its seemingly real contents had completely captured my interest, and consequently its true nature, *as an image*, had been overlooked. Now the situation was different. The new effect was exactly as if there were a slide-projector located somewhere just over my shoulder projecting pictures on to the path before me. I watched fascinated as each retracing revealed my thoughts as a "slide-show."

I now modified the mindfulness of breathing practice, meditating thenceforth with my eyes open and, if at night, always with some form of lighting. The effect was even more striking than it had been in the walking practice. I saw that the slide-show analogy was very apt: each image was a faint but nevertheless very realistic reproduction of an earlier visual experience. Consider, for example, the experience of recalling the stout cellist. At a certain time in the past I had had the visual experience of seeing the cellist. Now there was a fainter re-presentation of that visual experience: a picture of the cellist appeared, as if projected on to the wall before me. The images that appeared in any particular thought sequence were a tiny selection from the vast number available. It was as if (pursuing the slide-show analogy) I had an enormous album of slides depicting my past experiences, from which a few appropriate ones were selected for viewing on any particular occasion.

Curious about the nature of images, I went on to develop a method that enabled me to examine them more closely. I found that after retracing a thought sequence, I was able to cause any one of the component images to arise again. Then, in much the same way as I had retraced the whole sequence, I could now "retrace" that single image. This procedure was in fact a kind of insightful looking at the image, seeing it in the new way that I was now learning to see images: as a slide projected on to whatever was in my field of vision. When looked at in this way the image would promptly disappear. However, I found I could then cause it to arise again, and repeat the process.

Thus any chosen sample image could be called forth several times in succession and subjected to repeated insightful examination.

This repeated examination of single images consolidated my new ability to see images as images, rather than as the things they depicted. I found it deprived images of their affective charge. For example, one fairly frequently recurring image, depicting a certain annoying man who sometimes visited me at the wat, had previously been seen *as that annoying man*, and had tended on each occasion to evoke further annoyance. Now it was seen *as an image*, and evoked no such reaction. When an image was seen as an image rather than as the things it depicted, it lost its power to evoke an affective response. Under such conditions all images were equal. The judgements "annoying," "attractive," etc., appropriate enough for the contents of images, were not applicable to the images themselves. The contents carried affective charge; the images themselves, as mental events, were neutral.

I was reminded of an experience I had had in childhood, when, on looking closely at the pictures in a newspaper, I had discovered that they were made up of patterns of dots. This had caused the pictures to assume a very different status. Their content had lost its appearance of reality and importance. Looked at in that way, as patterns of dots, all the pictures in the paper acquired a certain sameness; none was better or more interesting than another. Similarly now, my mental images seen in this new way, as process rather than as content, were in effect all the same. Consequently, any form of affective involvement in them would have been totally inappropriate.

Under normal circumstances we see images not as images, but as people, places, things, or whatever else they depict; and we react to them accordingly. Each time I retraced an image sequence, I realized that I had, up to the moment of retracing, been completely involved in its content. I realized that under normal circumstances I was as if absorbed in watching an endless television show. I had first become conscious of the existence of the mental television show (the endless stream of thought) on the day I had begun practising concentration, but I had never before realized with what fascination and emotional involvement I watched it. Now that I had learned to see thought as process rather than as content, I realized the extent of my former involvement.

It occurred to me that in my normal waking condition I was actually involved in a long, very realistic dream. I then felt that I understood the significance of a statement I had come across in my early superficial reading on yoga. The gist of that statement was that, despite appearances to the contrary, our normal waking state has the quality of a dream. Just as one sees, on waking in the morning, that one's dream during the night was unreal, so one will see, on attaining the yogic awakening, that one's former everyday condition was a waking dream, an illusion, *māyā*. At the time this had made little sense to me, because I had assumed that it referred to the nature of the physical objects around us, so that the yogic awakening would presumably reveal those objects as insubstantial and unreal, more or less as subatomic physics had shown them to be. But now it occurred to me that the reference must be to the thought-stream. *That* was the waking dream, the cosmic illusion, the māyā. Previously I had hardly been conscious of its existence, let alone of its omnipresence and its remarkable power to delude. Now I had seen it in its true nature – which, however, did not prevent my being taken in by it again and again. Insight into its nature had to be renewed each time, by retracing followed optionally by the more intensive technique of examining individual images.

The shift of attention from content to process resembled the experience of suddenly realizing, in the middle of watching an absorbing television drama, that it is *just* a television drama. Most of the time the drama is perceived as real. One lives it, reacting with fear, joy, etc., as the plot develops. Then suddenly (perhaps as a result of some external disturbance) one realizes that the drama is merely a moving pattern of lights on a glass screen, which one is watching from the armchair in one's living-room. Seeing images as process rather than as content entails much the same insight, and it produces the same feeling of having seen through a very realistic illusion.

Continued practice revealed that my earlier model of thought, as made up of pictures from a mental photograph album, had been an over-simplification. Not all images were re-presentations of former visual experiences. Some were new combinations of fragments from several different experiences, as, for example, when I imagined how my room would look if I were to rearrange the furniture. Others were abstract diagrams, as when I drew mental graphs to facilitate comprehension of mathematical relationships. But such constructed images proved to be extremely rare in comparison with simple re-presentations.

The Inner Voice

Another over-simplification that I later realized was the assumption that images – more precisely, visual images – were the only elements of thought. I had not suspected there was any other component present until one day, while engaged in the walking practice, I had a novel experience which made me realize my error. Having caught myself in the middle of a train of thought, I found that this had happened because I had been "stuck for a word" while carrying on a mental conversation; and the reason I was stuck for a word was that my mental conversation was in Thai, which language I had still only very imperfectly mastered. Up to that time my introspective examination of thought sequences had revealed only images. Now, for the first time, I became aware of a second component: mental verbalizing, "the inner voice." It seemed astonishing that I had not noticed the inner voice earlier, because it proved thereafter to be a conspicuous component of the thought-stream, and I knew very well it had been there all along. I repeatedly found, on retracing an image sequence, that one or more of the images, and sometimes also the stimulus that had initiated the sequence, were accompanied by mentally verbalized comments. For example, in the sequence leading from the ache in my back to the problem of inadequate shelves, the ache was accompanied by the comment, "Bad posture!" and the final image of the cluttered office by, "How can I work with stuff everywhere like this?" Usually what I heard was my own voice, as I addressed some implied listener; and where necessary the language used would switch to suit that listener. In the case of the interrupted mental conversation in Thai, the listener was a Thai monk whom I knew well, and whose face was depicted in the accompanying image. Less often it was the implied other party who was speaking, in which case the inner voice was generally a partial replay of an earlier actual conversation. With this second layer in the thought-stream recognized, the resemblance to a slide-show became even closer, for the slides were now found to be accompanied by a pattering commentary.

Now fully conscious of the thought-stream as a combination of images plus the inner voice, I soon realized that thought could sometimes be very intrusive. I observed, for example, how my quiet enjoyment of a magnificent view was marred as soon as the inner voice began making comments. The effect was similar to that of a noisy group arriving with a radio playing loudly. The arising of images was equally disruptive. The images, perceived as if projected on top of the scene before me, obscured my view. They got in the way of visual perception; I was seeing the view as if through a veil. I found, however, that the veiling effect could be eliminated by developing concentration. This suppressed the imagery and verbalizing, yielding a refreshing clarity.

In this way I found the answer to a question I had asked myself during the vipassanā course: What is responsible for the remarkable subjective effects often experienced after a successful session of concentration practice? What causes the heightened sensory perception, the feeling of newness in everything, the sense of living in an eternal present? I now saw it clearly. These subjective effects come about when, by some means, such as perfecting concentration or becoming absorbed in the beauties of nature, the usual flow of mental imagery and verbalizing is halted, thus eliminating interference with incoming sensations. Normally the stream of thought flows on almost incessantly, like an endless, tiresome television program. Day and night – except, presumably, in deep sleep – sequences of images run on, one after the other, and the inner voice chatters away. This constant mental activity interferes seriously with perception. We see objects through an ever-changing veil of images, and hear sounds above the constant mental chatter. But we are unaware of this because it has always been so. When, through some means, the imagery and verbalizing are stopped, perception is altered. Colours and shapes, seen directly without the imagery, appear remarkably vivid. Sounds heard without interference from the inner voice are heard with great clarity. Objects which under normal circumstances would evoke associated images (the memories of previous experiences with similar objects), or comments by the inner voice, are now seen simply as they are, without reference to previous experience. This produces the sense of newness in everything. Without the repeatedly flashing images and the constantly droning inner monologue, one is deprived of an important in-built mental reference for judging temporal duration. Consequently one's other experiences become timeless; one seems to live in an eternal present moment.

Having recognized how imagery and verbalizing interfered with perception, I thereafter observed again and again how this phenomenon impaired performance of everyday tasks, particularly the more mechanical ones. For example, if I was typing, accuracy remained high as long as imagery was absent and verbalizing was limited to the words actually being typed. But as soon as some word in the text or some external stimulus set in train a sequence of imagery, I began making mistakes. When there was imagery, my attention was divided. I had, as it were, one eye on the text and one eye on the images. I was able to effect a marked increase in proficiency by consciously suppressing imagery. Almost any given task could serve in place of mindfulness of breathing or slow walking as the foundation for concentration – and for the retracing practice. For example, I would set about typing with the intention of keeping imagery suppressed; and then, whenever an image sequence did arise, I would retrace it. The retracing caused only a minimal delay because I was now able to retrace very rapidly, and also because I often caught the first image before it had time to evoke another and give rise to a full sequence. In this way I managed to integrate many kinds of daily activity into the practice. Even serious reading could be done in this way. Like most readers, I was familiar with the experience of suddenly realizing, on reaching the bottom of a page, that I had little idea what that page contained, attention having shifted from the content of the page to the content of a train of imagery. I now made a practice of retracing each such digression before re-reading. This usually led back to a word on the page that had initiated the digression.

Earlier it had distressed me, both in the vipassanā course and during my initial practice of mindfulness of breathing, that reading and writing, and even serious conversation, were considered inimical to progress in meditation, and were therefore banned. Now such activities had become part of my practice. The earlier dichotomy between practice and everyday life had, to some extent, been broken down.

Positive Value of Imagery and Verbalization

Up to this time imagery and verbalizing had always seemed "undesirable." They impaired efficiency in the performance of daily tasks; they obscured perception of the world; and it was they that were responsible for the relatively boring, humdrum quality of the normal, unconcentrated condition. Certainly imagery and verbalizing, as the objects of my introspective observation, were the source of all insight. But that insight had so far revealed no desirable qualities in them.

Increasing integration of the meditation into my daily activities led me gradually to revise this judgment. On one occasion, as I was setting out from the wat to attend a talk in the neighbouring town, it suddenly occurred to me that I ought to take a flashlight with me, as it would be dark when I returned. Retracing revealed the course of mental events that had led to this useful thought. The beginning point was my seeing a lizard scamper off into the grass beside the path. Then came a sequence of images depicting the following: a small snake seen a few days earlier; the old stone steps beside which I had seen that snake; myself stumbling on those steps while returning to my hut in semi-darkness the previous night; and, finally, my flashlight on the table in the hut. This kind of experience was repeated many times. Again and again I observed that image sequences could be *useful.*

Another, more sophisticated function of imagery revealed itself during a session of formal walking practice. I heard a strange yet vaguely familiar sound coming from behind some trees a short distance to my right. It lasted a few seconds then stopped. The experience that ensued could be loosely reported as follows. "I could not at first identify the sound. Then I realized: it was the sound of a load of gravel sliding off the back of a dump-truck." However, a rigorously phenomenological description would go as follows. "Initially no image was present, there being nothing in conscious-ness but primary sensation, in particular the strange sound. Then there arose a mental image depicting a dump-truck discharging a load of gravel." Without the image the sound was just a sound; with the image the sound was identified, recognized. The recognition *was* the arising of the image, and vice versa. Such experiences proved common, especially in conversation. If my partner in a conversation mentioned, for example, the name "Mr. Somphong," there would arise – usually – an image depicting Mr. Somphong as I knew him. Failure of such an image to arise coincided with partial incomprehension on my part, a situation of which we might say, "I couldn't recall who Mr. Somphong was." Similarly in the reverse situation, where I was the one speaking, I found that my words were usually accompanied by images, and that the words were largely descriptions of what the images contained.

In this way I noticed more and more frequently that imagery and verbalizing were an indispensable part of life. This tempered my earlier negative judgement of them. It now seemed that the question was not how to eliminate imagery and verbalizing, but rather how to keep them under constant observation so that (a) they would not get out of hand, and (b) they could be suppressed at a moment's notice if necessary. Increasingly, then, I felt that what was needed was to perfect the technique of observing images, so that one could live with them yet not be dominated by them. I did not know how to modify my practice in order to achieve that. It seemed that the practice of observing images-as-process was as far as it was possible to go with the technique of retracing. I saw too that retracing had certain inherent defects and limitations. One defect was that the insight attained through retracing was always retrospective and intermittent. Retracing brought insight into the nature of the image sequence, but only after the original sequence, the original mental event, was already over. I was never aware of the original sequence; I saw only a later reconstruction of it. Again, retracing always entailed drastic interference with trains of thought. It entailed, as it were, dissecting out sample sections from the flow of thought and examining them *in vitro*. I sometimes felt, after retracing, that it would have been interesting to know what might have come next had the image sequence been allowed to run on unimpeded.

I could not at that stage see how these defects might be overcome. With such feelings of mild dissatisfaction about the efficacy of my practice and uncertainty about where to turn next, I started experimenting with something different. It began as merely a variant version of retracing, but soon evolved into a new meditation technique.

Link-watching

In my early experimentation with retracing I had noted with interest the apparent logicality of the order in which images arose. This can be seen in the sample sequence cited earlier: aching back → slouching pianist → stout cellist → friend playing cello near shelves → shelves in garage → office with inadequate shelves. Each link between consecutive images, though by no means predictable, did seem to be obeying certain "laws." At that time I had not pursued the matter further because it had seemed relatively unimportant. To examine the nature of the links between successive images entailed a certain amount of attention to the content of the images. It had therefore seemed to me that, as regards level of insight, this was inferior to the practice of viewing images-as-process, whereby one saw beyond the content to the event. Consequently, in returning to this practice after pursuing retracing to its limits, I felt I was taking a step backwards; having attained penetrating insight into the elements of thought, I was now in part relinquishing it.

My investigation into the nature of the links between successive images depended on the following technique. Suppose a sequence of images A → B → C → D → E → F. I begin to retrace this sequence,

F → E → D → . . .; but I stop at some arbitrarily chosen image, say the image C, and permit attention to turn, in a relaxed manner, toward its content. As a result the sequence tends to resume its original course, as image C is again replaced by image D. But before it can go further, I again retrace to C. I then repeat, several times over, this process of alternating between the images C and D, thereby giving myself ample opportunity to observe the nature of the link C → D.

Repeatedly examining the linking process in this way, I came to perceive the "laws" that guided it, which, as I later learned from reading in the history of psychology, were formerly called the "laws of association." However, such obvious cases as "contiguity in experience" (exemplified in the sequence: slouching pianist → stout cellist – the two had been performing together) and "similarity" (stout cellist → friend playing cello) seemed of relatively minor importance. Far more important was another process which appeared to be determined by the images' affective charge. This process is illustrated in the transition from the image depicting the friend playing his cello near a set of shelves, to the image depicting a set of shelves in the garage at home. Of the many details of content in the first of these two images, it is the set of shelves that claims attention and becomes the cue for the next image; and this clearly reflects a current concern over the problem of inadequate shelves in my office. Had I not had this problem at the back of my mind, some other detail of content, such as the friend himself or the tune he was playing, might well have become the cue for the next image. I repeatedly saw this process operating, especially toward the end of an image sequence. Near the beginning of a sequence, the linkages were usually guided by contiguity in experience, similarity, and so on; but as the sequence developed, the linkages were increasingly guided by current interest or concern. It followed that the direction my image sequences took was indirectly determined by my earlier affective involvement in situations, for it was through that involvement that certain details of content became endowed with their particular emotive charge.

But such discoveries about the mechanism of linking, interesting though they were at the time, proved in the long term less important than the meditative technique that yielded them. My practice of causing a pair of consecutive images to re-arise alternately several times over, entailed two distinctly different phases. Phase 1 was simply a special case of retracing, going back from image D to image C, going upstream against the natural flow of thought. Phase 2 was the reverse of this. It was, in effect, a re-enactment of the original mental event: image C was allowed to link again to image D, more or less as had happened in the original thought sequence. It was a relaxed downstream movement, a going along with the natural flow of thought. Repeatedly practising these two phases in rapid succession, I became very conscious of the difference between them. Phase 1 entailed effort and attention, and yielded penetrating insight into the nature of image-as-process. Phase 2 entailed relaxation and a diminution of attention, and a partial switch of focus from image-as-process to image-as-content. However, care had to be taken to ensure that the relaxation was only partial, that the diminution of attention did not go too far. If I let go completely, the second image would link to another image, and another, and the flow of thought would resume without insight. I therefore learned to relax attention just sufficiently to permit a single linkage to take place. The result was a delicately balanced form of insight which saw image-as-process and image-as-content simultaneously.

In time I abandoned phase 1 and developed phase 2 as a technique in its own right. I found that by preserving the delicate balance, I could move with the stream of thought, observing successive images as they re-arose in the forward direction, always seeing image-as-process and image-as-content simultaneously. It was therefore possible, after retracing a full image sequence, to observe it without interference as it then repeated its original forward movement. The earlier technique of retracing had involved a cycle of three stages; with the perfecting of this new technique, a fourth stage was added:

1. concentration on a chosen object;
2. a short thought sequence, as the mind wanders from the object;
3. retracing this thought sequence to its starting point;
4. watching the same thought sequence with insight, link by link, as it again moves in the forward direction.

This new technique (stage 4) overcame what seemed to me a major defect of retracing (stage 3). With retracing it had only been possible to observe thought sequences in reverse order. With this new technique it was possible to observe each thought sequence a second time as it again moved in the natural forward direction. It remained true, however, that what was revealed was not the original unimpeded flow of thought. It was still a reconstructed version of a sample sequence dissected out of that flow. Further refinement was needed.

Awareness

In the event, the required refinement in technique came of its own accord without being sought. I found that when practising stage 4, the mind had a tendency to run on after arriving at the end of each sample sequence. Thus an original sequence A → B → C → D → E → F, after being retraced and observed as it moved again in the forward direction, often would not stop on reaching image F, but would continue into a new sequence: → F → G → H → . . . . Provided I maintained the delicately balanced insight of stage 4, I could have the continuing thought sequence without losing awareness of its true nature as process. I was therefore observing thought continuously, *as it happened*. Images arose one after the other, sometimes in very rapid succession, sometimes slowly. In themselves, and in the manner of their linking together, they were as I had come to know them in the earlier practices. But now, instead of looking at re-plays of artificially isolated segments, I was observing the original, undisturbed process itself. The inner voice was also clearly heard. I listened as it made its intermittent comments, or at times took over as the dominant component of thought. I was now listening in on, and watching, the processes of thought while they were going on, and without interfering with them. This, I was certain, was the ultimate in insight, the ideal technique in insight meditation. To refer to it I later adopted the term used by some of its best-known practitioners and advocates: *awareness*.

The only defect in awareness, as I was practising it, was that I usually could not maintain it for more than half a minute at a time. The collapse of awareness coincided with, and indeed was identical with, losing sight of the process and becoming involved again in the content. Whenever awareness broke down in this way, I was able to re-establish it by again going through the lead-up stages of retracing and link-watching. However, as I became more familiar with the practice, I found I could dispense with those preliminaries, and establish awareness directly. I therefore lived in a continual alternation between two different conditions: awareness and unawareness. Awareness would last until the mind reverted – through a kind of fatigue, it seemed – to its normal unaware condition. That condition would then last until something, usually difficult to identify, reminded me that I ought to be practising – whereupon I would re-establish awareness.

I found that awareness could be practised in any situation, regardless of what activity, physical or mental, I was engaged in. This was to be expected, since awareness coexists with the flow of thought and in no way impedes it. Even intensive study and complicated problem-solving activities proved compatible with the practice of awareness. Indeed, awareness seemed to contribute to greater efficiency, by enabling me to notice immediately any irrelevant digression and correct it,

However, it was not for these practical benefits that I valued awareness, but for the unobscured insight which it yielded into the ordinary everyday workings of the mind. It was as if the dark, mysterious room of my mind, into which the earlier practices had occasionally sent flashes of light, was now completely lit up for lengthy periods. At the level of process, what I saw was an essentially simple, orderly mechanism. Images, drawn from the vast mental photograph album of memory, appeared one after the other, usually according to the principles of linking already observed (but sometimes spontaneously and randomly), while the inner voice kept up its commentary. At the level of content, much of what I saw could be best described as useless. It seemed that most of the images stored in my mental album were of little intrinsic value, and the affective charges inhering in them were such that the most useless images were the ones likely to arise most frequently. However, my only response on seeing all this was detached amusement. Observing the antics of my mind often evoked a smile. This detached attitude was not cultivated. It was the only one possible, since affective involvement in the content of thought always caused awareness to collapse. Awareness and affective involvement were incompatible. For example, I could observe with awareness and detachment an image that would normally be conducive to an angry reaction; or I could react angrily to that image and lose awareness; but I could not do both at once. Awareness could not coexist with anger or with any other such reaction. Awareness entailed detachment. It seemed as if the mental energy normally squandered in emotional reaction to images was now being deployed instead as awareness.

The Nature of the Self

While there was much of interest in the details of content and process revealed under the spotlight of awareness, it all seemed of minor importance compared with one over-riding insight which constituted the very essence of the experience. That insight provided the answer to a number of interrelated questions, some of which had preoccupied me since my earliest encounter with meditation: Who –

or what – is doing the thinking? What is it that is aware? Who is observing all these processes? What is the nature of this observing?

It seemed natural to describe awareness with the statement, "I am observing the mental processes." But at the same time, that statement was self-evidently misleading. It suggested a situation analogous to that of a spectator watching a street parade, which was not at all the situation that existed in awareness. It was not a case of an observer, "I," engaged in observing a spectacle, "the mental processes." Rather – and this was *the* central insight of awareness – the observer *was* the mental processes. Instead of saying, "I am observing the mental processes," one ought to say, "I *am* the mental processes." In fact I verbalized this startling revelation in more or less the following words: "Good grief, this is *me*! I'm *all this*!" The supposed observer was identical with the object being observed. And the same was true of the supposed act of observing: the observing of the mental processes was nothing other than those processes. Observer, observed, and observing were all one and the same.

The moment awareness broke down, this vision was lost. Without awareness the split returned; there was again the sense of being "I, the thinker"; and there were again the mental contents or thoughts that I was thinking. While there was no awareness, there existed the feeling of being an "I" or thinker, separate and distinct from the thoughts. But when there *was* awareness, this feeling vanished, and it became self-evident that there was no "I" or thinker separate from the thinking process. The feeling of being an "I" separate from the thoughts coincided with failure to see thoughts as process. The seeming reality of "I, the thinker" coincided with the seeming reality of the contents of the images. The two arose and ceased together, as two aspects of the same fundamental illusion.

Awareness was, I was certain, the ultimate meditative technique. As long as awareness was maintained, there was uninterrupted insight into the functioning of the mind. It was not exactly the case that that functioning was not thereby interfered with. Clearly, mental events did not go on just as they would have done in the absence of awareness. Awareness implied recognition of the true nature of images, and hence absence of any affective involvement in their contents; and this would certainly influence the direction taken by thought sequences. Nevertheless, awareness was a maximally non-intrusive technique for observing the thought-stream in operation.

In retrospect I saw that my four years of meditative effort had in one respect led me in a circle. I had begun by attempting to stop the thought-stream (through concentration), then I had tried making it go backwards (retracing), and finally I had let it flow normally again (link-watching, awareness). The mind had thus arrived back at its starting-point. However, in the process it had acquired an important new skill: it had learned to be aware of itself in action.

As for the way ahead, that now seemed clear and beyond doubt: awareness must be perfected. The intermittent, brief periods of awareness must become progressively more frequent and must last progressively longer. Other techniques learned earlier in my meditative career still had their place; basic concentration, together with general mindfulness of the body, feelings, and emotional states, would always be valuable as a foundation. However, awareness of the thought-stream was the real practice. The practice would be perfected when the mind had become fully and uninterruptedly aware of itself. The achievement of that condition would surely be the culmination of the entire meditative endeavour.

Abbreviations

Pali Text Society's editions of Pali texts in roman characters:

A: *Anguttara Nikāya*
D: *Dīgha Nikāya*
M: *Majjhima Nikāya*
S: *Saṃyutta Nikāya*
Vism: *Visuddhimagga* of Buddhaghosa

Other:

PED: T. W. Rhys Davids and W. Stede, *Pali-English Dictionary* (London: Luzac, 1959).
T: *Taishō Tripiṭaka.*

Notes

1 The Middle Way

1 *Dukkha*, perhaps better translated "unsatisfactoriness."
2 *Pañcupādānakkhandhā*, the five component elements of samsaric existence: the body, feeling, perception, mental activities, and consciousness.

2 The Eightfold Path Explained

3 *Vitakka-vicāra*, here translated "applied and sustained thinking" in deference to common practice, though according to PED (p. 620, note) its meaning in the suttas is just "thinking" or "thought."

4 The Sublime States

4 That is, the five unwholesome states just listed: desire, ill-will, slackness-and-drowsiness, distraction-and-worry, doubt.
5 *Mettā*. The remaining three "sublime states" (compassion etc.) are: *karuṇā, muditā, upekkhā*.

5 The Foundations of Mindfulness

6 *Satipaṭṭhāna*.
7 Mindfulness of breathing = *ānāpānasati*; see Reading 6.
8 Some say "inwardly" refers to the meditator's own body-mind complex, "outwardly" to other people's.
9 *Dhamma*.
10 The four elements (*mahābhūta*) of early Indian philosophy.
11 *Vedanā*, hedonic tone.
12 *Citta*, which also has the wider meaning "mind."
13 *Dhamma*, a word with many meanings: "phenomenon" (note 9), "mental image," "nature," "truth," "the Buddha's teaching" (Dharma, cf. note 15). Here the translation "mental objects" seems not to fit with the items that follow (the hindrances, etc.). This discrepancy is apparently due to editorial elaboration of this portion of the sutta, on which cf. Johannes Bronkhorst, "Dharma and Abhidharma," *Bulletin of the School of Oriental and African Studies*, 48.2 (1985), 305–320, pp. 310, 312.

14 The mind (*mano*) is reckoned a sense-base on a par with the eye etc.
15 Or "investigation of mental objects"?
16 The *anāgāmin*, one stage below the fully liberated *arahant.*

6 Mindfulness of Breathing

17 Joy (*pīti*) in stage 5 and pleasure (*sukha*) in stage 6 are two of the *jhāna* factors; cf. Reading 7.
18 Or "mental states" (*citta*).
19 Fading away (*virāga*) of greed, hatred, and delusion; similarly for cessation and relinquishment in stages 15 and 16.
20 The sutta goes on to explain how cultivation of the four foundations of mindfulness brings to perfection the seven factors of enlightenment, and thus brings liberation through insight.

7 The Jhānas

21 Many accounts of the jhānas describe a further attainment, "cessation of perception and feeling."

8 The Meditator's Progress

22 *Sati-sampajañña.* The practice described here is the third exercise under observation of the body (Reading 5).
23 The simile that follows (examining one's face in a mirror) suggests knowing one's own mind rather than the minds of others. The practice parallels exactly that for the third foundation of mindfulness: observing mental states (Reading 5).
24 This knowledge and the next two (knowledge of the passing away and arising of beings, and knowledge that destroys the influences) form a frequently mentioned triad. They are the "three knowledges" (*tisso vijjā*) that were attained by the Buddha immediately before his enlightenment.
25 *Āsava*, often translated "corruption," "intoxicant," "bias," "canker," etc.
26 That is, no more of samsaric existence.

9 Concentration on the Earth Disk

27 The *kasiṇa*, in this case a clay disk that serves as concentration object. This is the artificial "sign of earth" referred to above; for a natural sign the meditator might use a cleared circular patch of ground. Ten *kasiṇas* are usually recognized: earth, water, fire, air, blue, yellow, red, white, space, and either consciousness or light.
28 *Nimitta*, in this case a mental image of the disk.
29 Transience, suffering, and non-selfhood.
30 *Vitakka, vicāra, pīti, sukha, cittekaggatā* (applied and sustained thought, joy, pleasure, mental one-pointedness). According to the Abhidhamma version, which Buddhaghosa follows, these are all present in the first jhāna.
31 More literally, "factor of becoming"; often translated "life-continuum," "subconsciousness," etc. A problematic Abhidhamma term for a certain karma-resultant mental function.

32 Another problematic Abhidhamma term, denoting the karmically effective
    stages in a "thought process."
33 Verse translation from Ñāṇamoli Bhikkhu (trans.), *The Path of Purification*
    (*Visuddhimagga* of Buddhaghosa) (Berkeley & London: Shambhala, 1976),
    p. 132.
34 The jhāna factors; see note 30.
35 The five hindrances; see note 4.

10 Self-Protection through Mindfulness

36 *Citta*. Often the reference is to "emotions," though *citta* has a much wider
    scope.

11 Calm and Insight

37 Calm = *zhi*, "stopping," i.e. samatha; insight = *guan*, "looking," i.e. vipassanā.
38 Walking, standing, sitting, reclining.
39 A set of six different flavours traditionally recognized in China.

13 Some Zen Kōans

40 *Mu* (Chinese: *wu*) means "there is not" or "has not."
41 "Gateless gateway."

14 Fastening the Mind

42 The first jhāna.
43 Quoted from *Śrāvakabhūmi*.
44 In India twenty-four minutes was one half of a *muhurta*, of which there were
    thirty in a full day and night; three hours was one watch.

15 A Spectrum of Meditative Practices

45 S v 321.
46 See Reading 3.
47 M i 115.
48 Kamalañjali 17–20.
49 The following recollections (on generosity, friendship, death, and peace)
    were composed by Dhammika himself.
50 A v 336.
51 A v 334.
52 Cariyāpiṭaka Aṭṭhakathā 292.
53 Dhammapada 372.
54 D i 73.
55 Vism 142.
56 Vism 143.
57 D i 74.
58 M i 57–59.
59 S v 181.
60 S v 332.

17 Insight by the Nature Method

61 The way of practice (*magga*) and the fruit of that practice (*phala*), as developed by each of the four *ariyas* or "noble ones": stream enterer, once-returner, non-returner, and fully liberated being (*sotāpanna, sakadāgāmin, anāgāmin, arahant*).

20 Watching Thoughts and Emotions

62 A pause of about one minute follows each paragraph.

23 Meditation in Tantra

63 Literally "enlightenment-mind."

24 Experiences in Meditation

64 Author of Reading 15.
65 Nyanaponika Thera, *The Heart of Buddhist Meditation* (London: Rider, 1972), p. 108.
66 D i 73; Maurice Walshe, *Thus Have I Heard: The Long Discourses of the Buddha (Dīgha Nikāya)* (London: Wisdom, 1987), p. 102.
67 D i 250–251; Walshe, p. 194.
68 D i 74; Walshe, p. 103.
69 D ii 71; Walshe, p. 229.
70 Ibid.
71 Walshe, pp. 11–12.

25 From a Meditator's Diary

72 Monasteries.
73 Monk's hut.
74 Traditional gesture of respect.
75 Mindfulness.
76 Buddhadasa Bhikkhu, *Towards Buddha-Dhamma* (Bangkok: Siripat), pp. 32–33. Buddhadasa is author of Reading 17.
77 Ibid., p. 33.
78 See Reading 4.

28 Experiments in Insight Meditation

79 See Reading 18.
80 See Reading 6.

Index

Achaan Chah, 81
activities, mental (citta-sankhāra), 27
adepts, 187
affective charge, 234–236, 251, 258, 261
affective involvement (*see also* emotion), 251, 258, 261–262
aggregates (khandhas), 11, 23, 94–95, 107, 266
analytical meditation, 159–162, 164, 169
ānāpāna-sati, *see* mindfulness of breathing
anattā, *see* non-selfhood
anger, 142
anicca, *see* transience
anuloma (conformity), 46
anussati, *see* recollection
appanā-samādhi, *see* concentration, fixed
applied and sustained thought, *see* vitakka-vicāra
applied thought, *see* vitakka
arahant, 30, 107–109, 267, 269
arūpa, *see* jhāna
āsava (influence), 7, 123, 267
Avalokiteshvara (Chenrezig), 164, 169–170
awareness, 31, 70–71, 76, 94, 101, 125–127, 129–130, 132–134, 136, 149, 178, 180–181, 220–221, 226, 228, 239, 260–263

bhavanga (stream of becoming), 45, 48–49, 267
bindu, 190

bliss, 183, 188, 191, 201, 216
bodhicitta, 175, 184, 269
body, 13, 19, 33–34, 50, 52, 166; mind-made, 34; movements of, 20, 50; repulsiveness of, 20
boredom, 200–201, 222, 255
brahma-vihāra, *see* sublime states
breathing, 19–20, 86, 98, 113, 140, 143, 148–151, 153, 155, 159, 168, 172, 203, 221, 230–231
Buddha, 7, 30, 42, 84, 109, 131, 147–148
Buddhadasa, 81, 217
Buddhaghosa, 41
Burmese satipaṭṭhāna, 82, 244, 247

cakra, 166, 171–173, 188, 190
calm (*see also* samatha), 55–60, 63, 70, 104, 154, 220, 234
canon, Pali (Tipiṭaka), 1–3, 7
cemetary meditations, 21
cessation (nirodha-samāpatti), 9, 267
chakra, *see* cakra
channel (nāḍi), 171–173, 188, 190–191
characteristics, three, 221, 247
Chih-I (Zhiyi), 41
citta, *see* mind-state
cittekaggatā, *see* one-pointedness
colour, 182, 213–214, 216–217, 224, 267
compassion (karuṇā), 8, 17, 32, 91, 164, 167–171, 218
concentration (*see also* samādhi), 8–9, 11–13, 29, 32, 41, 44, 58, 85, 94, 100, 104, 106–108, 112, 114,

116, 151, 165, 172–173, 183, 199, 202, 210, 221, 226, 245–247, 249, 254–255, 262–263; access (upacāra-samādhi), 44–46; fixed (appanā-samādhi), 44–46
conditioning, 123–127, 132–133, 138, 142, 236
consciousness, 33, 64, 124, 126, 177–179, 183, 188; endless, 29, 206
content, mental, 241, 251–252, 257, 259–262
contentment, 31
counting, 56, 85–86, 151, 208–209, 222, 224–225, 231

ḍāka/ḍākinī, 189
daydreaming, 139–140, 222
death, 99, 191
defilement (kilesa), 57, 109, 213
deity, 164, 166, 186–189
delusion, 9, 14–15, 53, 61, 157
desire, 14–17, 22–23, 31, 35, 46, 53, 56, 61, 93, 100, 109, 130; sensual, 29, 43
destruction of the influences, see knowledge
detachment, 13, 29, 32, 46, 93, 218, 261
Dhammika, 81, 197
Dharma/Dhamma, 30, 58, 100–101, 131, 141–142, 201, 266
dharmakāya, 189
Dhiravamsa, 82
dhyāna, see jhāna
disidentification, 240
disk, see kasiṇa
distraction, 17, 23, 32, 52, 70, 74, 134
divine ear, 9, 34
divine eye, 36
Dōgen, 41–42, 82, 84, 152, 156
doubt, 17, 23, 32
drowsiness, 17, 23, 32, 43, 73, 120, 200–201
drugs, 100
dukkha (suffering, unsatisfactoriness), 8–12, 16, 25, 36, 94, 98–99, 101–102, 104, 108–111, 129, 135, 139–140, 145, 151, 163, 169, 202, 214–215, 221, 247, 266

Dzogchen, 3

eightfold path, 8–12
ekaggatā, see one-pointedness
elements, 21, 33, 56, 266–267
emotion (see also affective involvement), 15, 82, 133, 136–138, 140–145, 171, 177–178, 183, 198–200, 202, 220, 230, 236, 239, 251, 261
empathic joy (muditā), 8, 17, 91, 218
empowerment, 184, 187
emptiness, 98, 104, 160–161, 163, 175, 177, 184, 191, 245
energy, 171–174, 187, 189–191, 212, 261
enlightenment, 9–11, 25, 65, 100, 107, 126, 144–145, 160, 167, 184, 232; seven factors of, 24, 26, 101, 267
equanimity (upekkhā), 8, 49, 91

fantasy, 229–234, 240, 248
fatigue, 129, 249, 260
feeling (vedanā), 13, 19, 22, 53, 101, 115, 117, 173–174, 266
fetter, 24
focusing, 137, 140, 145
fruit, see path and fruit

Gelugpa, 42
ghost in the machine, 242
gotrabhū (change of lineage), 46
guru, 76, 126, 184–189

hallucination, 232, 234
happiness, 93–94
hatred, 14–17, 22, 32, 35, 53, 56, 61
Hīnayāna, 3, 7
hindrance (nīvaraṇa), 17, 23, 32, 44, 93, 216, 266
"I, me", 114–115, 128, 145, 148–149, 161–163, 210–211, 238–241, 262.
identification, 236–241
ignorance (avijjā), 126
ill-will, 23
illusion (see also māyā), 125, 232, 252
images, 14, 99, 151, 153, 163–165, 169, 188, 199–200, 202, 214–216, 245, 250–262, 266; sequence of,

251, 253, 257–259; and
verbalizing, 253–254, 255–256
impermanence, *see* transience
impulsion, *see* javana
impurities, 20, 56
initial application/thought, *see*
vitakka
initiation, 184, 187
inner heat, 171–173
inner speech, 230–232, 253–254,
260–261
insight (*see also* vipassanā), 9, 11,
55–57, 59–61, 63, 66, 94, 98, 106–
108, 110, 112, 163, 222, 252, 255,
257, 259–262
insight meditation (*see also*
vipassanā), 228, 244, 246, 260
interest, 201
introspection, 106–107
itching, 117, 209–210

javana (impulsion), 45–49, 268
jhāna (dhyāna), 9, 13, 29, 32–33, 46–
47, 58, 93–94, 198, 206; factors of
(jhānanga), 45–46, 267; first 13,
29, 32, 46–47, 93–94, 204–205;
fourth, 13, 29, 33, 49, 69; material
(rūpa jhāna), 9; non-material
(arūpa), 9, 205; second, 13, 29,
32, 47–48, 94, 205; third, 13, 29,
33, 48–49
Jōshū, 66–68
joy (*see also* pīti), 13, 27, 29, 32, 46,
48, 93–94, 107, 201–202, 205,
217.
judging, 138, 145, 251

kāma (sensuality), 46
karma, 50, 57–58
karuṇā, *see* compassion
kasiṇa (disk for meditation), 41–43,
267
khandhas, *see* aggregates
knowledge, 33; of death and rebirth
of beings, 9, 36; of former
existences, 9, 35; of other's minds,
9, 34–35; that destroys the
influences (āsavas), 9, 36;
threefold, 9, 267
kōan (Zen riddle), 42, 66, 83, 155

labelling, 82, 233, 247
lamrim, 42
laws of association, 258
liberation, 9, 26, 111, 123, 128, 134,
141, 152, 176
light, 166, 168, 170, 188, 190–191
lineage, 76, 185, 187–188
link-watching, 257–258, 260, 263
linking, 221, 257–261
love/loving-kindness (mettā), 8, 17,
56, 91–92, 109, 181, 197–203, 205,
218

Mādhyamika, 41
Mahāmudrā, 3, 139, 191
Mahasi Sayadaw, 81, 244, 247
Mahāyāna, 7, 41
maṇḍala, 186
mantra, 97, 103–104, 169–170
mastery, 47
māyā (*see also* illusion), 231–232, 252
McDonald, Kathleen, 83
meditation, *see under specific categories*
meditative mind, 128–133
memory, 125, 234, 261
mental objects, 13, 19, 23, 28, 54
mettā, *see* love/loving-kindness
middle way, 8, 11, 211
mind-state (citta), 13, 19, 22, 28, 53–
54, 98, 120, 142–143, 201, 266,
268; unwholesome, 8, 12–13, 29,
32, 46; wholesome, 12
mindfulness (sati), 8, 11–13, 17, 19,
26, 28–29, 31, 33, 41, 49–52, 70–
72, 74–77, 95, 98, 101, 104, 203,
211, 219, 230, 241; four
foundations of (satipaṭṭhāna), 95,
219; of body, 19–21, 27–28, 52, 95;
of breathing (ānāpāna-sati), 9,
26–27, 81, 85, 95–97, 143, 169,
197, 199, 208–209, 219, 247, 249;
of feelings, 22, 28, 53, 95, 115; of
mind-objects, 23, 28, 54, 95; of
mind-states, 22, 28, 53–54, 95,
114, 267; of walking, 102, 118–
119, 226, 249
morality, 30.
mu, 67–68, 268
muditā, *see* empathic joy
Mumonkan, 42

neither perception nor non-
  perception, 29
nimitta, see sign
nirodha-samāpatti (cessation), 9, 267
nirvana (nibbāna), 11, 19, 107,
  110–112, 115, 177
Nishimura Eshin, 219
noble truths, 8, 11, 13, 25, 185
non-duality, 176–178, 181–182, 191
non-returner (anāgāmin), 25, 267,
  269
non-selfhood (anattā), 94, 98, 101,
  108, 110, 221, 241, 247
nothingness (ākiñcañña), 29
noting, 113–122
Nyanaponika, 198

observer, 239, 241–242, 262
observing death and rebirth, see
  knowledge
once-returner (sakadāgāmin), 269
one-pointedness of mind (ekaggatā,
  cittekaggatā) 46, 48–49, 94, 202,
  204–205, 245
oxygen consumption, 86

pain, 118, 209–211, 221, 223–224,
  226
parikamma (preliminary), 46
path and fruit (magga-phala),
  106–107, 110, 120, 269
Path of Purification, see
  Visuddhimagga
patience, 116
perceptual enhancement, 225, 233,
  237, 242, 245, 254
pīti (see also joy), 46–48, 93, 107, 267
pleasure (see also sukha), 13, 27, 29,
  32–33, 46, 48–49, 69, 173, 183;
  sensual, 11
posture, 20, 50, 104, 115–118, 136,
  146–148
prāṇa (energy winds), 190–191
process, thought as, 252, 257,
  259–260, 262
purification, 166–167

reaction, 123, 127, 133, 180, 251
recollecting former existences, see
  knowledge

recollection (anussati), 86–87; on
  Buddha, 87; on death, 89–90; on
  friendship, 85–89; on generosity,
  88; on peace, 90
renunciation, 175, 184
repression, 138, 142–145
retracing, 221–223, 248–253, 255,
  257–260, 263
retreat, 198, 201, 228, 233
right effort, 8, 11–12, 132, 151
Rinzai Zen, 41–42

sādhana (spiritual exercise), 186–
  187
sakadāgāmin, see once-returner
samādhi (see also concentration),
  69–70, 72–75, 97, 211
samatha (see also calm), 41–42, 51
Samararatne, Godwin, 82
samsara, 177
Sangye Khadro, 83
Śāntideva, 41
sati, see mindfulness
scanning, 137
seat, 43, 64, 97
selfhood, 56, 114–115, 125, 161–163,
  261–262
self-mortification, 11
sensation, 101, 137
sense doors, 24, 31, 61, 100, 184
sign (nimitta), 43, 214–217;
  acquired (uggaha-nimitta), 44,
  215–216; counterpart (paṭibhāga-
  nimitta), 44–45, 216, 267
sleep, 120
Sobhana Dhammasudhi, 219
sotāpanna, see stream-enterer
Sōtō Zen, 41–42
stabilizing meditation, 164, 169
stream-enterer (sotāpanna), 102,
  269
stream of becoming, see bhavanga
stream of consciousness, 177, 229
sublime states (brahma-vihāra), 91,
  266
suffering, see dukkha
sukha (see also pleasure), 46–48, 93,
  267
Sumedho, 206
supernormal powers, 9, 34

sūtra/sutta, 2, 7, 42
Sutta Piṭaka, 7
Suzuki Shunryu, 82
synaesthesia, 237–238, 245

tantra, 164, 175, 182, 184–185, 198–190
Tārā, 164
tension, 133, 145
Theravāda, 2–3, 7, 219
thinker, 128, 145, 173, 262
thinking, 13, 56, 68, 114, 126, 128, 133, 145, 152, 179, 222, 224, 248, 262
thought, 16, 64, 71–73, 75–76, 82, 85, 93–95, 101, 126–127, 130, 134–140, 153, 162, 173, 177, 179, 183, 198–199, 201–202, 204–205, 221–224, 233, 236, 238–239, 248–250, 253, 262; sequence of, 224, 249–250, 253, 259–260; stream of, 252–253, 259; unwholesome, 14–15
Tiantai, 41
time, 152, 254
Tipiṭaka/Tripiṭaka, see canon
transience (anicca), 27–28, 94, 98–99, 101–102, 104, 108, 110, 221–222, 247
truth, 125–126

Tsongkhapa, 42

unconscious, 145
unsatisfactoriness, see dukkha
upacāra-samādhi, see concentration
upekkhā, see equanimity

vajra body, 190
Vajrayāna, 164
Vasubandhu, 72
vicāra (sustained thought), 46
vipassanā (see also insight), 8–9, 41–42, 113, 116, 228, 244, 246
visions, 98–99
visualization, 163–166, 168–170, 172–173, 182, 187–188, 202
Visuddhimagga (Path of Purification), 41
vitakka (initial thought), 46–47, 93
vitakka-vicāra (initial and sustained thought), 29, 32, 46, 93, 266

wisdom (paññā), 58, 104.

Yeshe, Thubten, 83

zazen, 42, 64, 146–148, 150, 155–158, 219
Zen, 41–42, 68, 82, 151, 221, 224
Zhiyi (Chih-I), 41